Interrupting the City
Artistic Constitutions of the Public Sphere

Sander Bax, Pascal Gielen,
Bram Ieven (eds.)

Antennae
Valiz, Amsterdam

Interrupting the City

Artistic Constitutions of the Public Sphere

Sander Bax, Pascal Gielen,
Bram Ieven (eds.)

With contributions by
Sander Bax
Bojana Cvejić
Lieven De Cauter
Pascal Gielen
Odile Heynders
Bram Ieven
Vanessa Joosen
Jennifer Miller
Tessa Overbeek
Gerald Raunig
Gregory Sholette
Erik Swyngedouw
Rennie Tang
Sarah Vanhee
Geertjan de Vugt
Sara Wookey

Contents

Part 4
Common Public Space

Introduction
A Public Sphere, For Example

Sander Bax, Pascal Gielen, Bram Ieven

In 1869, in the immediate aftermath of the Boshin War that started the Meiji Renovation in Japan, the Shinto shrine known as Yasukini was built. Originally the shrine was meant to pay tribute to those fallen in the Boshin War. Today, however, it honours those who have fallen in any of the twelve wars fought since that time. Since 1978, when the souls of a dozen Class A war criminals were enshrined in Yasukini, the shrine has been highly controversial. Its yearly memorial service, traditionally held at the beginning of July and attended by most state officials of the Japanese government, has been strongly criticized by China, Taiwan, South Korea and others (all of whom have suffered under the military rule of Japan).

The memorial service, not surprisingly, is a highly publicized, public, and political moment, taking place right at the heart of Tokyo. Immediately bordering on the Imperial Palace and next to the Imperial War museum, the memorial connects the urban with the national, the rituals of a constitutional democracy with those of an empire (the Boshin Wars were – and this is what makes this shrine so significant, what at some point made it the chosen site for the memorial service for all war casualties – the beginning of the Renovation that was so important to Japan). And of course the commemoration is also an economic and cultural affair: it attracts the small entrepreneurs and owners of market stands selling trinkets, souvenirs, religious attributes and pickled vegetables; it attracts tourists and nationals, and so on and so forth.

The annual memorial service at the Yasukini Shrine is an excellent case study for how the authors in this book approach the idea of the public sphere. In general terms, the essays understand the public sphere as a volatile field in which the different powers of society intersect. None of the powers has complete control over the situation, which is what makes the situation volatile but also makes it a site of political struggle and socio-economic emancipation. The annual ritual taking place at the Yasukini shrine is an example of how these different powers intersect. We can see different economies at work here, vying with each other and/or conspiring together: the micro-economics of the market stands selling trinkets, the macro-economics of the multinational corporations sponsoring the event, a religious economics of paying tribute to the dead whose souls are enshrined in Yasukini, the political economics of state officials visiting Yasukini and thereby paying tribute to war criminals, and the cultural economics of creating a tradition and a cultural identity that traces modern Japan back to the Meji Restauration. And of course, all of this is broadcast, publicized, and becomes a topic for public debate on a national and international level.

Such a public sphere, the Yasukini example makes clear, is not only a volatile intersection of different powers in society; it is also something that must be 'kept alive', so to speak, it must be reiterated, reaffirmed and reinstated in order to exist: the media must keep on broadcasting, the economic forces must keep looking for dominance, and so on. For a public sphere to exist it must be *constituted* in each and every moment, through each and every gesture, through each and every institution that adopts its principles and aspirations. The public sphere, in other words, is constituted by the continuous intersection of different societal powers, usually in the city. The question for this book is: how can art contribute or interrupt this process of constituting a public sphere?

Interruption and Constitution

Interrupting the City wants to contribute to our understanding of the ways in which art – or more precisely: artistic practices and interventions – constitutes the public sphere. Most contributors working with us on this book were kind enough to go along with us in assuming that *interrupting* the city is one way of forcing the public sphere to renew itself; or if not renew then at least to rehash itself. The essays engage with the question *how art might contribute to the constitution of a public sphere*. They provide different answers to this question, compelling the readers to make up their own minds about the contribution of art to the public or even to the political sphere. But to make all of this comprehensible and convincing we must clarify the premises and core concepts we are using. We need to answer questions such as: what do we mean by interruption and constitution? And if we assume that interrupting the city is a way to constitute the public sphere, then aren't we working with a rather minimal way of defining constitution?

To such questions we would respond: yes, why not try to approach constitution as the result of an interruption, as caused by a series of interruptions? That is indeed a minimal definition of 'constitution'. Precisely for that reason it allows us to take a fresh approach to understanding what constitution means, both politically and artistically. More importantly, how it helps us understand the relation between art and politics, art's intervention in the public sphere.

The reason why this way of understanding 'constitution' seems rather minimal is because we are used to the religious and political connotations that are deeply ingrained in the concept. In the English language tradition, constitution acquires its religious connotation clearly in the Douaye-Rheims Bible, the first English translation of the Latin Vulgate authorized and published under the auspices of the Catholic Church and published in several instalments between 1582 and 1610. The Rheims Bible mentions 'the constitution of the world'. A few decades later, in 1651, Thomas Hobbes' *Leviathan* emphasized not just the importance of political sovereignty, but also the *constitution* of that sovereignty in the social sphere. This is what made him act against the idea of natural rights, defended by contemporaries such as John Locke and Hugo Grotius: no one is born with certain minimal rights, and no one is born with absolute political power, that is to say sovereignty. Instead, for Hobbes, the constitution of sovereignty becomes a social affair forced upon mankind because of the brutality and unpredictability of the state of nature. The social contract marks the transition from the state of nature to civil society, but it does so precisely through the *constitution* of sovereignty; that is to say, the constitution of an authority that presides and rules over the social and political world.

We can make do without a detailed biblical and political exegesis to grasp the transference of meaning taking place here. Through its religious history, constitution references creation – the 'constitution' of the world, a classic case of *creatio ex nihilo*. Through its political history, constitution references a transition from one state to another, nothing short of the 'birth' of the political: we are moving from one state of affairs, the state of nature, to another state of affairs, society, which promises to be totally different, as it holds in store for us everything that was lacking in the state of nature: security, comfort, safety. Over the next couple of centuries these two definitions were at times played out against each other and at other times spliced together. Accordingly, its semantic and political field inflated, affecting every concept in its vicinity – and that includes everything from 'constitutional democracy' to the highly metaphorical (and equally ideological)

'Birth' of a nation. With these big expectations of 'birth' (the creation of something new) and 'change' (the effectuation of a real change) constitution became something very abstract, at least for the individual citizens going about their daily lives. Constitution, after all, is not something one can do on one's own.

As a matter of fact, it is not something anyone, as an individual citizen, can do. It thus quickly becomes a rarity, a myth of origin almost, and therefore out of the reach of individual citizens. In that sense constitution, albeit a core concept of modern political thought, was poorly developed: it has become strangely sterile, acceptable only in the most technical of legal documents on the one hand, and the most disproportionate social dreams of revolution on the other hand. Precisely for this reason a minimal definition of constitution that emphasizes the reiterative and performative aspect of the public sphere can be useful. In our reading, the *constitution* of the public sphere does not refer back to a myth of origin, the birth of the political, but to a process that takes place time and again, through a multi-rhythmic articulation and reaffirmation of local economic and political concerns. The concerns are shaped and expressed through local customs and rituals, in combination with the use of global media, national and transnational institutions and so on. The massive virtual space opened by social media is part of the public sphere, contributes to its constitution while altering it and opening it up at the same time. The same holds for the city squares, streets, shopping malls, subway stations, slums and suburbs. They are *all* a potential part of the urban public sphere. What will be decisive for the constitution of the public sphere, however, is how these different elements are connected, and which communication flows they allow for. An artistic approach to this constitution, then, would mean little more (and little less!) than interrupting these different elements by making them visible or by addressing the biases that they impose on us.

A concrete example of how such a constitution of the public sphere through a continued and reiterated interruption of an existing urban space might look like, can be found in Jennifer Miller's traveling circus. Descending upon parks and public squares to engage with the local community in setting up a circus act, Miller's *Circus Amok* presents in this book how art intervenes in the public sphere. But she also makes understandable that such a reclamation of the public sphere can only be done in close collaboration and negotiation with the existing conditions of the neighbourhood, taking into account its micro-economics and social and political tensions. The parks in which *Circus Amok* takes place are traversed by conflicting audiences, youngsters playing basketball on the courts, trucks that are parked in the parks, and so on. These material elements pair up with an institutional framework (the law) and together can begin to form a public sphere.

What is a Public Sphere?

One of the most pressing questions that this collection of essays tries to answer is: what shape does the public sphere take on today? How is the contemporary public sphere structured? And which political, social and economic forces determine what can or cannot happen within the public sphere? In answering these questions, the concept of interruption takes the lead over constitution. The hypothesis that the essays in this book explore, holds that the public sphere is constituted by a combination of social, political and media forces. But also, and primarily, we submit that this combination of forces is in a continuous flux, continuously in need of reiteration and subject to institutionalization, but also, and most significantly, continuously being interrupted. So what does interruption mean in this context? Interrupting these forces can mean that they are brought to a temporary halt. This is what happens during a demonstration or a public sit-in or occupation, for example. At the same time, such an interruption can be the starting point for a reorganization, a re-evaluation and creative recombining of the social, media and economic forces that make up the public sphere. Such a reorganization, the idea goes, can only be achieved through interrupting the already existing structures of the public sphere. Such an interruption, indeed, is never a real stand-still but rather an activity that must be undertaken collectively. In the city nothing ever really comes to a halt. Quite to the contrary, the moment a square is occupied city life is intensified: police are sent out, media pay attention, passers-by take an interest in what is going on, discussions take place. Interruption means first and foremost the interruption of the solidified structures according to which public life in the city takes place day in, day out. These activities can lead to a reorganization, indeed a (re)constitution, of the various forces that make up the public sphere.

We wish to distinguish this conceptualization of the public sphere from a more conventional, albeit authoritative and important reading such as the one developed by the German philosopher and sociologist Jürgen Habermas in his classic essay *The Structural Transformation of the Public Sphere* (1962). For Habermas, the public sphere came about in modern times, after the onset of capitalism and the rise of media within civil society. He traces back the genesis of the public sphere to the broader, more encompassing development of a new economic and political system during the fourteenth and fifteenth century: proto-capitalism. With the rise of capitalism came the rise of a 'sphere of commodity exchange and social labor'.[1] This sphere of commodity exchange was, in Habermas' own words, 'privatized, but publicly relevant'.[2] In other words, it was a public sphere and needed to be treated as such, but it should not be regulated by the state (it is, after all, privatized).

A negative way to approach this observation would be to point out that this situation holds all the key ingredients for neoliberalism. Something along those lines was done by Michel Foucault in his argument on the relation between sovereignty and economic liberalism during the seventeenth century.[3] A more optimistic approach, chosen by Habermas, would argue that this opens up an alternative site for politics. In so far as this is the site where a free discussion on the direction society should take can take place, this is a site for genuine democracy, perhaps even making democratic politics as we know it possible. Habermas adds that this public sphere was itself already prepared and performed by the literary public sphere which 'provided the training ground for a critical public reflection still preoccupied with itself'.[4] When, finally, the rise of the mass media took on steam, with journals and later newspapers facilitating the discussions and debates that belonged to the public sphere, the public sphere that still up to a large extent acts as the main site for political and social discussion began.

In more recent publications, Habermas has acknowledged that the emancipatory potential of the public sphere, the freedom to speak one's mind and to discuss publicly one's ideas and beliefs – in short: the Enlightenment ideal of the public sphere that was sketched by Habermas in his publications from the early 1960s – has not been realized. As early as the 1970s he began to warn his readers that the rise of technological communication media and the control exercised by various political and commercial parties over these communication media were posing a threat to the independence of the public sphere. Worse even, it seems as if this independence, this so-called *separateness* of the public sphere may have always been a fictive idea. This is where our idea of the public sphere diverges from Habermas. Whereas Habermas maintains that the public sphere is separate from other spheres, such as the political and the economic sphere, we suggest that the public sphere is built up out of the economic and political vectors that come together in the public domain. More concretely, and at the risk of oversimplifying things, what can be said and thought today is largely dependent upon the structures of contemporary capitalism. Mass media such as television and (online and offline) newspapers adjusted their publication policies to commercial successes, indicated by viewer ratings and the number of clicks and mentions received.[5] The upsurge and influx of 'infotainment' in news media emphasize this reorientation of the public sphere on the basis of market concerns.

Despite its hegemonic hold over the contemporary public sphere, the market and its obsession with economic gains is just one element that constitutes the public sphere. It competes with other elements, which often try to counter the influence of the market on the ideas that circulate in the public sphere, and it is this struggle that creates a vibrant public sphere in which we can intervene in political, aesthetic or economic ways. In our reading, then, the public space is neither 'open' nor free. More than anything else, the public sphere today is a site of struggle: a struggle both in the sense that participating in the public sphere revolves around continuously trying to open up to new, divergent ideas and actions, and a struggle in the sense that the public sphere is constantly being shaped and transformed by 'external' economic, social and political forces. It is also this struggle which can explain the importance we attach to interruption. These struggles must be understood as activities that lead toward an interruption of the public sphere and, as a result, a reconstitution of that public sphere.

Although the ubiquity of digital communication networks suggests otherwise, the last two decades have not seen a democratization of the public sphere. The conditions that determine who has access to the public sphere by means of public fora, newspapers and broadcasting time have remained largely unchanged: they are still exclusive, obfuscating or downright ignoring many of the events and political and social concerns that people are struggling with in their daily lives. The essays collected in this book attempt to chart the conditions under which one is able to develop a voice in the public sphere, to analyse them and to ask in what way these conditions could be altered by means of artistic interventions. Likewise, the contributing authors ask questions such as: to which restrictions are artists, writers and intellectuals who engage with the contemporary public sphere subjected? And how do they deal with these restrictions? At the same time, however, *Interrupting the City* asks which voices, actions and bodies remain inaudible, ineffectual or invisible in the public sphere. And what sort of aesthetic or artistic strategies would enable these slighted voices to become audible?

Just as we argue that the public sphere is not properly a 'separate', let alone autonomous sphere, but that it is determined by social, political and economic forces within society, so too we argue in this book that the contemporary public sphere is not led by (or even focused on) the production and exchange of rational arguments. Today, the public sphere is structured and dominated by emotions and affects, sentiments and feelings of hope and fear rather than by colloquial reasoning. 'Public spheres', Lauren Berlant has suggested, 'are always affect worlds, worlds to which people are bound ... by affective projections of a constantly negotiated common interestedness'.[6] Public debates not only revolve around overcoming disagreements or addressing political conflicts; they are also, in the final resort, spectacles, performances and aesthetic (and most certainly rhetorical) interventions. People are not only attracted to these performances and interventions because of their cogent articulation of political ideas and visions, but just as much because of the affectual impact they have upon listeners and viewers. The aesthetic or sensory performance in political debates, as much as the context in which these debates take place, determine to a large degree how people will relate to them; that is to say, whether they will be able to project their own social affects onto the issues and ideas that circulate in the public sphere. As Berlant has it:

> In liberal societies, freedom includes freedom from the obligation to pay attention to much, whether personal or political – no-one is obliged to be conscious or socially active in their modes and scenes of belonging. For many this means

> that political attention is usually something delegated and politics is something overheard, encountered indirectly and unsystematically, through a kind of communication more akin to gossip than to cultivated rationality.[7]

For Berlant, however, the 'freedom from the obligation to pay attention to much' does not result in a loss of political agency for individual citizens. People are simply not moved by arguments that appeal to their rationality, but by issues that speak to their immediate personal or social concerns and desires. 'Amidst all of the chaos, crisis and injustice in front of us, the desire for alternative filters that produce the sense – if not the scene – of a more livable and intimate sociality is another name for the desire for the political.'[8] In short, the political – that is to say, the public sphere in which political discussion and action take place – rather than being based on rationality and sound argumentation, is primarily driven by public passions, affects and shared emotions. These passions and affects, coming about at the intersection of the personal and the public, is what provides the public sphere its specific dynamic. This is, as Berlant has it, the *desire* for the political.

The desire for the political, then, is composed out of wider social concerns that are addressed in the public domain proper as well as out of personal, vernacular concerns of individual citizens. On the basis of this insight we may arrive at a more precise characterization of the public sphere as composed out of both public and personal affects and ideas. On the one hand, the public sphere concerns public debates which take place on public fora (on television, in the marketplace, or on the internet). On the other hand, the vernacular public spaces of our daily lives (the neighbourhood, the shopping mall, the pavements and local parks) have an equally important role to play in the constitution not only of the public sphere, but also of our social and political desires. Judith Vega's essay 'Imagining the City: The Difference that Art Makes' (2013) addresses this issue.

When Vega speaks of the public space, she is referring to the various bodies that can be found in the public space: 'Mere empirical presence in the public space does not suffice as an indication of presence in the public sphere: whether we "see" presence in the public sphere depends on a conceptualization of what counts as being-in-public.'[9] This is important because for Vega the city is a 'difference machine', a generator of inequality. Whereas in the public debate argumentation takes place discursively, there the force of art, she argues, is that it is able to show us the 'actual "embodiments" of urban subjectivity and interactions' such as they take place in the city.[10]

These different views of how the public sphere can be defined are related to how one defines politics. The starting point in this is the distinction that Rancière makes between 'politics' and 'the political', in *Disagreement* (1999).[11] In the classical sense, 'politics' is the political debate as held in parliaments, so it is about how parties, through negotiations, convert their interests into policy and about the way in which this is discussed in the ritual conversation that a parliamentary debate is. Once every so many years, this ritual is performed in the form of elections and the associated spectacle. The underlying thought is that the people only interfere in politics at these moments but in the interim leave it to specialists.

Rancière posits a different definition of the political: the political is a struggle about what can be seen and can be said within a community. Lauren Berlant, quoted earlier, again situates this in the sphere of affect: 'This locates politics in a commitment to the present activity of the senses. It sees the work of citizenship as a dense sensual activity of performative belonging to the now in which potentiality is affirmed.'[12]

Artistic Practices in the Public Sphere

So where does art come in? Could it be as simple as saying that certain artistic practices, if well-prepared and performed at the right time, can interrupt this public sphere either through an intervention in the material conditions of the public sphere or through an intervention in the legal and institutional frameworks that hold this public sphere in place? In one way, yes; but in another way most certainly not. Because although this is indeed the sort of interruption we believe art can set in motion in the public sphere, thereby forcing it to reshape and reconstite itself, we also recognize that the ways in which this can be done (through art or by other means) are far from simple. They necessarily intervene in a complex constellation of institutional, material and cultural constraints.

What the effect of an artistic interruption will be is often hard to predict. But art that takes place in the city, that positions itself within a city and takes a stand with regard to this city, interrupting it where possible, not just hiding in its museums but moving into its suburbs and slums, does contribute to the constitution of the public sphere. In *Interrupting the City*, various aspects of the relations between art and the public sphere will be discussed: reflecting, criticising, constituting, interrupting, disrupting but also transforming and imagining. For this reason we have brought together artists, academics, geographers, art historians, philosophers and sociologists. We are convinced that the complexity of art's relation to the public sphere, one of its vested entries in becoming political, cannot be studied from just one angle. This book tries to unravel the complexity of this seemingly simple relation between art and the political as mediated through the public sphere. They try to make it tangible by analysing concrete examples.

The various contributions to this book represent the continual exploration of the relations between artistic practices and the public space, including the various relations between art and politics. The first of these is that of 'representation'. An artwork or a literary text is always a representation of reality (or the illusion thereof). This representation quickly becomes a comment or critique on that reality. This is relevant when we think about writers and artists who take on the role of public intellectual or of an engaged writer in order to directly – explicitly or otherwise – intervene in the rhetoric of the public debate.

But there are other relations as well. For instance, artworks or other cultural expressions may provide 'alternative scenarios'. In that case the work of art is not opposed to or juxtaposed with reality but offers another reality that may as well have been 'real'. In that scenario, the work of art creates the other possible realities (and thereby also comments upon and criticizes reality). Art and literature create imaginary spaces that shape reality in a different manner or present a new reality. In this context, various contributions to this book mentioned the phenomenon of 'embodiment'. How can we, through the imagination, give a body, a face, a voice to what remains in visible or hidden in the discursive-rhetorical public debate?

One may wonder whether criticism and comment suffice. Especially in thinking about art in the urban, public space, more direct forms of political engagement come to mind. Art made and provide an interruption or intervention that compels the public to look in a different way, the making things visible that would otherwise remain invisible. If one does not define politics in the classical manner, but rather in the manner of Rancière, then art in the public space can enforce a different distribution of the visible. In that context, there is also mention of an intervention that aims to disrupt the flow of neoliberal capitalism. This may be art that intervenes intentionally, but also spontaneous the servicing initiatives for which spaces are created in the city for a brief period; spaces that are owned by no one and where something is made visible. These are tactical, always changing creations that reveal moments of freedom and escape. As one of the contributors asks: does the city of today still have space to *play*?

Finally, another relation between art and politics is that in which art thinks that it has detached itself from reality. In the spirit of Adorno and Blanchot, people speak of 'autonomy' or the 'space of literature' is a place where the things that take place in political reality are actually totally absent and precisely in creating this absence – which may also be seen as destruction – life to critical potential of art. It is perhaps remarkable that in the contributions to this book, this view on art is conspicuously *absent*. In her contribution, Odile Heynders says that such an interpretation of Italo Calvino's *Invisible Cities* is quite possible but that and other interpretations, in which Calvino's novel is a fictional prediction of the urban experience of today, is much more productive.

The Digital City

Today, the rise of the megacity and the recent emergence of a digital social sphere probably make up the two most important transformations of the public sphere. Of old the city has been the central site for public and economic interaction and debate, the public sphere that emerged in the wake of this. With the advent of the first cities in the late Middle Ages, West European culture gave rise to the idea that the square or market square was the place where public opinion was formed and literature was practised. It wasn't until the seventeenth and eighteenth century that the idea of this market square would develop into what we now call public space: a 'media space' in which various political voices can interact, a situation that is generally assumed to have been reflected in the magazine and pamphlet culture of the eighteenth century.

What seems to be central to both the capital mega-cities that today form the nodes of contemporary global capitalism and social media is that they are both about *circulation* and *flow*. This may sound abstract but it is in fact very easy to grasp. With the expansion of the urban living environment toward the end of the seventeenth century and during the nineteenth century, it became increasingly important in these urban megalopolises is that the people would circulate. What needed to be avoided was people getting cramped in the streets, or in large public spaces; that would interrupt the daily flow of the city. Such interruptions could be simple traffic jams, but could also be political revolts. To sit down and occupy a public space and thus to lay claim to the public sphere and the debates taking place there, is not a new strategy. But as Occupy has shown, it remains a relevant strategy, one which only gains strength by the emergence of social media.

As far as social media are concerned, the digital megacity so to speak, there too an interruption of a flow may constitute a real space for public discussions. In the same vein, a contemporary media scholar such as Jodi Dean has argued that today we are in a form of capitalism that is best described as *communicative capitalism*. In communicative capitalism, Dean argues in *Democracy and Other Neoliberal Fantasies*, 'the use value of a message is less important than its exchange value, its contribution to a larger pool, flow, or circulation of content. A contribution need not be understood; it need only be repeated reproduced, forwarded.'[13]

It is in this context that the concept of interruption can reveal its significance. To interrupt the city (be it digitally or materially) means to arrest the flow or circulation that the city consists of. The tactics by which this interruption is achieved may vary, ranging from a media offensive to riots in the streets, but each and every time it will mean that the activity that has been undertaken somehow affects the public sphere, maybe even *makes* the public sphere. For example, it could affect the media that co-constitute the public sphere, by using them and commenting upon them.

The Contributions

Interrupting the City is divided into four parts. The first part, 'Artistic Imagination of the City', analyses how the city is imagined by artists. Sander Bax compares how writer Tom Lanoye and journalist Joris Luyendijk tried to influence discursive-rhetorical debate in the public sphere. It is interesting to see how the writer applies journalistic-rhetorical techniques, whereas the journalist is rather using 'embodiment'. Odile Heynders rereads Italo Calvino's

Invisible Cities as an imagining of urban experiences of today, showing that reading classic literature may induce a new relation to our own day and age.

In an interview with the artist Sarah Vanhee, Bojana Cvejić makes it clear that the city can be imagined in various ways. No matter how varied the artistic strategies that Vanhee applies are, she always tries to provide a stage or rather a medium for things that are also present in the city but have a low public profile. Cvejić and Vanhee discuss for remarkable projects by the artist in which she stepped out of the comfort zone of the pre-programmed theatre space. To interrupt the city first and foremost means that the artist herself allows to be interrupted too by what is not encountered in traditional theatre.

By way of 'intermission', architect Rennie Tang and choreographer Sara Wookey speak about their performance *ActionScape*, which they realized in Grand Park, Los Angeles.

In the second part, 'The City and Its Politics', we stay with the imagining of the city, but this time by giving the floor to philosophers and academic thinkers. How do they imagine the city in theoretical discussions? Bram Ieven concentrates on the political imagining of the public space in the city and how it is kept under control by and mechanisms of repressive tolerance and at the same time can be broken open. Thanks to the influence of technological developments, according to philosopher Gerald Raunig the city no longer consists of individuals but of 'dividuals' and therefore the city and the role of the public space must be fundamentally redefined. Even more so: the old distinction between private and public space is no longer relevant for imagining contemporary urban life. Erik Swyngedouw poses the question what the political and the artistic having common in their relation to the city and concludes that both perform aesthetic interventions. 'Art and politics', he argues, 'dwell in the register of the aesthetic.' But what does that mean and what does it imply?

The artistic interruptions are not always evident however, becomes clear in the third part, 'Struggle with the City'. In this part, Vanessa Joosen, in her essay 'Poet Interrupted', illustrates how artistic urban interventions can sometimes 'backfire' and hit the artist in the face like a returning boomerang. Featuring Bart Moeyaert as her protagonist, Joosen shows how this writer was driven into a

corner after being appointed city poet of Antwerp. What is tolerated, what is not? How autonomous are writers in their own work? Should they explicitly engage in politics or not? In short, what are the uncertainties of a sudden public artistic existence for someone who is used to sitting at his writer's desk in relative isolation? Joosen's text is certainly shocking: the city as a stage is an unsavoury place where artists have to fight tough battles.

The New York founder of Circus Amok, Jennifer Miller, seems better equipped. Although she made a conscious decision to bring the circus to New York parks, she nevertheless fights an uphill battle to make the public space public and keep it that way. Amok is not a regular circus, as soon becomes clear from the interview she gave to Tessa Overbeek: '... topics such as racial profiling or radical feminism may fly back and forth between jugglers'. As a critical commentator Miller has been following city life for two decades. Here, circus is a public chronicler of the city, about the city and in the city. Each time Amok 'pitches its tent' she makes that space public again for a while and therefore also political.

Miller's power sharply contrasts with the story of her fellow New York artist and theorist Gregory Sholette. He reveals how altruistic artistic and active is to get initiatives such as REPOhistory are easily usurped by the so-called creative class. The struggle over public space is a risky and tiresome undertaking indeed, whereby sometimes the artist scores a point but much more often capital prevails. 'Struggle with the City' makes clear that public art is an energy consuming business but also shows that clever artistic practices exist that succeed in evading prevailing paradigms time and again.

In the fourth and final part, 'Common Public Space', we take leave of the daily struggle of artists and explore the possibilities in a more speculative manner. How to escape the pitfalls of the neoliberal creative city? Geertjan de Vugt takes a look at the cultural-historical importance of the notion of 'play' in the work of Huizinga and shows how Huizinga, as a cultural pessimist at the start of the twentieth century, mainly observed the loss of play in the modern city. At the end of his essay he has Huizinga walking through Paris together with that other great cultural critic of the early twentieth century, Walter Benjamin. Benjamin shows him that there are definitely still possibilities of play, also in the modern city shaped by Haussmann – Benjamin's own, unfinished 'Passagen' being a case in point. After some pessimism, this reopens a more hopeful perspective.

Philosopher Lieven De Cauter and sociologist Pascal Gielen elaborate this hopefulness by exploring the possibilities of the common. Perhaps the struggle in the twenty-first century is not so much about the public sphere, but rather about a common place that transcends the dichotomy between private and public, between market and state. De Cauter sees 'commoning' as the challenge for the coming era. Following a clear exploration of what exactly the common is – including a very useful distinction between Common with a capital 'C' as the universal property of everyone and no one, and common in with a 'c' as an everyday, concrete praxis – De Cauter, in his contribution, posits relatively optimistically, as does David Harvey (2012),[14] that for every instance of gentrification there will be 'a thousand practices of communing, from a simple pick nick in the park to urban activism'.

Armed with the work of Richard Sennett and Michel de Certeau, Pascal Gielen concludes *Interrupting the City*. In 'Performing the Common City' he outlines the relation between art, public space and urban life in a sharp analysis, resulting in a typology of four possible relations between art, city and politics: the monumental, the situational, the creative and the common city. Gielen's argument shows that the fashionable creative city has had its day but that the struggle for the common city has still only begun. This struggle requires completely new strategies and even a completely new attitude from artists. Artists can only 'perforate' the city if they allow themselves to be 'perforated' too.

Interrupting the City connects reflections on artistic practices with theoretical perspectives, thus exploring the constituting role of art in the public urban space. Perhaps this space will no longer be called 'public' as that notion is too much linked to the state, or because it is too rigorously contrasted with private space. One thing is certain, however: only a physical, mental and virtual common city can be the challenge of the twenty-first century. How can it be organized politically and how can we build a solid constitution for it?

In any case, *Interrupting the City* shows that writers and artists are thinking critically and self-reflectively about the city, about how they imagine it or how they try to interrupt the flow of the city through deliberate political projects. Whatever tactic they choose, artistic work testifies to the possibility of an always possible different way. These alternative constitutions for the urban public space are what we had in mind with this publication.

Those who dare to trust the imagination know which directions they *also* could take in their thinking and acting. With the imaginary city, artists and speculative spirits feed the energy and drive of those who try to convert words into concrete actions. Not seldom, they do so by suiting the actions to their words and their fictions. Those who interrupt the flow of the city generate imagination: how could it be otherwise? *Interrupting the City* attempts to articulate that imagination in the hope of a different liveable city, even in the hope of an artistically and politically effervescent urban life.

Notes

1 Jürgen Habermas, *The Structural Transformation of the Public Sphere: An Inquiry into a Category of Bourgeois Society*, trans. Thomas Burger with assistance of Frederic Lawrence (Cambridge, MA: MIT Press, 1991), p. 27.

2 Ibid.

3 See Michel Foucault's *Society Must Be Defended: Lectures at the Collège de France 1975–1976*, ed. Mauro Bertani and Alessandro Fontana, trans. David Macey (New York: Picador, 2003), p. 13 and further, and *The Birth of Biopolitics: Lectures at the Collège de France 1977–1978*, ed. François Ewald and Alessandro Fontana, trans. Graham Burchell (New York: Pallgrave Macmillan, 2008).

4 For a concrete research into the waning independence of news media and the rising pressure of advertisers and market policies, see the recent research published by the Dutch Commissariaat voor de Media in 'Onafhankelijkheid van nieuwsredacties' (June 2015), online: www.mediamonitor.nl/analyse-verdieping/onafhankelijkheid-van-nieuwsredacties-2015/.

5 Habermas, *The Structural Transformation of the Public Sphere*, p. 29.

6 Berlant, *Cruel Optimism* (Durham, NC: Duke University Press, 2011), p. 226.

7 Ibid., p. 227.

8 Ibid.

9 Judith Vega, 'Imagining the City: The Difference that Art Makes', in *Contemporary Culture: New Directions in Art and Humanities Research*, ed. Judith Thissen, Robert Zwijnenberg and Kitty Zijlmans (Amsterdam: Amsterdam University Press, 2013), pp. 51–61, p. 54.

10 Ibid. p. 55.

11 Jacques Rancière, *Disagreement: Politics and Philosophy*, trans. Julie Rose (Minneapolis: University of Minnesota Press, 1999).

12 Berlant, *Cruel Optimism*, p. 261.

13 Jodi Dean, *Democracy and Other Neoliberal Fantasies: Communicative Capitalism and Left Politics* (Durham, NC: Duke University Press, 2009), p. 108.

14 David Harvey, *Rebel Cities: From the Right to the City to the Urban Revolution* (London and New York: Verso, 2012).

Part 1

Artistic Imagination of the City

Voices of Finance
The Joris Luyendijk Banking Blog and Tom Lanoye's Novel *Gelukkige slaven*

Sander Bax

Introduction

For his 2013 novel *Gelukkige slaven* [Happy Slaves], the Belgian writer Tom Lanoye, by his own account, partly leaned on the blog that the Dutch journalist Joris Luyendijk wrote for *The Guardian* from 2010 to 2013. In this blog, Luyendijk collected and reported on stories he heard from London City bankers and conversations he had with them. Lanoye read this blog with enthusiasm, fascination and amazement and then offered a new perspective in the shape of a novel. Each in their own way, Luyendijk and Lanoye attempted to penetrate into the heart of the financial sector. The former used a new journalistic method, the latter regarded literature as the most suitable weapon for interrupting the city.

In September 2013, both writers were interviewed by the Belgian daily newspaper *De Standaard*. Luyendijk suggested doing the interview in the Coq d'Argent, a London lounge bar on one of the top floors of an office building and more than once the site from which disillusioned bankers jumped to oblivion. Lanoye enjoyed being introduced to this spot. Apparently, they both thought it was a good idea to profile themselves as tourists/observers in a place where bankers spend some of their time.

> ... In the morning, you see them on their way to work, this *jeunesse dorée* of the City, this international mercenary army of overtalented youths living out their dreams. Forty years ago, they would have been obese smokers, but now they look extremely healthy. They cycle to work wearing designer helmets or very expensive headsets. They quickly swing by Pret A Manger for their breakfast, as if performing a ballet in which the waiters serve them their healthy snacks with the same flourish.[1]

Gelukkige slaven has two protagonists, both named Tony Hanssen. One is a lover boy who has fallen on hard times and now works for the Chinese businessman Bo Xiang, the other is a fallen banker, once a successful econometrist at a Brussels bank. When the bank goes belly-up, he flees to South Africa where he becomes involved in the ivory trade, also in the employ of Bo Xiang. So, for this novel Lanoye made extensive use of the columns that Joris Luyendijk wrote for the newspapers *NRC Handelsblad* and *De Standaard* and of his blog for *The Guardian*. Lanoye did this because 'it is such essential work, comparable to what the *Holinshed's Chronicles* were for Shakespeare's history plays'.[2] Through Luyendijk's blog the reader is brought into contact with real people and their experiences and those stories feed literature. Luyendijk in turn points out the importance of creating literary fiction about the banking world.

> Very soon after starting my blog, I realized that the whole issue was too big and too complex to solve from within. It required new concepts and metaphors, just like *1984* injected the notion of privacy into the collective imagination at the time.[3]

Lanoye explains why he took the banking sector as the subject of a novel. In Luyendijk's columns he found the story of 'young people, temptation, big money, moral dilemmas'. In his novel, he links these elements to two fictional characters wandering around aimlessly in the world of big finance. Lanoye feels this is not nearly done often enough: 'It is frankly amazing that so little fiction is published about the financial crisis.'[4]

This raises the question what role journalist Luyendijk and author Lanoye adopt when looking at and writing about the world of bankers. That of observer, obviously, but Luyendijk – as will soon become apparent – is also a confessor and an intruder. Besides, he comments on what he sees and tries to interpret it. With Lanoye things are different. He too observes – intriguingly enough mainly through Luyendijk's documentation – and transforms the stories of the bankers into material for his own creation: a fictional world in which various elements from the real world resurface, but at the end of the day is still an alternative, created world that wishes to comment on the world of bankers, albeit in a literary fashion. In this essay I intend to analyse both forms of commentary.

Literature and Journalism in the Public Sphere

What happens when the same issue – the current banking sector, the contemporary banker – is described and commented upon in two different genres: one a journalistic project, the other a literary novel? What are the various and perhaps different rhetorical and artistic strategies deployed by the journalist and writer? What part do they really play in the public sphere? With his blog in *The Guardian*, Luyendijk may influence an international public sphere, but he is also active as a columnist in Dutch media. Lanoye promotes his new novel by giving a series of interviews in which he profiles himself as a social critic. What is the position of both men in this?

A second issue is the question of how the banking sector is represented in both texts. Journalist Luyendijk offers a glimpse of what goes on in the City in London. He introduces us to the residents of this city-within-a-city and also reveals the laws and rules of this city, which is of course a public sphere in itself. We will probably never visit this city and even if we do, we will only be looking at the huge office buildings from the outside. But Luyendijk wants to place us inside the heads of the people roaming this city.

One might expect Tom Lanoye to write a novel in which the City of London is the scene of the action, but the link with Luyendijk's project is not that straightforward. The cities and countries featuring in Lanoye's novel are in various corners of the world (Belgium, South Africa, Argentina, China). Lanoye picks up elements from the journalistic work and places them in a fictional context: Luyendijk's London banker becomes a Brussels banker who has various shady adventures in South Africa and China. Via the literary construction of the doppelgänger this banker is then linked to a male prostitute cum haggler travelling from Argentina to China.

Luyendijk and Lanoye use two different 'truth systems'. A literary writer writes differently about reality than a journalist would. Literary non-fiction uses all kinds of narrative and stylistic techniques, but focuses mainly on the techniques of realistic literature.[5] After all, journalistic work (even if it is literary non-fiction) is not about creating a world, but about reflecting or describing it. It is no coincidence that the so-called 'new journalism' emerged at a time when the novel was no longer considered to be sufficient to write about the complex reality of the 1960s.[6] By contrast, there is the traditional idea that literature would proclaim a higher truth than discursive work. 'Fictionality' then makes up the essence of literature: 'in the mirror of the imagination' man can experience the freedom that in social life is limited by moral and legal restrictions.[7] It is precisely this freedom that gives literature the impact that journalism supposedly lacks. These notions of disinterest, independence and uniqueness (in short: of freedom) are inextricably linked to the notion of fictionality.[8] The idea that literature is the domain of freedom, that writers have the freedom to create a world of their own, that is what gives literature its special status.

It looks as if that freedom simply cannot exist in literary non-fiction: the world that the non-fiction writer describes must be a truthful rendering of facts that have actually occurred in the reality outside literature. These writers may perhaps *borrow* the techniques of the literary writer, but can never apply them with the same freedom.[9] For journalists the possibility to use narrative and stylistic techniques is liberating, but for writers who start doing journalistic work this must at first feel like a limitation. These writers, used as they are to being able to create without any rules in their fictional work, now see themselves confronted with a story of which the contours are, to a degree, already established.

The difference between journalistic work and literary fiction also manifests itself if we think about the influence that the two projects at hand can or wish to exert on the public sphere. With his journalistic project, Luyendijk apparently wishes to position himself in the public sphere with an explicit argument and thus actively take part in the public debate. Lanoye, on the other hand, by writing a novel, appears to align himself more with the artistic projects as featured in this book; projects that rather attempt to provide the public sphere with an alternative.

A case in point in relation to this thought is a recent publication by Lieven De Cauter and Michiel Dehaene, in which they develop Foucault's concept of 'heterotopia' as a 'third space' between what is called *oikos* (private sphere) and *agora* (public sphere) in Greek theory. Between these two lies a space which the Greek call the holy space (*hièran*), but which De Cauter and Dehaene call 'heterotopia'. To them these are spaces for play, in the sense that Johan Huizinga used the term in his *Homo Ludens*. These are liminal spaces that are unstable and therefore contain an alternative to the existing order. Within these heterotopian spaces we find mainly nomadic figures. 'Some people, however, dwell in heterotopia: priests, gurus and wandering philosophers, actors, artists, bohemians, musicians, athletes, entertainers and even architects or urban designers ... .'[10] These people are either deeply hated (outcasts) or highly popular in the city.

At first sight, this heterotopia seems to fit in quite well with the theatrical-literary work of the writer-poet Lanoye and less so with the journalistic and therefore partly descriptive work of Luyendijk. After all, the idea is that art and literature can make a special contribution to the public debate precisely because they can open up this third space through fiction, thus offering an alternative scenario – or, in the words of Rancière – they show how the perceivable may be distributed in a different way.

In her essay 'Imagining the City', Judith Vega subscribes to this idea: according to her, visual art provides 'an urban imagery of public subjectivity'.[11] Vega makes a distinction between public 'space' and public 'sphere' (the public debate). The public debate is about exchanging political opinions and concepts, but this debate offers only a very limited image of the public space. When Vega speaks of public space she refers to the various bodies that can be found there: 'mere empirical presence in the public space does not suffice as an indication of presence in the public sphere: whether we "see" presence in the public sphere depends on a conceptualization of what counts as being-in-public.'[12] This is important, because Vega sees the city as a 'difference machine', a generator of inequality. Whereas in the public debate the arguments are discursive, art demonstrates 'actual "embodiments" of urban subjectivity and interactions'.[13]

> In that respect, the visual arts critically engage with the dominant concept of the public sphere as an essentially 'argumentative', rationalist practice, premised on the political fiction of a unified citizenry. The specific contribution of the arts to thinking about urban culture and public sphere consists in the problematics it interpolates in such a conceptual focus: who is where and how are they present? This does not imply that these arts necessarily constitute a 'critical' discourse in substantive respects. As stated above, narrative clichés similar to those running through urban theories are indeed entertained by the arts. But the different kind of stories about the public sphere that the visual arts give us, effectuate a change in the ontological 'register' or 'feel' of urban experience. They orient us towards the public sphere as a realm of the sensory next to the discursive, a realm of physical next to linguistic confrontations.[14]

Vega argues that we should not only focus on discursive conceptualization in direct political media such as newspapers, television and the Internet (where public *opinion* is central) but we should also look at the artistic contribution of visual art that concerns itself with public *presence*.

The projects by Luyendijk and Lanoye undermine the contradistinction between discursive texts that supposedly mainly contribute to public *opinion* and artistic contributions that focus on public *presence* and *embodiment*. Luyendijk's project actually turns out to be an attempt – via a digital platform – to open up a space that until then did not exist in the City, a space on the borderline between public and private. We are introduced to individuals and their personal stories, so with Luyendijk we can definitely speak of the *embodiment* of a problem that is usually only discussed in the form of an exchange of opinions. By contrast, Lanoye's novel relates a fictional story of the demise of two outcasts – clearly nomads in today's globalized world – but his story is rhetorically structured in such a way that the novel indeed appears to be breaking into the public debate on the *agora*.

Joris Luyendijk

2008 saw the start of a global financial crisis. After the housing market in the US collapsed and banks such as Lehmann Brothers went under, the economies of countries elsewhere in the world also became vulnerable. Especially in Europe, a series of small crises spread like wildfire: Iceland, Ireland, Greece, Italy and Spain were hit, and the Netherlands, with the fall of the ABN Amro/Fortis bank, could not avoid the malaise either. In the wake of these acute economic crises, many European countries laboured under draconic austerity measures caused by the fact that their national governments had spent billions to bail out the banks.

From 2010 onwards, this led to the awkward situation that the banks were slowly beginning to recover from the crisis but that the citizens in the various European countries were feeling the crisis all the more in their wallets: the bailout of the banks was financed by cutting back on health care, culture, education and, in some instances, on the police and the military as well. As this austerity policy was carried out, the news came that some bankers were again receiving higher bonuses. The discussion about the 'bonus culture' was symptomatic for the public debate during these years about the role the banks had played in the crisis. After all, had it not been the egocentric top bankers who were only after their personal gain, who had sold products they didn't even understand themselves? And wasn't there an 'old boys network' in which these same fat cats were appointing each other in top positions that brought excessive bonuses?

At the start of the twenty-first century, the image of the investment banker was at an all-time low because of all this. Paradoxically, at the same time the interest in this figure increased dramatically. Joris Luyendijk observed a growing number of myths in this respect and in 2011, at the request of the British newspaper *The Guardian*, he started writing a blog about the City in London. His main objective was to meet real bankers in order to reveal how these people lived. He was looking for a more truthful representation of the people in banking in order to counter the mythologization in the international media.

It was a project that fitted well with Luyendijk's journalistic body of work. After having studied Political Science and Arabic in Amsterdam in the 1980s and 1990s, in the mid-1990s Luyendijk started working as Middle East correspondent for the Dutch newspaper *de Volkskrant* and later for *NOS News* on TV. By his own account, he owed this second job to his debut book *Een goede man slaat soms zijn vrouw* [A good husband sometimes beats his wife] (1998), in which he relates his experiences during the year that he studied in Cairo. It is a portrait of Egyptian society from the inside by which he questions the Dutch and European view of the Arab world.

After having been a correspondent for five years, Luyendijk published the politically much more outspoken book *Het zijn net mensen* [They are just like humans] (2006). It is an account of how he gradually lost all his idealistic notions about journalism after being stationed in Cairo as the correspondent for an area that was much too vast to be covered by a single journalist, an area also where the truth was always being shaped by the machinations of Information Ministers. As journalists don't have enough time, money or influence to do any real investigation themselves, their agenda is set by a few press agencies that distribute news reports which are then replicated in all media. Finally then, the correspondents' main task is to say a few words 'on location', giving viewers the illusion is that there are journalists 'on the ground'. The book ends on a note of disappointment: 'In Europe as well, all audience ratings and circulation figures show that people empathize with the familiar face of the anchor man rather than with the dull-looking expert.'[15]

According to Luyendijk, the media, including the quality media, have been taken in by the market thinking of – repressive or neoliberal – capitalism and are influenced by something as intangible as 'viewer demand' and therefore by 'audience ratings and circulation figures'. In 2009, in his Johan de Witt Lecture, Luyendijk again made the point he also made in *Het zijn net mensen*.[16] With this lecture Luyendijk states his view of the journalism of the future. He criticizes the 'infantile' model: holding on to traditional methods and genres, but now with increasingly fewer words and ever bigger photographs. This model should be replaced by 'other means of gathering and representing information', because the world has fundamentally changed. 'We should reinvent journalism as a profession and once again learn to survive financially by selling what we are good at: information and insight.'[17]

Luyendijk articulates a model of 'three-dimensional information'. Journalism is concerned with one-dimensional statements ('The climate is changing') and two-dimensional statements ('Is the climate really changing? Watch tomorrow's programme with a believer and a denier.') Luyendijk argues for a third dimension in journalism, a dimension that puts the 'apparent dispute' in the above example in a wider perspective and knows that this generally accepted journalistic approach is really just 'a way to frame/ represent the world'.[18]

> The media are increasingly inclined to present the State with the answers of the Street. A current affairs programme sets up a camera in a busy high street and then all and sundry are allowed to voice their opinion on what should be done about health care. As if all and sundry know anything about that. I would say: find out what the questions are that all and sundry are struggling with, and try to answer those.[19]

In September 2010, Luyendijk was allowed to be a 'fly on the wall' in the press centre of the Dutch parliament 'Nieuwspoort' for a month. He therefore spent some time in what the Dutch often refer to as the 'ivory tower of The Hague'. He wrote down his observations in *Je hebt het niet van mij, maar...* [You didn't hear it from me, but...] (2010), about the entanglement of politicians, journalists, lobbyists, press officers and spokespersons.

> Anthropologists know that taboos practically always serve established interests, which also seems to apply to the taboo on the question whether or not the real power lies

> with Parliament. Because all the groups around that parliament benefit from the image that power lies with politics. The lobbyists because they can ply their trade with the civil servants in this manner, away from the annoying searchlights of the press. The journalists because they can justify and sell their stories with the argument of checking on those in power. Politicians want to look important, and the more power is accredited to them by the outside world, the grander their stature. Finally, spokespersons and PR strategists are hired to further enhance this image.[20]

After reading Luyendijk's report, one is left with the image of an introverted world where only one thing matters: how a politician, a party or politics in general are represented in the media. This means that, through journalists and press officers, the entire media logic that is the result of the audience ratings doctrine discussed earlier now dominates politics. Luyendijk also argues that this whole entertainment circus serves first and foremost to hide one thing: that the real power no longer resides in The Hague but in Brussels, London or New York. Either with European politics – which decides much more than most Dutch people realize – or with the international business world and banks that even transcend the European domain.

In 2011, Joris Luyendijk left the Netherlands for London to work for *The Guardian*. At the time, he was a rather well-known public figure who had been the cause of considerable controversy. He was offered the job by Alan Rusbridger, editor with *The Guardian*, whom he had met at a conference where Luyendijk had spoken about his 'ideas, experiences and plans for innovations in journalism'.[21] As *The Guardian*, together with *The New York Times*, is the largest online newspaper in the world, it was an easy decision. Going to work in England had its risks, as he would now be operating on an international platform where he had no clear status as yet.

Luyendijk sees himself as a critical journalist, but he is of course also a media theorist and a public intellectual. 'I see myself as a writer who has chosen the media as his working field and subject, like others choose history or travel. I think we are all public intellectuals as soon as we speak about ideas in public, but the notion has become somewhat tainted.' He has a simpler view of a journalist's function: 'Personally, I try to go back and forth between experts and interested laymen, in an attempt to close that gap. Explaining to people how the world seems to work; that is a fine assignment for journalists. Meanwhile the press agencies can do the news.' And as to the question whether there is room for criticizing the media system: 'There is certainly room for criticism, just look at my career. Many sectors ostracize whistle-blowers, but that has never happened to me.'

In most of his projects, Luyendijk opts for the role of a relative outsider, which he often labels as an anthropologist. That label refers to the ambiguous attitude of distance (an anthropologist does not belong to the population he studies) and involvement (an anthropologist engages in detailed research by immersing himself in the world he is trying to describe). 'Fieldwork, observation, starting with the perception of the players in the field, looking systemically at power relations and power dependencies, taboos, conventions.' Central to his new project are the personal stories of people. The blog thus becomes a kaleidoscope of little stories. By using this method he tries to reveal what kind of people bankers really are. 'That they are people and not monsters. It is interesting that someone like Tom Lanoye has used my blog as the raw material for his novel about a banker. There was simply almost nothing else that betrayed bankers as people.'

By choosing to work for *The Guardian*, Luyendijk seemed to favour a new approach in journalism, a digital and international work method. Digital journalism provides an opportunity to work in a different, more investigated manner for which there is hardly room any more in traditional media. 'I regard journalistic innovation as an opportunity. Things that were never possible before are possible now, as my blog shows. The people volunteering to speak with me would never have come forward if they had had to post a letter to me. And those interviews could not be published on paper because they gathered their readership along the way, in the long tail.'

Tom Lanoye

The Belgian literary author Tom Lanoye's development has been quite different from Luyendijk's. In the early 1980s he was already working on his career as a writer, poet and performance artist, initially labelled as 'angry young Belgian' together with his contemporary Herman Brusselmans. Both writers broke through in the 1990s with their statements against the literary establishment.

They opposed the prevailing poetics of post-modernism and stated explicitly that they wanted to produce literature that would appeal to a large audience.[22] In the 1980s, Lanoye published his collection of short stories *Een slagerszoon met een brilletje* [A butcher's son with glasses] (1985) and the novel *Alles moet weg* [Everything's got to go] (1988), but his first real success came with his novel about the youth of a burgeoning homosexual boy *Kartonnen dozen* [Cardboard boxes] (1991).

Before that, Lanoye had already made a name for himself as a poet. At the beginning of his career he drew attention with his spectacular public performances. In interviews he stated that literature also had to be entertaining and that he himself, as a poet, should be regarded as a 'literary vaudeville artist, producer of entertainment, manager of the multimedia company 'Lanoye Inc'.[23] It explains why he modelled his first collection of poems *In de piste* [In the ring] after the circus. Bertram Mourits, in an essay in the Dutch literary magazine *De Revisor*, said that the poet Lanoye has a twofold problem: he wants to reconcile poetry and life, but this means that his faith in poetry is constantly tested: 'He would prefer to write with everything he has, but he can only do so if he *believes* in art. Life and art are in each other's way and that is a problem for a writer who puts so much life into his poetry.'[24]

In 2003 Lanoye was appointed poet laureate of Antwerp, a position that is only partly about writing poems. Lanoye embarked on a number of theatrical projects in which he involved various artists: designer Gert Dooreman, visual artists Fred Eerdekens and Panamarenko, and the Antwerp singer of popular songs La Esterella.[25] 'As Antwerp's 'city poet', Lanoye was down to earth and concrete, but he doesn't see this in terms of making concessions to being a poet.'[26] On the contrary, according to Mourits he has more or less resolved the problems of his being a poet: 'He portrays daily life in Antwerp in a poetic manner, a recognizable and accessible manner – poetry and politics, word and image, life and art actually coincide here effortlessly. As poet laureate he adopted a helpful attitude: he wanted to reflect the city's unruliness in poems.'[27]

In the 1990s, Lanoye wrote his 'Monster' trilogy about Belgium as the land of Marc Dutroux.[28] Because of his controversial work and his frequent appearances in the media and at festivals such as Behoud de Begeerte [Hold fast to desire], Lanoye became a well-known public figure in Belgium. With his high-profile novels, his socially committed plays (such as *Fort Europa*

[Fortress Europe] from 2005) but also with his columns in the satirical weekly magazine *HUMO* and provocative statements and interviews, Lanoye became a political voice in the Flemish (and party also Dutch) public debate. Nonetheless, he sees the role of literature as a modest one.

> I have said this before, but to me art and writing are like dreams and nightmares: useless except during the night, when they lighten the burden of the stone that weighs down on our hearts every day. Likewise, art can resolve tensions, including existential ones. But this stone always returns, so there is always a recurring need of art, of writing and of reading.[29]

This emphasis on 'uselessness' contrast strongly with the enormous drive that is also a hallmark of Lanoye's writing. He does not confine himself to one genre, he writes prolifically and calls himself a 'supply business of texts' and 'a strong brand'.

> And this brand is a feel for life, a world view. I strive to be the best medium to present a text and automatically my greatest pleasure is to mix things. This is also my strong point: why deny it? Why deny my political heart, why only go for aesthetics? That is not my forte, and it's boring. A column that only deals with innermost feelings is a missed chance.[30]

By his own account, Lanoye's career took a decisive turn when he adapted Shakespeare's history plays for the stage as *Ten oorlog* [Battle cry] in 1997. The publication marked a phase of deepening in Lanoye's work that resonated in his novels *Het derde huwelijk* (2006) [The third marriage] and *Sprakeloos* (2009) [Speechless] but also in new works for the stage and in collections of poems. *Sprakeloos*, which sold quite well, is the story of his mother's deterioration after she suffered a stroke. It marked a return to the autobiographical writing of his early years.[31]

In interviews from the beginning of the twenty-first century, Lanoye also manifests himself as a rather explicitly engaged writer calling bankers and managers to account.

> What I find shocking is that even today, knowing what we know about the nature of this crisis, there are still no

> political consequences. An architect who builds a house remains accountable for any flaws in his construction for a period of ten years. Why does this liability not apply to bankers and managers? When will these bank Molochs be broken up so people's savings can no longer be tainted by speculation? Who is going to temper the omnipotence of the credit rating agencies?[32]

With *Gelukkige slaven*, Lanoye comments on the financial world in a literary form, which is different from voicing one's political views in an interview or interpreting the situation in a journalistic column or blog. Lanoye could also have opted for expressing his views in a pamphlet or writing a column, to directly intervene in the public debate, but he chose the form of the novel.

> ... Because I wrote a novel, not some political-philosophical pamphlet against capitalism. Although, in one of the best and most important books in Dutch literary history, *Max Havelaar*, Multatuli did have the courage to blow up the structure of his narrative and enter the stage himself to deliver a personal indictment against the excesses of colonialism. Maybe I lack the courage to write a book such as *Max Havelaar* or *What Is the What* by Dave Eggers. Perhaps I am too much of a theatre author who always puts the psychology of his characters first, even if they are wicked. Theatre is about being torn by dilemmas, about the inconsistencies of life. Personally, I love to be inconsistent. And so I write an emphatic, balanced book about a theme that actually enrages me. (*laughs*)[33]

What exactly did Lanoye wish to show with this novel? We have seen how, in the passages that concern Tony Hanssen's past as a banker in Brussels, he more or less aligns himself with the views of Joris Luyendijk.

> I have learned a lot from the columns that Joris Luyendijk writes from the London City: in *Gelukkige slaven* I use a lot of anecdotes that I pilfered from his pieces. In these pieces he depicts a world that has become too complicated, a world in which no one has the power to change anything about the system. And that is why no one feels responsible anymore.[34]

Voices of Finance/Opinions about Bankers

For his banking blog, Luyendijk interviewed almost 200 people over a period of two years, all of whom came to him voluntarily. The result was a profile of the typical banker.

> The interviewee was a man in his mid-thirties. Down-to-earth, friendly and shy, ostensibly the sort of man everyone would wish for a neighbour. He worked for one of the top banks as a 'structurer', which means that he constructed financial tools so complex that his clients didn't understand that they didn't understand them. He had made millions for himself and even more for his bank. Now he had quit his job and was even considering working for one of the financial authorities.[35]

Luyendijk quotes one banker who compares himself to Faust, who had sold his soul to the devil: he had cast aside his moral considerations in exchange for financial gain. After a while, he began to ask himself what he would tell his children about the work he was doing. In his analysis, Luyendijk not only refers to Goethe but also to Hannah Arendt: he speaks of 'the banality of evil' he has encountered. After these 200 interviews, he could only conclude that nothing has structurally changed in the banking sector since the financial crisis of 2008.

On his banking blog Luyendijk has published short interviews he had with bankers who came to him of their own free will. In all, over 70 of the interviews come under the heading 'Voices of Finance', a section containing 'anonymized self-portraits'. The individuals featured here have no names, they are only assigned roles: 'former senior analyst at Moody's' or 'ex-central risk manager'. On his homepage, Luyendijk has included a link to a page 'How to use this banking blog'. One can either go down the entire list of interviews, or follow a selection made by the journalist himself. For instance, there is a page about the former head of the 'trading department', a department that made financial products of such complexity that only a few staff members knew how they worked.

> If you can stomach it, then read about this banker. He was in charge of a computer algorithm when it began to produce inexplicable losses big enough to sink his bank: 'This was a bomb and I was the only one who could defuse it.'[36]

Most of these people will initially not have been overly keen to speak with a Dutch journalist. Many of those interviewed made contact by sending an email to the blog or to the journalist himself. This guarantee of anonymity was crucial. 'Without anonymity, they would either have to bring a PR person or lose their job immediately after publication.'[37] In another interview, Luyendijk says: 'The PR and communication departments of all the banks monitor the press every day to find out if any of their people have spoken to the press without authorization. And then they fire them.'[38] So gathering data was a risky operation, especially for the people who dared to come forward with their stories, which makes it quite amazing that so many bankers dared to take that risk.

Luyendijk used this particular approach to reveal a little about how 'everyday' bankers live. He had two, rather dissimilar questions: 'Who are these people?' and 'Can this happen again?' With his search into how bankers work and live in the current system he hoped to discover in what condition the banking world of today is. Have his questions been answered?

In spite of everything, bankers still enjoy a rather high status, Luyendijk concludes in hindsight, if only because they can afford so much. People may disapprove of individuals who work in finance, but anyone who owns a large house and drives a big car soon finds himself the object of admiration. 'So in spite of all the anger and outrage about finance, I think that if you have a lot of money you'll win almost every discussion.'[39] Clearly people could take risks that made them a lot of money because they knew the government would bail them out eventually, but you can't really call them 'bad' people.[40] These bankers weren't evil or immoral, but they had developed a mechanism of denial, a 'functional stupidity'. It is precisely the world of banking that demonstrates the ineffectiveness of economic theories based on the notion that people act rationally. People lie to themselves and choose not to know what they do not want to know. And there, according to Luyendijk, lies the biggest risk of a new crisis.[41]

To conclude his project, Luyendijk wrote a long article in the Dutch daily *NRC Handelsblad*, summarizing his findings. He shows that the crisis is not over yet. It is a fairly gloomy piece. In his view, the essence of the crisis is financial as well as political and moral. What should be done?

> Rehabilitation of politics, which must re-establish free market rules in the sector, so that amateurs go bankrupt, and fees and therefore financial rewards are lowered by competition. A moral problem lies underneath: the sector, like the entire economy, is organized in an a-moral way. This is not something you can blame bankers for, but this amorality is detrimental in such a complex, dynamic and opaque world where consequences of actions sometimes only become clear after many years and may then turn out to be catastrophic to a great many others.[42]

The financial sector has made itself invincible because it has eliminated all forms of criticism: accountants, financial authorities, top universities and even the media have been encapsulated by the system.

> Well, the Internet has robbed traditional quality media of their business model, while many newspapers have been bought by investors who primarily seek a return on their investments, not quality. Public channels or stations suffer the same fate. ...
>
> If people want cauliflower, we give them cauliflower and for shopping you go to the supermarket. That's how commercial types in information media think, and their mentality increasingly dominates public opinion. I'm sure the financial lobby is grateful to them.[43]

And so the media and the financial world become ever more entangled. And politics, according to Luyendijk, is also incapable of putting up any resistance. Not just because politicians start earning their money in the financial sector after their political careers (take Tony Blair and, in the Netherlands, Wouter Bos), but also because national parliaments have very little influence on the global economic system on which they are totally dependent.

Luyendijk concludes that banks are 'inherently unstable'. They cannot be compared to hierarchically structured armies, but rather to renegade groups of mercenaries. People join a company for such a short time, either because of job hopping or because they are dismissed, that nobody feels responsible for the tiny island they happen to find themselves on. And if things go wrong there is always the financial authorities or the government to solve the problem. While during the 1990s we believed in 'the end of history' and after 2001 were preoccupied with Al-Qaeda, Afghanistan and Iraq, the banks got rid of government interference and created this 'gated swamp', is Luyendijk's conclusion.

In the novel *Gelukkige slaven* everything revolves around Chinese billionaire Bo Xiang. 'From Beijing to Guangzhou, formerly Canton, Mr Bo Xiang was known as the most powerful entrepreneur in construction with the most strongly pursed lips. His fortune was immeasurable, his ruthlessness legendary.'[44] One of the two Tony Hanssens falls into the hands of this tycoon when trying to escape from a life as a toy boy on cruise ships. He incurs gambling debts, which he has to pay back by entering into the service of Bo Xiang. His job is to accompany Bo Xiang's wife on her luxury trips.

At the start of the novel they are on a trip to Buenos Aires. When Tony finally gives in to the woman and goes to bed with her, she dies during the act. Then follows a hilarious description of Hanssen's attempts to have the body repatriated. Meanwhile, we read how the other Tony Hanssen is busy killing a rhinoceros – or rather, shooting the poacher that threatens to steal the animal from him because of his dilly-dallying. After many fumbles and doubts he makes off with two horns, which he has promised to deliver to Bo Xiang.

The two Hanssens meet in a hotel where the billionaire has arranged accommodation for both of them. A police detective, Khumalo, erroneously warns the first Tony that he has been spotted smuggling the rhinoceros horns into the country. He informs him that these horns are poisoned in order to discourage smuggling. It slowly dawns on 'toy boy' Tony that this is a case of mistaken identity and before long he has sought out his namesake and compatriot. They feel a connection and decide to negotiate the deal about the horns with Bo Xiang together, hoping it will enable them to set themselves up in business, a mission that actually seems to be going quite well.

When the deal is done – seemingly, as Bo Xiang's business empire has crumbled – a Chinese tea ceremony is held in which the rhinoceros horn is grated and mixed with the tea. Former banker Tony even drinks two cups, while toy boy Tony knows the tea is now poisonous and refuses to drink it. In this Hamlet-like fashion he causes the death of all those present. All of the other protagonists die, with banker Tony thinking he has finally prevailed and can return to Belgium.

When the surviving Tony tries to escape to the Cayman Islands, he is accosted at the airport by a former colleague of his namesake. This man asks him to accompany him to Brussels, where the bank is meanwhile back in business and doing well. '"We have changed our name," says Diederik, "other than that we have stayed the same. Except for one thing."' (p. 291) As it happens, they miss their irreplaceable former colleague, because 'there is no-one to equal your algorithmic insights'. (p. 297)

> 'Make us happy, Tony,' Diederik insisted. 'Come back to the bank you once helped make great. We will start from scratch. Together. As if nothing has happened.'
>
> 'And that would make you happy?' Tony looked at his sealed suitcases. Then he looked at Diederik again.
>
> 'It will make you happy as well,' said he. 'I will do whatever it takes. I promise you.'
>
> Tony looked his successor in the eyes for a long time. 'Very well then,' he gave in, once again. 'In that case, I'm your man.' (p. 300)

Thus Lanoye ends his novel with a scene that illustrates one of the conclusions Joris Luyendijk had drawn from his project: the banks start all over again. They change their names but not their methods. As a result, someone is given an important position in banking, someone who throughout the novel has been dabbling in crime and unsavoury activities, someone we have seen handing out bribes, someone who has only recently caused the death of four people. On top of that he is a weakling, as he didn't kill by actually doing something (as his namesake has) but by keeping silent and giving in. We could interpret this ending as a rather explicit condemnation of the figure of the banker.

Lanoye represents his view of the financial sector in these two characters, but also in the self-reflection of one of them on his past as a banker. We see the financial world through the eyes of ex-banker Tony Hanssen, a person not unlike the former head of the trading department interviewed by Luyendijk. Tony Hanssen made products so complex that years later they wish to hire him again because he is one of the few people who actually understands how these products work. His reminiscences quite faithfully copy the trail of Luyendijk's blog. Undoubtedly, Lanoye also uses the actions of the Hanssens to make a statement about 'men in times of haute finance'. Here we have two renegades, displaced figures living in a world in which everything is trade. Their only assignment is to survive, and while doing so they leave a trail of disaster. 'He had learned to live like a nomad, a compulsory drifter, a stowaway without purpose, and it was a fate that suited him well.' (p. 27) This is what 'toy boy' Tony says when reminiscing about the 'one-horse town' where he was born, but of course it applies just as well to his namesake who fled Brussels and says he is living 'in exile' (p. 48). Their lives consist of continually running away from responsibility: it seems they will not be or cannot be accountable for anything.

We have gotten to know the ex-banker Tony Hanssen as the type that would very much like to be ruthless but is constantly reluctant to do the 'manly' deeds that are expected of him: shooting a rhinoceros, chopping off its horn, kicking his double from the room. But in spite of his hesitations, his actions are brutal: he shoots a poacher and even finishes him off with an axe, and he smuggles two horns from South Africa to China. He is quite the successful 'hunter', a career that suits him well after his years as a banker, the novel seems to imply. When his bank failed, also because Tony's prognoses turned out to be incorrect, he had gone into hiding taking twelve memory sticks with company secrets with him. 'Toxic investment products mixed with clean ones which were then sold in great numbers as reliable derivatives.' (p. 46)

> Now, looking back, he could no longer imagine it but as long as he had worked for the bank he had let gratitude for his job prevail over the doubts about his role. He had shown respect because he imagined he was given respect. Proud as a peacock he had been, of his career, his earnings and his domestic bliss, even though he rarely came home before 11 at night and was usually on his way to the office again by 7 in the morning. (p. 47)

He is loyal as a dog to his employer. He even creates several aliases on social media to counter any slander directed against the company. In Tony Hanssen, Lanoye outlines the problem of the financial sector: only Tony and a few others grasp the details of the econometric computer models used.

> It would not be long now before they would be tumours operating independently, autonomous digital organisms driven algorithmically to ever higher gears until they would become a perpetual motion machine with unprecedented buying power and not a single braking mechanism. (p. 50)
>
> Trading had finally freed itself of its two shackles: the merchandise and the money. The products of the Earth and the means of exchange to procure them? These had simply become redundant. Just like *l'art pour l'art*, trading was now solely for the sake of trading. After the poets and the conceptual sculptors, now the bankers and the traders had entered the era of pure lyricism in which you didn't have to show any consideration with anyone, least of all with your public or customers. Money became hermetic poetry. Even real estate could be a bubble. (p. 50)

These developments led to the rise of a 'nouveau aristocracy', a 'coterie of untouchables'. (p. 51) This had never sat well with Tony. The things he had to do in his 'banker's uniform' clashed with his ethical and political awareness and at heart he had always remained a rebel. 'An autonomous hinge between the ordinary people from which he came and the *Herrenvolk* of haute finance that would never accept him.' (p. 52) At the same time, he is evading his responsibility in a predictable manner. 'They should have supervised him better, and corrected him. But they hadn't even been capable of that. That was the essence of the whole crash.' (p. 49)

In the end, Tony Hanssen internalizes the law of the banking world: help yourself, no one else will do it for you. He goes off the radar, taking said banking secrets with him. In his new life he becomes part of another financial system: that of the underground, criminal circles that raises tycoons such as Bo Xiang. The implication is that Hanssen only appears to flee but that in a sense he simply continues his 'criminal' behaviour, but this time undisguised. How thin is the line, is the question the novel begs, between a smuggler in South Africa and an econometrist at a Brussels bank?

Lanoye illustrates the harshness of the 'elite corps' of international bankers with the phrase 'Go get a teaching job!', which the bankers snap at anyone who is about to collapse. It is a system of natural selection: burnouts, nervous breakdowns, suicides. 'It strengthened the survivors' motivation and pride. One man's sickness is another man's jewel.' (p. 120) 'The hefty pay check was a nice bonus, but honour was the real reward. In spite of everything, they were still standing. The weaklings had succumbed.' (p. 122)

In the plot of this insane story Lanoye uses an important analogy: how things are done in banking and in the world of criminals. Both circuits are all about power, money and surviving. The character of Bo Xiang is the link between these two worlds. The novel's irony lies perhaps primarily in the fact that the tycoon's empire collapses in the end, whereas the European banking sector simply goes on with business as usual. Lanoye denies that his novel therefore represents a pessimistic view of the world.

> I am actually a rather cheerful pessimist who keeps getting enraged and wants to debate. My book ends with the message that the circle is closed: banks change their names and then continue to do business as usual. This shows that we now have a new aristocracy, just like we used to have counts and dukes. When they go bankrupt, they are saved by us. The profit is theirs, the losses are for the rest of us. How else could my book end except on an almost cynical, desperate note?[45]

Public Sphere/Public Space: City, Blog, Novel

In 2015, Luyendijk published his book *Dit kan niet waar zijn* [This cannot be true], based on his digital project. Like the blog, the book focuses on what bankers themselves say: we meet a lot of the characters that were already introduced in the blog. This time, however, their voices become part of a story that is controlled by Luyendijk himself as first-person narrator. He uses a lot of spatial metaphors: 'the City as a Village', 'Planet Finance', 'the World of Zero Job Security', the bank as an 'Island Empire in the Fog', and, finally, 'the City as a Bubble'. Still, the book contains hardly any descriptions of actual spaces. Luyendijk invariably meets the people he speaks with in the same anonymous pubs and watering holes where bankers tend to gather. This anonymity is partly due to his operating method but also illustrates how detached the City Bubble has become from the world around it.

Luyendijk was not able to take a direct look inside the banks themselves – he could not get access – so he has had to rely on the pictures that others painted for him. His is not an insider's perspective, but one from the outside.

> I did get into a few banks a few times, because people took risks and pretended they didn't know who I was. But broadly speaking, it meant meeting people from the tribe outside the village and asking them what was going on in the village. So that's primarily research into how people see themselves and others rather than into what actually goes on, because what actually goes on is shrouded in fog.[46]

The bankers he interviewed all lived in London, where the housing prices are many times higher than in the rest of the country and where the luxuries of city life perhaps also contribute to their idea that the world of the City is *the* world and not an anomaly. Also, these companies' offices are so close together that it is much easier to hop from one job to the next and this creates an anonymous bubble: 'The City is a bubble and you are either in it or not.'[47] Bankers in London work so many hours and so hard that there is no distinction between work and leisure any more. Also, in their personal lives they socialize only with partners and friends from the same class.

> They work double-full time. One of the problems is that they overdo it at work. Most of them, even the ones in support functions ... all of them work more than they'd need to in similar jobs. ... The actual bankers, they work and they work and they work. This, I think, is one of the problems: that they're living in a bubble and they're surrounded by people who live in the same bubble. They usually marry someone from that bubble, and over time they lose touch with the rest of society.[48]

This is why in London you find a group of people who behave like a tribe with established hierarchies and where everything is about status. 'I think on the whole it's a misunderstanding to think that it's about money; I think it's primarily, for bankers, a status game, and the amount of money they make marks their position in the hierarchy.'[51] This results in a specific type of social behaviour.

> Yes – and this is really important – it's about where you live in London, and how you live, where you send your children to school, the clothes you wear, the kind of holidays you take. ... The way you do this [show commitment – SB] is by essentially spending everything. You send your children to the most expensive school within your means, you go on the most extravagant holiday you can, you live in the most expensive house you can, because by doing so you signal: 'Yes, I'm in it for the long run. I'll do anything in order to keep my job, and to grow.'[50]

The fact that these bankers all live in a specific part of London is part of the problem:

> The city does have an impact on the banking sector, for instance through the system of private education, which means that people are really chained to their jobs. Add to this the real estate bubble plus the class system which, at least for the British, very strongly determines their social status.[51]

In his book, Luyendijk illustrates how the lifestyle in London's City coincides with the lives of people working in banks:

> So there you are, a British father or mother. Some religious schools are very good, but they are only for religious people. Some of the free state-run schools are good enough, so you won't squander your chances of a place at one of the elite universities. But the houses near these schools are astronomically expensive. ... London has created an even bigger real estate bubble than Amsterdam, even though bank employees often get a discount on their mortgage interest. If they lose their job, they also lose this discount and they cannot be absolutely sure they will quickly find work elsewhere. In any case, jobs outside the sector pay at least 20 per cent less. Can they then still afford the tuition fees? People with children of school age are really struggling in that respect.[52]

It is in this light that we must interpret the statement of one of the former bankers in Luyendijk's book, who says that the City seems to be almost designed to 'detach people from society'. Another interviewee associates the evaporation of moral judgement – so central to Luyendijk's analysis – explicitly with living in the City:

> It is all very dense. All those pubs and bars around the corner where people can meet quickly and discreetly. It becomes an enormous playground, a social network within easy reach. Colleagues become buddies. Add alcohol and entertaining clients, when you are fêted by someone who has a business agenda, and you have an explosive mix. Lines are easily crossed.[53]

The motive underlying this sidestepping of moral barriers is not so much 'greed' but keeping up the now achieved social status: 'money comes and goes, but lifestyle stays'. (p. 65) People become prisoners of the lifestyle they have grown accustomed to. After all, the system works like this: within the space of an hour anyone's status can change from being very important to being totally unimportant. Without any employment protection you may be dismissed at any moment and immediately lose your high income. Then you have to leave your social environment because it is based on your salary, which you earn in competition with all your colleagues and people like you who live in the same part of London. Fear and maintaining social status are the key words. These bankers do not regard themselves at all as 'masters of the universe', as is sometimes alleged. 'They are not even masters of their own fate. Because they can be out of the door within five minutes. But they like to believe they are masters of the universe, and they are in total and complete denial about the fact that they can be fired in five minutes.'[54]

London is far away in *Gelukkige slaven;* even more so as the story is mostly situated outside of Europe. Although Lanoye had already used the fictional character of Tony Hanssen in his debut novel, in this latest novel life in Belgium only figures as a longing. The one Tony Hanssen is on the run from the creditors of the bank he helped collapse and his only desire is to return to his wife Martine and daughter Klaartje. The other Tony Hanssen represses the thought of his pathetic parents until, at the end of the story, he suddenly has a Skype session with his father's young girlfriend.

From her he learns that his mother has died and this shakes him to the core. 'What he had hated suddenly turned out to no longer exist. It made his hatred look ridiculous, and him too.' (p. 245)

Both Hanssens are globetrotters, but Lanoye also presents them as people who are on the run in a globalized world – a world that is never in their grasp. This results in a continual longing for home, for security, for a rootedness that seems no longer possible. They resign themselves to their nomadic existence. 'A man should feel at home somewhere, if need be in nothingness.' (p. 28) In Africa, at the rhino's feeding ground, Tony even feels a longing for Brussels. 'The reality around the office towers. Too little had he enjoyed its overwhelming, multi-coloured chaos, it cacophony of languages, its range of striking faces from all over the world. ... Brussels was an unruly but great city. He felt at home there more than he cared to admit.' (p. 117)

In any case, both Hanssens have a complex relationship with the public space of the city. They are never 'at home' anywhere, as we already saw. They always find themselves in semi-public, urban spaces: hotels, airplanes, taxis, cruise ships, ambulances, hospitals, South African game parks, restaurants and airports. These places make up a middle ground between the private space ('home') and the public space (the 'street' or the 'media'). That both Tonys seek out these 'interspaces' is related to the fact that they are always on the run: they wish to be present as little as possible, to avoid the danger of being detected by businessman Bo Xiang or the authorities. Both Tonys do have a 'home' in Belgium, but it is alienated, and unreachable except as a fantasy.

Both Hanssens are very much world citizens of today, and so Lanoye places them in a context of tourism. When the ex-banker Hanssen gets ready to shoot the rhinoceros, he remembers a vacation he once had with his wife and daughter in South Africa when he was still working for the bank (p. 64). The other Tony, as we have seen, worked for a while as 'host and later as cruise director on the most luxurious cruise ships of the world' (p. 82), presenting us with a far from positive image of today's tourists:

> They gorged themselves on food and drink, danced and fornicated all night long. The next day they rotated their fat bodies in the sun by the on-deck swimming pool like almost hairless seals, lazy and bloated from feeding. Their lifelong existence of neglect and stress had to be compensated by

> three weeks of excessive inactivity, in an Ark that could have survived the Flood twice over. (p. 82)

In his private life too he is a tourist: he accompanies Mrs Xiang on her pleasure trips across the globe. He compares Buenos Aires with another place they visited together:

> Monaco had turned out to be a façade, a Disneyland for billionaires, a cardboard skyline, a flashy quarantine zone for upstart louts, sanctimoniously clean and hilariously chic, an architectural neurosis for extras in a light opera. But this city, Buenos Aires, was a true city. Unashamedly dirty, sincerely impure, unruly and unavoidable. (p. 36)

While the one Tony Hanssen experiences the South African game reserve as a jungle that he prefers to his working environment in Brussels, this Tony prefers the impure Buenos Aires to the fake worlds of millionaires. It is no coincidence that Lanoye situates both characters on historically 'polluted' ground: there are references to the history of apartheid in South Africa and to previous dictatorships in Argentina.

In contrast with these places that are in a sense embedded in world history, there is the country where Bo Xiang resides and where the grand finale of the novel unfolds: China. In the novel, cities such as Macau and Ghuangzhou resemble Joris Luyendijk's London the most. This is already evident from the similarities between the covers of *Dit kan niet waar zijn* (featuring the skyline of the London City) and *Gelukkige slaven* (which has a picture of Shenzhen in China). Lanoye describes Macau as follows:

> Fashionable towers lured visitors with either a rotating restaurant on the top floor or water gardens on the ground floor where – all through the night and to constantly changing music – computer-controlled fountains performed multi-coloured ballets of water and light. The world's largest gambling palace, The Venetian, was a city within the city. (p. 85)

Just like the City in London is a 'city-within-the-city', here 'the largest gambling palace' is just that. The analogy speaks volumes. These gambling halls make up Bo Xiang's real empire. This is how he enslaves people: by first treating them like royalty, but once they fall and incur debts they are in his power.

> Row after row of symmetrically placed slot machines bleeped their welcome to hundreds of players or advised them to double their bets in metallic voices. The women had eyes that betrayed either madness or drug use, the men chain-smoked and hawked like fishwives. They all had popcorn buckets full of coins in their hands. (p. 86)

The second part of the novel ('Union') takes place exclusively in China, in the city of Guangzhou, to be precise, on the 50th and 81st floors of the hotel where Bo Xiang has placed both Hanssens. Their rooms overlook the Pearl River as well as the busy traffic flows of the city. What does Tony see when he looks out the window?

> A labyrinth of fly-overs and boulevards filled with Western cars, thousands of pedestrians, cyclists, trams and taxis united in double flows of traffic, coming and going, linked to each other by the zipper of the crash barriers. ... The whole thing was surrounded by a forest of skyscrapers. (p. 154)

In this part, Tony stays in a hotel room almost all the time, so we do not get to see much of the city except the generic interior of the hotel room, 'the invariably fresh room climate of international hotel chains'. (pp. 153 and 207) Then, at the end of the novel, the Tonys go to a restaurant to negotiate with Bo Xiang. Here, the picture changes dramatically.

> It was a mortifying sight. Mr Bo Xiang squinted and looked quite drunk. His eyes, beady to begin with, swam behind his swollen, watery eyelids. A bubble of snot protruded from one nostril, sweat was dripping from his forehead, his mouth hung open in misery. (p. 260)

Toy boy Tony (consequently referred to by his namesake as 'that moron') understands that something is wrong, but banker Tony thinks only of the deal of a lifetime he is about to make. At the end he all but floats through the streets, proud of his achievement and in love with the city. Never again does he want to go back to 'that odorous navel of a worn-out continent' where 'everything is stuck'.

> The further he walked and the more he looked about, the clearer he understood what was going on. He had fallen for this city. Not even for the city itself. He had fallen head over heels in love with the life it promised him, like the animals the cooks had offered him to eat. Abundant, within reach, inexhaustible and trembling with life force. His future was here. (p. 275)

That turns out to be an ironic truth. On the next page he drops dead. The other Tony looks at the banker and suddenly realizes that he is just as big a moron as he himself is: 'This was a shrimp who thought he was a swordfish.' (p. 278)

> 'I looked up to him too much,' concluded Tony, 'because I knew nothing of his domain. Then admiration comes easily. But he too,' Tony thought, 'was out of his league tonight. A brilliant computer linguist, but an absolute beginner when it came to real trading.' (p. 278)

While the swordfish-deluded Tony exclaims that 'the bubble should never have burst' and that 'we should have just kept going' he finally loses his way forever and falls down on the pavement. This is also the end of this part of the novel, which brings us to the third part, ironically entitled 'Hope'. It is the part where the remaining Tony is recruited at the airport to continue life as a banker, posing as his former companion.

Conclusion

The case of Luyendijk and Lanoye presents us with two contrasting ways of responding to social reality: the discursive-argumentative approach of the journalist Luyendijk and the fictional-imaginary one of the writer Lanoye. It would seem that of these two Lanoye comes closest to what Odile Heynders, in her contribution to this collection of essays, calls 'urban imaginaries' or what Judith Vega calls the 'actual embodiment' of human life in the city: fictional/artistic works that present an image of social or urban reality, thus offering an 'alternative scenario' for reality.

This theory offers an interesting perspective on what Luyendijk and Lanoye have to say about the banking sector. With his blog, Luyendijk makes an explicit contribution to the argumentative, political debate about the financial crisis. In interviews and columns, Lanoye too contributes to this debate, but he also makes it very clear in interviews that *Gelukkige slaven* is a work of fiction. He even states explicitly that he does not regard his novel as contributing to the political debate (as *Max Havelaar* is supposed to have done in its day), but that by writing it he actually became more empathic towards his characters.

Because it consists of language, the literary novel finds itself by definition between public *sphere* and public *space*, or between *public* space and *private* space. Novelists do indeed enter the discursive debate because they use words and voice opinions, but since they fictionalize and 'imagine', they often just show things rather than take up a position. If the latter is true, novels can contribute to the embodiment of public presence, as Judith Vega advocates. Can we observe the Tony Hanssens in *Gelukkige slaven* from that perspective?

Is Lanoye showing us people who are not visible to us in the public sphere? Both Tonys seem more like embodiments of the (futile) attempt to be absent from the public space. They emphatically avoid the public space of the cities they are in, just like Luyendijk's bankers favour the anonymity of the bars in their own city-within-the-city. It is no coincidence that the novel ends with the one Tony being recognized and taken back to his past. Also, the narrator in the novel *Gelukkige slaven* shows a lot less empathy than the interviewed author would have us believe. The narrator actually adopts a quite detached attitude, framing himself as part of a 'we' watching what happens to both characters from a distance. Besides, he is an ubiquitous almighty narrator ('that is still to come', 'things would turn out differently').

Thus both characters are not so much embodied as constructed. What we see here is mostly 'theatricality', behaviour that is being 'performed'. The characters are constructions of a narrator and serve primarily to support his argument. Eventually he bestows on the two characters all kinds of qualities that in the public discourse are reserved for 'evil bankers': greed, egotism, lack of morality. By avoiding the public space in their attempts to survive, the two Tonys embody the banker's cliché as people beyond morality, as instruments of a global criminal capitalist network. Lanoye applies the cliché-like templates readily available within the public debate to colour his characters and in a sense denies them their presence as people in the public space.

Joris Luyendijk treats 'his' bankers (the 'voices of finance') with a lot more empathy than Lanoye does in his novel. Luyendijk came into contact with real bankers and made an effort to listen to their personal stories. This allowed him to paint a much more nuanced picture of the causes of the economic crisis and make the bankers look a lot more human. Luyendijk took up the position of the impartial (virtually invisible) interviewer and published their words on his website without immediately subjecting them to a prescribed, and ideological, narrative. Also, in his columns and essays, he has stressed that we cannot speak of 'the banker' as a stereotype but should always look at individual cases.

Luyendijk gives a voice to people who, for various reasons, have remained invisible in the public discourse about the financial crisis, and shows which bankers are in what positions and how they act. His project opposes cliché-like sketches of bankers in the public *sphere* and gives them a face in the public *space*. Lanoye uses his freedom as a writer to make up his characters and bestow them with all kinds of qualities copied from the people in Luyendijk's blog. It is remarkable that the writer Lanoye reduces these characters in this novel to the cliché image of the 'happy slave', whereas the journalist Luyendijk with his journalistic project makes much more of a contribution to the embodiment of subjectivity in the public space, thereby offering, in a sense, more of an 'artistic intervention in or constitution of' that public space.

Notes

1 Sjoen Lieven, 'Het voelt lekker om hier te zijn', *De Standaard*, 7 September 2013. (all passages from originally Dutch texts are translated for this essay by Leo Reijnen).
2 Ibid.
3 Ibid.
4 Ibid.
5 About realism, see Sander Bax, *De taak van de schrijver: Het poëticale debat in de Nederlandse literatuur (1968-1985)* (PhD diss., Tilburg University, 2007) (Den Bosch: Next Academic, 2007), pp. 225-30, webwijs.uvt.nl/publications/481908_ext.pdf. Cf: Frank Harbers, 'Defying Journalistic Performativity: The Tension between Journalism and Literature in Arnon Grunberg's Reportage', *Interférences littéraires/ Literaire interferenties* 7 (2011), pp. 141-63.
6 Tom Wolfe, *The New Journalism* (London: Pan Books, 1980), pp. 20-21.
7 Frans Ruiter and Wilbert Smulders, 'Van moedwil tot misverstand, van Dorleijn tot Vaessens: Kritische kanttekeningen uit het veld', *Tijdschrift voor Nederlandse Taal- en Letterkunde* 126 (2010-2) 1, pp. 63-85; Frans Ruiter and Wilbert Smulders, 'The Aggressive Logic of Singularity: Willem Frederik Hermans', *Journal of Dutch Literature* 4 (2013) 1, pp. 4-42.
8 I use the terms disinterest, independence, uniqueness and fictionality for easy reference to the four forms of autonomy that I distinguished in Sander Bax, 'Over literatuur, engagement en autonomie: De literaire schrijver als onruststoker', *De Leeswolf* 16 (2010-6) 4, pp. 278-81. See also: Sander Bax, *De Mulisch mythe: Harry Mulisch: schrijver, intellectueel, icoon* (Amsterdam: Meulenhoff, 2015).
9 Frans Ruiter, 'Wat is er eigenlijk literair aan het literaire essay?' (paper presented at the Third Cross-Over Conference at the Leiden University, 12 January 2011), p. 12.
10 Lieven De Cauter and Michiel Dehaene, 'The Space of Play: Towards a General Theory of Heterotopia', in *Heterotopia and the City: Public Space in a Postcivil Society*, ed. Michiel Dehaene and Lieven De Cauter (London: Routledge, 2008), pp. 87-102, p. 96.
11 Judith Vega, 'Imagining the City: The Difference that Art Makes', in *Contemporary Culture: New Directions in Art and Humanities Research*, ed. Judith Thissen, Robert Zwijnenberg and Kitty Zijlmans (Amsterdam: Amsterdam University Press, 2013), pp. 51-61, p. 53.
12 Ibid., p. 54.
13 Ibid., p. 55.
14 Ibid.
15 Joris Luyendijk, *Het zijn net mensen: Beelden uit het Midden-Oosten* (Amsterdam: Podium, 2006), p. 210.
16 Joris Luyendijk, Johan de Witt lecture 'Naar een nieuwe journalistiek' [Towards a New Journalism'], Dordrecht, 15 October 2009, www.villamedia.nl/docs/johan%20de%20witt%20lezing.pdf.
17 Ibid.
18 Ibid.
19 Ibid.
20 Ibid.
21 Interview in writing of Sander Bax with Joris Luyendijk, 7 November 2014. All citations in this and the next three paragraphs were taken from this interview.
22 Hugo Brems, *Altijd weer vogels die nesten beginnen: Geschiedenis van de Nederlandse literatuur 1945-2005* (Amsterdam: Bert Bakker, 2006).
23 Quoted from: Bertram Mourits, 'Niet bij poëzie alleen: Tom Lanoye als dichter', *De Revisor* 34 (2007), pp. 55-65, p. 56.
24 Ibid., p. 61.
25 Ibid., p. 64.
26 Ibid.
27 Ibid.
28 Marc Dutroux is a Belgian serial killer and child molester, convicted of having kidnapped, tortured and sexually abused six girls from 1995 to 1996, ranging in age from 8 to 19, four of whom he murdered. (Source: Wikipedia)
29 Bertram Mourits, 'Je kunt ook zwijgen: Een gesprek met Tom Lanoye', *Passionate* 12 (2005), pp. 37-41, p. 39.
30 Ibid., p. 40
31 Cyrille Offermans, 'Een Vlaamse Rabelais', in *Wat er op het spel staat: Literatuur en kunst na 1945* (Amsterdam: Cossee, 2014), pp. 255-59.
32 Bart Eeckhout, 'Waar is de schaamte van rechts?', *De Morgen*, 4 September 2013.
33 Ibid.
34 Arjen Fortuin, 'Ik ben een blije pessimist', *NRC Next*, 6 September 2013.
35 Joris Luyendijk, 'Het kan zo weer gebeuren', *NRC Handelsblad*, 2 October 2013. (www.nrc.nl/nieuws/2013/10/02/het-kan-zo-weer-gebeuren/, accessed 16 December 2014).
36 Bax, interview.
37 Ibid.

38 Arjen Mulder, 'The City People Tribe: An interview with Joris Luyendijk by Arjen Mulder', in *Giving and Taking: Antidotes to a Culture of Greed*, ed. Joke Brouwer and Sjoerd van Tuinen (Rotterdam: V2/NAi Publishers, 2014), p. 57–77, p. 57.
39 Ibid., p. 68.
40 Ibid., p. 60.
41 Ibid.
42 Luyendijk, 'Het kan zo weer gebeuren'.
43 Ibid.
44 Tom Lanoye, *Gelukkige slaven* (Amsterdam: Prometheus, 2013), p. 89
45 Ann Peeteman and Hubert van Humbeeck, '"Ik blijf liberaal, en ik geloof dat Tom Lanoye dat ook is": Dubbel en dwars: Paul De Grauwe and Tom Lanoye', *Knack Magazine*, 4 September 2013.
46 Mulder, 'The City People Tribe', p. 58.
47 Bax, interview.
48 Mulder, 'The City People Tribe', p. 62.
49 Ibid., p. 64.
50 Ibid., p. 65.
51 Bax, interview.
52 Joris Luyendijk, *Dit kan niet waar zijn: Onder bankiers* (Amsterdam: Atlas/Contact, 2015), p. 142.
53 Ibid., p. 176.
54 Mulder, 'The City People Tribe', p. 66.

Cities & Signs
Rethinking Calvino's Urban Imaginaries

Odile Heynders

A Hybrid Literary Text

Italo Calvino's *Invisible Cities*[1] (1972) can be characterized both as exploratory fiction and a narrative without a conventional plot, and as a tale in which the various images are pieces of a meticulously composed puzzle. The 55 city miniatures can also be considered prose poems, as the texts present words that hint rather than describe, addressing imagination over reference, and showing the potential of density and subversiveness. The pieces contain a philosophical insight that is expressed poetically, which implies that things that we find in the world are reordered here. The notion of reordering is used by philosopher Simon Critchley in his essay on the work of American poet Wallace Stevens, who writes poetry on things *as they are.* This evokes, as Critchley underscores, an anti-realist interpretation in which poetry is read as an 'act of the mind'.[2] Calvino's prose poems on cities, on the contrary, are rather fairy-tale like and enigmatic, but they invoke an interpretation, I argue in this paper, that brings the emphasis back to reality.

Invisible Cities, definitely a classic of European literature, not only consists of the 55 prose poems, but in the framing dialogue it also is a text on meeting the other, bringing together different cultures, fantasies and attitudes. The text is structured around the conversation between two historical figures: the Venetian adventurer Marco Polo (1254–1323) and the Chinese emperor Kublai Kahn (1215–1294). Their fictional dialogue is on cities, and even though it seems clear that Polo is the one who has travelled and is reporting all the time, the reader immediately senses that the act of speaking as such is more mysterious. The conversation is mixed up with dreams, hallucinations, and critique. As Kathryn Hume observes, *Invisible Cities* 'turns out not to be the travelogues of one middle-aged man reporting to another ... but rather the occasional words, the silent interpretations of emblems, and even the Khan's re-creations of what Polo might have said had Polo spoken'.[3] Hume suggests that we do not really know what is and what is not said, what is imagined and what is seen and by whom. The reader has to find a particular method or strategy of interpretation for this text.

Calvino makes us aware of the fact that when we read, we have to *do* something: construct a meaning, be active in building an understanding and in assembling all the various ideas, perspectives, speech acts and fantasies. Where are the boundaries between the words of the author, the narrative construct, or the two conversation partners? How to notice one aspect and not deliberately oversee another? To illustrate the complexity in particular in regard to the narrative frame of the text, let us take a passage from the conversation at the end of chapter three:

> The Great Kahn has dreamed of a city; he describes it to Marco Polo:
>
> 'The harbor faces north, in shadow. The docks are high over the black water, which slams against the retaining walls; stone steps descend, made slippery by seaweed. Boats smeared with tar are tied up, waiting for the departing passengers lingering on the quay to bid their families farewell. The farewells take place in silence, but with tears' ...
>
> 'Set out, explore every coast, and seek this city', the Khan says to Marco. 'Then come back and tell me if my dream corresponds to reality.'
>
> 'Forgive me, my Lord, there is no doubt that sooner or later I shall set sail from that dock', Marco says, 'but I shall not come back to tell you about it. The city exists and it has a simple secret: it knows only departures, not returns.' (p. 47)

Italian entrepreneur Marco Polo is at the court in China and has reported on the cities he has travelled through. The emperor, in reaction to all the tales and stories, exposes a dream city, and imagines the ceremony of departure. His conversation partner recognizes this vision, but counters the Kahn's dream by arguing that although the city *exists*, one cannot come back from it. This mystifying image of a city from which one can only depart, immediately elicits interpretations of human life as ending; after passing away there is no chance on re-entering the city of life again. However, this connotation is challenged by the meticulous descriptions of the cities: they are depicted in all their details.

The reader has to take the conversation between the emperor and the traveller seriously, but at the same time will be aware of the willing suspension of disbelief, as Samuel Taylor Coleridge has called it.[4] This implies that one accepts that this is a fictional narrative and, thus, that one has to take a distance from the logical, discursive dimension of the dialogue. We cannot but take notice that Marco Polo is not answering the question asked by the Kahn, whether the dream corresponds to reality, and it could be argued that what we read could be taken as 'the inner workings of one or of two minds', whose exchanges are sometimes wordless.[5] Hence, reading Calvino encourages counter-intuitive thinking, taking other paths, so to say, through the text. We will never arrive at a truth located *within* the text, yet we will become aware of the potential of meaning and of our ability to create and experience it.

The main question of this publication is how art may contribute to the constitution of a public sphere, and this question definitely comes to the fore when discussing Calvino's masterpiece and the various perspectives from which it can be interpreted. Significantly, all descriptions of the 55 cities, with enchanting women's names such as Octavia, Eudoxia, Fedora, Isaura, Cecilia or Berenice, more or less vaguely remind us of the Italian city that Marco Polo departed from. Venice, obviously, is one of the historic Italian city-states, which in the early-modern period established a socio-economic and political power and became a republic with global influence. In the Middle Ages it already was a powerful urban space, and from the thirteenth to the sixteenth centuries it became a leading maritime power. The singularity of Venice, however, is not only political, but geographical or architectural as well. The city, indeed, is built in the lagoon of the Adriatic, on numerous islands separated by canals and connected by bridges. As a fantastic *real* construction of stone, water and mud, the city is portrayed by famous authors such as Joseph Brodsky or Thomas Mann,[6] as a dying city, slowly sinking in the salt water, and as such representative of the European culture and heritage in decline.

But Calvino's imagination of the 55 cities, or 55 Venices, is also representative of the prosperous modern city; among them are trading cities with a continuous 'voluptuous vibration' (p. 44), in which we observe architectural highlights with 'alabaster gates transparent in the sunlight' and 'coral columns supporting pediments encrusted with serpentine' and 'villas all of glass like aquariums'. (p. 95) A critique of the consequences of Western modernity is provided too, for example in the counter-image of globalized cities looking similar: 'I was landing at the same airport from which I had taken off. The suburbs they drove me through were no different from the others.' (p. 116) Furthermore, Calvino depicts consumerism as polluted cities drenched in garbage: each year 'the city expands ... the bulk of the outflow increases and the piles rise higher'. (p. 102) And next to these we observe cities as fortresses: 'pale buildings back to back in mangy fields, among plank fences and corrugated-iron sheds'. (p. 141) All these different cities can be recognized as representations and critical interpretations of contemporary urban spaces, demonstrating the actuality of the text, as if the author could foresee in the 1970s how the world and cities would transform rapidly in the coming decades. So, to present a first answer to the question posed in this book – how does art contribute to the public sphere? – I would argue that Calvino's literary work discusses various topics regarding modern urbanism, and as such the author critiques contemporary culture and politics.

But, intriguingly, we could just as well argue the opposite. Calvino might not have been interested in participating in public debates at all, and that is why he depicts cities as more or less abstract fantasies and imaginary spaces, which the identifiable protagonist – the historical figure of Marco Polo the traveler from Venice – does not regard as a continuity of places. In the fairy-tale construction, in the framed dialogue and the mathematical composition of the work, Calvino undermines the functioning of a critical multi-voiced public sphere, and encapsulates himself in the position of the subversive modernist author who does not believe at all in the power and opinions of the public. We will see how both arguments can be further elaborated, once we follow one path through the text, reading the parts on 'Cities & Signs'. In what follows, I will scrutinize these pieces to discover the various levels and consequences of representation and, for that matter, of critiquing the public sphere.

An Itinerary through the 'Cities & Signs'

The five 'Cities & Signs' all appear in the first half of the book: two pieces in chapter one, the other three in the subsequent chapters. The orderly arrangement of the text and the taxonomy of the various cities are captivating. In his *Il Milione*,[7] the historical Marco Polo classified cities by religion, political affiliation and particular features such as trade or crafts. For example, in Tinanfu people make horse harnesses and wine, and in Hekienfu they have silk.[8] That categorization was not rigidly ordered. The mathematical arrangement of cities with Calvino has the function to structure the text, to keep it together as an urban project, since an explicit plot is missing. This is what Calvino himself explained:

> When I began writing *Invisible Cities* I had only a vague idea of what the frame, the architecture of the book would be. But then, little by little, the design became so important that it carried the entire book; it became the plot of a book that had no plot.[9]

The Fibonacci-inspired[10] composition of the book is based on sets of cities grouped together, as an urban plan or global network. Next to the Cities & Signs we find: Cities & Memory, Cities & Desire, Thin Cities, Trading Cities, Cities & Eyes, Cities & Names, Cities & the Dead, Cities & the Sky, Hidden Cities, and the Continuous Cities. These eleven categories of cities are spread over 9 parts of the text in which 55 prose poems are collected, and as such the text appears like an urban grid, recognizable in modernized cities but labyrinthine in medieval ones.

This architecture of the book as a whole underlines the explicitly formulated ideas on signs and signification in the five segments of 'Cities & Signs', which can be taken as a semiotic theory on the understanding of various features and characteristics of cities.[11] In these texts, Calvino sharpens his ideas on language, meaning and representation. But in the expressions on signs and signification another perspective becomes clear as well, one that points at imaginaries as mental constructions on how someone observes his surroundings. The idea is that watching and seeing are always influenced by images, stories, and legends. This implies that what we see is rooted in what we have seen before, or have read, or have heard from others. Of relevance here is the notion 'social imaginary', as it was coined by Charles Taylor (2004),[12] based on Benedict Anderson's *Imagined Communities*,[13] and elaborated by Andreas Huyssen (2008) with a special focus on the experiences of urbanization in a globalizing age. Huyssen explains – with an explicit reference to Calvino's *Invisible Cities* – that urban imaginaries,

> differ depending on a multitude of perspectives and subject positions. All cities are palimpsests of real and diverse experiences and memories. They comprise a great variety of spatial practices, including architecture and planning, administration and business, labour and leisure, politics, culture and everyday life.[14]

In regard to the specific pieces of 'Cities & Signs', imaginaries seem an appropriate concept to understand the ideas on sign, representation, and memory that Calvino underlines. Let's take a route through the five cities.

The first 'Cities & Signs' brings us to Tamara, with streets 'thick with signboards jutting from the walls'. (p. 11) We could imagine here a lively urban space such as for instance Besiktas in Istanbul, Kreuzberg in Berlin, or Montmartre in Paris, although there is almost no reference to people acting in Calvino's text. The city is reached after days in the wilderness. The contrast between trees and stones outside of the city, and the buildings within is big; it is the difference between what *is* and what *means*, as Marco Polo as focalizer emphasizes. This is how the distinction is indicated,

> You walk for days among trees and among stones. Rarely does the eye light on a thing, and then only when it has recognized that thing as the sign of another thing: a print in the sand indicates the tiger's passage; a marsh announces a vein of water; the hibiscus flower, the end of winter. All the rest is silent and interchangeable; trees and stones are only what they are. (p. 11)

In Tamara the eye does not see things, but images of things that mean other things. Pincers point out the tooth-drawer's house, a tankard points at the tavern, a halberd refers to the barracks, and so on. There are signals warning what is forbidden and what is allowed in a particular place. Marco Polo observes religious buildings, and edifices without a 'signboard or figure', thus establishing their special function as palace, prison or brothel. Everything in the city seems to be a sign of other things, with the consequence that 'your gaze scans the streets as if they were written pages'. (p. 12) But noticing all these signs does not bring one closer to 'however the city may really be ... whatever it may contain or conceal'. (p. 12) Somehow the signs keep us away from the things as they are. Hence, what the reality of nature is, does not relate to the reality of the city: a culture constructed by humans.

The point Calvino is making in all the five 'Cities & Signs' pieces, is that language does not refer to the reality of a city that exists *as such*. This idea can be understood in the context of the work of the American rhetorician Kenneth Burke,[15] who developed the idea of man as the symbol-using animal.[16] We are familiar with using many different terminologies, Burke (1966) explains, and much of what we mean by reality has been only built up through our symbol systems: maps, magazines, newspapers and so on. Man clings to a kind of naïve verbal realism that refuses to realize the full extent of the role played by 'symbolicity in his notions of reality',[17] writes Burke, and he continues with a relevant example,

> A road map that helps us easily find our way from one side of the continent to the other owes its great utility to its exceptional existential poverty. It tells us absurdly little about the trip that is to be experienced in a welter of detail. Indeed, its value for us is in the very fact that it is so essentially inane.[18]

Marco Polo's variant is this: 'the city says everything you must think, makes you repeat her discourse, and while you believe you are visiting Tamara you are only recording the names with which she defines herself and all her parts'. (p. 12) So, staying or living in Tamara means that one takes up the signs as symbols. It implies being encapsulated in a specific discourse or symbol-system, but it never leads to the core or essence of what the city *is*.

This brings us to the second and shortest piece of 'Cities & Signs', in which Zirma is visited. Zirma is an estranging memory and repetitive description of peculiar people: a blind black man, a lunatic, and a girl walking with a puma. Then, the memories are erased with the sentence: 'the city is redundant: it repeats itself so that something will stick in mind'. (p. 16) This, obviously, ties in with the words in the previous piece; the individual is part of the discourse of the city but can also disconnect from it. Subsequently, the narrating and experiencing 'I' – whom we presume to be Marco Polo – asserts that he is returning from Zirma, and he reveals his memory of dirigibles flying in all directions, tattoo shops and obese women in underground trains – we can easily imagine an American subway scene here. His travelling companions however – Marco Polo the historical figure did travel with his father Niccolò and uncle Matteo[19] – only saw a separate dirigible, one tattoo artist and one fat woman. This leads to the conclusion: 'Memory is redundant: it repeats signs so that the city can begin to exist.' (p. 16)

Again the emphasis is not on what a city *is*, but on how it starts to become real once it is described in words and visualized in images. Cities are imaginaries and experiences. Huyssen's description is helpful at this point:

> an urban imaginary is the cognitive and somatic image which we carry within us of the places where we live, work, and play. It is an embodied material fact. Urban imaginaries are thus part of any city's reality, rather than being only figments of the imagination. What we think of a city and how we perceive it informs the ways we act in it.[20]

The point made by Calvino in regard to Zirma, is that no one who becomes part of a city, who enters it and strolls around, can do without imagination and memory by which the signs, images and discourses are collected and interpreted. In the description of each specific city, within the narrative context of the conversation between Kahn and Polo, Calvino interweaves ideas on signification and mediation. In prose poems he thus develops a theory on signs and meaning in regard to urban experiences.

What Marco Polo tells about Zoe, in the third piece of 'Cities & Signs', again puts the emphasis on imaginaries. The suggestion is that every traveller has a general idea about a city:

> The man who is traveling and does not yet know the city awaiting him along his route wonders what the palace will be like, the barracks, the mill, the theater, the bazaar. In every city of the empire every building is different and set in a different order: but as soon as the stranger arrives at the unknown city and his eye penetrates the pine cone of pagodas and garrets and haymows, following the scrawl of canals, gardens, rubbish heaps, he immediately distinguishes which are the princes' palaces, the high priests' temples, the tavern, the prison, the slum. This – some say – confirms the hypothesis that each man bears in his mind a city made only of differences, a city without figures and without form, and the individual cities fill it up. (p. 29)

If we continue this line of thinking, we could argue that everyone who has grown up in Europe knows the typical model of a city: a church, a central marketplace, a city hall, streets, outskirts, green surroundings. Zoe, however, does not fit in this mind pattern of a city. The traveller 'roams all around and has nothing but doubts:

he is unable to distinguish the features of the city, the features he keeps distinct in his mind also mingle'. (p. 29) If there is no element that can be recognized, the conclusion must be that Zoe is a place of 'indivisible existence' and it is not clear what separates the inside from thc outside. What Calvino is describing here, it may be argued, are two different experiences. The first is the experience of someone who has grown up somewhere and has typical features and patterns of that specific culture in mind, who then travels elsewhere and discovers that things are not the same. Patterns do not match. But the meeting of cultures, or even a *cultural clash*, motivates the traveller to adapt his presuppositions, to assimilate (or not) to new standards. The second experience refers back to the real Venice as the a-typical European hometown of Marco Polo. Because Venice is a floating city, built in the lagoon, it does not fit into the regular model of a European city. What is inside and outside if water, light and air are everywhere?

Hypatia, the fourth part in 'Cities & Signs', at first sight seems idyllic: a magnolia garden is reflected in blue lagoons, but the opposite is the case: 'at the bottom of the water crabs were biting the eyes of suicides, stones tied around their necks'. (p. 40) This surrealistic scenery[21] leads to other panoramas: a palace, six tiled courtyards, a hall with chained convicts, a great library, and finally a sage seated on a lawn, saying the cryptic words: 'Signs form a language, but not the one you think you know.' (p. 40) Everything is turned upside down or in juxtaposition in this scene, as becomes clear in the final passage:

> True, also in Hypathia the day will come when my only desire will be to leave. I know I must not go down to the harbor then, but climb the citadel's highest pinnacle and wait for a ship to go by up there. But will it ever go by? There is no language without deceit. (p. 41)

Surrealism, of course, can be considered the ultimate pole of imagination. It leads to unconscious fantasies or fantasies of the unconsciousness, and to the experimental activity in everyday life. We can take as example André Breton's character Nadja, strolling through Paris. The focus is on active exploration of the city space, and thus on making visible what is probably there (or not). The real comes with the force of hallucination, the surrealists thought, and they called this *la pensée sauvage*.[22] This is what comes to the fore when the narrator in the Hypatia prose poem constructs an erotic fantasy about naked women on horses, who, as soon as a young foreigner approaches fling him on piles of hay and press their firm nipples against him.

The final 'Cities & Signs' piece is on the city of Olivia and follows immediately on the dialogue that opens the fourth chapter of the book, in which the changing moods of the emperor of the Tartars are depicted. Sometimes he is depressed and believes that his empire is rotting like a corpse in a swamp; at other, euphoric moments, it feels as if the empire is made of crystals, with molecules arranged in a perfect pattern. When Marco Polo takes the floor again, he does not talk about changing moods, but about words that can frame the city and influence or manipulate our perspectives and expectations. 'No one, wise Kublai,' Polo says, 'knows better than you that the city must never be confused with the words that describe it.' (p. 53) Olivia can be characterized as a city of luxuries: the prosperity of the filigree palaces, and of ladies who glide at night in illuminated canoes. But a description of the 'grease that sticks to the houses' and of a pedestrian crushed against the wall by the shifting trailers could be precise as well. The city could be characterized as a refined civilization, but also as the opposite in the description of men and women, who come back at night to the outskirts of town 'like lines of sleepwalkers'. (p. 53) Marco Polo explains,

> This perhaps you do not know: that to talk of Olivia, I could not use different words. If there really were an Olivia of mullioned windows and peacocks, of saddlers and rug-weavers and canoes and estuaries, it would be a wretched, black, fly-ridden hole, and to describe it, I would have to fall back on the metaphors of soot, the creaking of wheels, repeated actions, sarcasm. Falsehood is never in words; it is in things. (p. 54)

In particular the last sentence turns around the argument under construction about words and representation. Polo suggests that words are not illusory, but things are. Apparently, the city of Olivia has different spheres, of extreme luxury and hard work, and the idea is that the people functioning in these spheres do not realize that they are living in an illusion.

The critique expressed in this description of Olivia, is very recognizable for the twenty-first-century reader, familiar with shining city centres full of Chanel or Louis Vuitton flagship stores, but with the depressing outskirts of cities as well: the Parisian *banlieues*, slums around Mumbai, *favelas* in Rio de Janeiro or parts of Naples currently overcrowded by migrants from Africa seeking refuge. Almost every global city could be taken in mind as representative. This brings us back to the doubleness of argument in *Invisible Cities*: we could argue that it is an engaged message that is underscored here by Marco Polo, to be understood as critique on the social inequality in global cities: falsehood as unbalance and inequality is not in words but in things. But it could as well be argued that what Marco Polo explains here is that Olivia does not exist at all, neither the wealth, nor the poverty. Whatever metaphor is chosen to describe it, the city is just virtual, based on the cognitive images we carry within us.

This latter interpretation encapsulates the concept and practice of urban imaginaries as generated by customs, languages, everyday practices, as well as by images, film, music, literature or social media. In regard to the latter we could demonstrate how the websites of cities effectuate certain ideas and characterizations of urban places. Venice today, for instance, brands itself as a place of 'sustainable cultural tourism', and offers special information for twelve types of people, from 'older person', to 'woman', or 'sportsman'. Interestingly, the 'foreigner' is mentioned as type before the 'tourist'. The foreigner is the potential migrant, as evidenced by the picture of a young black child writing. The Venice website gives foreigners the addresses where to go when entering the city, thus establishing an identity of the city as a place of hospitality.[23]

To sum up, the route we took through the 'Cities & Signs' illustrates Calvino's ideas on signification and meaning as new forms of semiotic practices in cities. A city is not considered a vast entity or place, but is thought of as a process of negotiation of signs and experiences. Roaming through a city implies distinguishing the features and trying to keep them distinct while they also mingle in the mind.

Opening the Space of Literature

The corpus of studies of *Invisible Cities* is impressive; many scholars have analysed and discussed the experience of *estrangement* ('Erfahrung der Fremde')[24] that seems inescapable when reading this book. Various interpretations consider Calvino a post-modern author and underline that although *Invisible Cities* centres on a dialogue between the traveller and the emperor, and offers fantasies of cities as well as ideas on intercultural exchange, the main focus is on the invisible and the never-to-be-reached arrival. The communication takes place within the context of a game of chess, as such a canonical literary theme,[25] and is underlined by the numerological composition of the book. This mathematical structure paradoxically functions as an open work in which 'writing keeps generating itself and where the notion of an ending is only a commercial necessity'.[26] The literary text opens up a space apart from the referential world we live in, and in order to understand the words, we have to accept the evasiveness, elusiveness and inscrutability of the text. What we are reading is 'the encounter between language, the self and reality'.[27] Calvino's text, thus, is the perfect example of what the French philosopher Maurice Blanchot described as the space of literature, that is, a space in which there is no fixed time and presence. Literature opens an interstitial zone in between, in which the meaning of absence is investigated.[28]

I do not want to critique the relevance of a postmodern or Blanchotian[29] perspective on Calvino, or undermine the self-reflective dimension of Calvino's work as literary space. In this article, however, I propose a counter approach to the work by (re)connecting the text to reality. I am interested in a reading of *Invisible Cities* as urban scenario, and I take the prose poems as commentary pieces on globalization. This is literature that in a way precedes reality; what Calvino described in the 1970s is gaining more and more relevance and significance in the twenty-first century where issues of increasing mobility and displacement transform our conceptions of cities as global cities, *supervilles*, world cities or informational cities,[30] that is, places of global economy marked by non-national firms and stock markets.

The five 'Cities & Signs' that we have visited in the previous paragraph can be read as a commentary on the mechanism of urban imaginaries, historical as well as contemporary. The city is not what it is, but is constructed by the way inhabitants see, experience and imagine the space as the place of everyday life, the site of traditions and continuities, as well as scenes of destruction, crime, greediness and conflicts of all kinds.[31] The global city is a grid of material, physical and strategic places.[32] What we read in Calvino's text, I argue, can be linked to experiences of current travellers, cosmopolitan tourist as well as migrants, entering cities and hiding in them all over the world, while encouraged and forced to interpret the various signs and discourses. Calvino's text challenges the idea of the authentic city *as it is*, while pointing at experiences of mobility and transformation that have to be negotiated by semiotic processes.

To give this a more solid foundation, I will discuss some experiences of European migrants moving to cities elsewhere in Europe. How do they describe the imagination, the visibility or invisibility of cities? The data are available at a fascinating website, *Migration and Integration*, organized by the Goethe Institut, and focusing on the European, relatively young urban traveller.[33] Zygmunt Bauman[34] distinguishes different types of travellers in the postmodern era: the stroller, tourist, vagabond and player, but these types have to be supplemented with the new adventurous but also economically driven type we find here: that of the 'European expat living abroad in Europe'. On the website we can find their personal stories on living in a new city. These travellers can be considered the Marco Polos of our age.

The first story I would like to focus on, is told by Tanja Nettersheim, 38 years old and born in Euskirchen, Germany. She has lived in Athens, Greece since 2000 and works there as a business manager. She writes,

> I often live as though in limbo, since I don't feel at home here or in Germany. Once a month I have a dream: I'm going down a winding road through no-man's land on my way to my hometown. Just before arriving, I have to open the gate to a garden. But I can't get it open. When I'm here I long for Germany. When I go there, I'm disappointed that people aren't the way I imagined them.[35]

The analogy with Calvino's text lies in the repeating dream of the winding road through no-man's land. Calvino's Marco Polo describes how he travels for days before arriving in a city, and in this story by the German expat a surrealist dimension is distinguished in the image of the gate that repeatedly cannot be opened. The limbo realm is a suggestive metaphor to describe the living *in between* cultures. There probably is some unconscious conviction of not belonging at either the one or the other place anymore.

A second correspondence to Calvino can be made from the story told by Corinna Lawrenz, 26 years old, born in Nuremberg, Germany, and living as a student in Lisbon since 2011. She tells how the first weeks and months in Lisbon were one big adventure, when every street, every smell, every sound was new and exciting. Then, after two months 'we went ... to a home of our own in what is to me one of the most beautiful neighbourhoods in the city, Graça – an old working-class district with the right mix of traditional life, a little tourism, a couple of bars and gorgeous views from several spots right on our doorstep ... – in a word: we have arrived!'[36] The temporary home is experienced as a place to stay, as 'a mental space where the ... silence [is] streaked by the rustling of leaves' (p. 93). Significantly, a mental space again points to an imaginary realm: this is not home but the idea or feeling of being at home. This is about mood and sphere, not about existence. The third Calvinean story on the website of the Goethe Institut is told by Ignacio Fernandez, 53 years old, born in Toledo and currently living in Brussels. He points at the feeling of immobility of his generation 'isolated within our walls of khaki and cassock-black nostalgia for so long with Europe's acquiescence and immobility'. He is convinced that the twenty-first century will be mobile, and that the population flows will no longer run along the north-south axis, but east-west. He describes Brussels through his Spanish eyes:

> The city looks different on the weekend when Brussels shines again, with its flea markets held on remote squares that are lined with the awnings of neighbourhood cafés, with sunshine – this is a treasure not to be missed. A green mantle envelops the avenues and parks. A tropical blue winds its way through the lanes. The city of illustrators, the Belgian School is renewing with graffiti in hidden local train tunnels and in abandoned factory buildings on industrial estates with no future. As the Bard of Saint-Josse puts it in his song *I like living in Brussels*: 'The city is what it is: a place where all sorts of things are happening and you never realize it.'[37]

The song of the bard sounds like one of Polo's sentences: 'we are allowed to withdraw here ... to ponder what we are seeing and living, to draw conclusions, to contemplate from the distance'. (p. 93) Maybe, they have been in a garden listening to each other's stories and dreams all the time. 'I, too, am not sure I am here' (p. 93)

Kublai answers, 'our dialogue is taking place between two beggars sifting through a rubbish heap.'

The last example of an expat story marking current European cities as 'invisible' in the sense that there is no pure, uncontaminated, monocultural, or monolingual locality, is written by cultural manager Sören Meschede, 36 years old and living in Madrid:

> My *Heimat* is Madrid. But I could probably feel equally at home in Stuttgart, or in Córdoba, Málaga, or in Nantes, Montevideo, Toronto, Bucharest, Beijing, Gijón or Setúbal. ... The point is not the place, but the emotion that connects you to the place. Chance and luck play a big part, and even the most sedentary homebody can probably feel homeless. I had to travel a bit to figure that one out.[38]

This reminds us of the final chapter in Calvino's book where Marco Polo explains to the Great Kahn that the city is discontinuous in space and time, now scattered, then more condensed, but always depending on the journey. And the lesson is this: 'seek and learn to recognize who and what, in the midst of the inferno, are not inferno, then make them endure, give them space.' (p. 148) The emphasis in the end is not on the place, but on the meaning that one might temporarily connect to it.

Conclusion: Literature is Always Contemporary

Reading Calvino's classical text implies making it into an event (Attridge, 2004)[39] and responding to it. Reading is based on a dialogue between author, text and reader, and requires the negotiation and re-contextualization of meaning. As Marjorie Garber (2011)[40] has pointed out, a literary text exist in at least three time zones: the time in which it was written (the early 1970s), the time in which it is set (the thirteenth-fourteenth century), and the time in which it is being read (spring 2015, in my case). All time zones have their effect on the construction of an interpretation of the text, and subsequently, it is the quality of Calvino's work that it intersects fluidly with these different times. In Garber's words: reading a literary work 'involves a kind of stereo-optical vision: one eye on the image of the past, the other on the present, the two eyes combining them into a vivid single picture.'[41]

In this chapter, I have argued that Calvino's text provides two juxtaposed arguments regarding ideas on signification and semiotic processes connected to the experience of arriving in cities. First, it provides a critique on social and cultural issues, and second, it escapes claims of reference and mimesis. Marco Polo is a historical figure, a sceptical stranger and uninvolved outsider as well as a baffled newcomer,[42] but he also is the focalizer who realizes that the signs and symbols of cities are ambiguous. No one will ever get to a point from which an overall and static view on what a city means is possible. This is what has been currently underlined by scholars on globalization, pointing at this idea of a dynamic process of signification in regard to cities and their imaginaries.[43] Calvino's *Invisible Cities* thus demonstrates that contemporary literature provides a scenario for understanding experiences of mobility and displacement. Subsequently, framed by Calvino, the personal stories of European expats look familiar as well as estranging. Madrid, Brussels or Athens are places to which the storytellers for some time *belong*, in the sense that these cities provide modes of being and temporary attachment.[44] The invisibility of the city becomes visible, once people recognize the patterns and the signs and are capable of responding and imagining.

My aim was to read Calvino's book as contemporary, that is, as an interruption of stories and experiences of migrants arriving in new places. Today's main travellers are no longer the discovery voyagers or cosmopolitan adventurers in search of an unknown world, but thousands of migrants, refugees, outcasts moving in search of freedom, safety, education, new job opportunities and peace.[45] They travel a dangerous route without a map or a set date for the landing in their minds, and undoubtedly, while on the road, they will fantasize and 'put together, piece by piece, the perfect city, made of fragments mixed with the rest, of instants separated by intervals, of signals one sends out, not knowing who receives them'. (p. 147) Calvino's classic can be read as a description of the realities and irrealties migrants face when crossing the borders of Europe from the mountains in the east or the sea in the south, hoping for the hospitality a Great Kahn might offer them.

Notes

1 I use the vintage edition: Italo Calvino, *Invisible Cities*, trans. William Weaver (London: Vintage Books, 1997).

2 Simon Critchley, *Things Merely Are: Philosophy in the Poetry of Wallace Stevens* (London and New York: Routledge, 2008), p. 26.

3 Kathryn Hume, *Calvino's Fictions: Cogito and Cosmos* (Oxford: Clarendon Press, 1992), p. 133.

4 The 'willing suspension of disbelief' is a formula for justifying the use of fantastic or non-realistic elements in literature. It was put forth by the poet Coleridge, who suggested that if a writer could infuse a 'human interest and a semblance of truth' into a fantastic tale, the reader would suspend judgment concerning the implausibility of the narrative. See: www.princeton.edu/~achaney/tmve/wiki100k/docs/Suspension_of_disbelief.html (accessed 17 May 2015).

5 Hume *Calvino's Fictions*, p. 133.

6 See Joseph Brodsky, *Watermark* (1989), and Thomas Mann, *Death in Venice* (1912).

7 After his return to Venice in 1295, Marco Polo took part in the sea battle at Korcula and was caught by the enemy, the fighters of Genoa. In prison he met the 'ghost writer' Rustichello, who wrote Polo's stories on paper. The original of this book was from 1298–1299, and got lost, though several extended copies appeared in later years and centuries. The title *Il Milione* was used for the first time in the fourteenth century and indicated the traveller Marco Polo d'Emilione (from Emilia). See: Marco Polo, *De wonderen van de Orient: Il Milione*, trans. Anton Haakman ('s-Hertogenbosch: Erasmus festival and Atheneum-Polak & Van Gennep), 2001, pp. 120–21.

8 Marco Polo, *De wonderen van de Orient, Il Milone*, 2001, pp. 62–63.

9 Calvino, *Paris Review interview* See: www.theparisreview.org/interviews/2027/the-art-of-fiction-no-130-italo-calvino (accessed 17 May 2015).

10 Leonardo Fibonacci (1170–1250), Italian mathematician from Pisa, who popularized the use of the 'new' Arabic numerals in Europe. (OED)

11 See for an analysis of the semiotics in *Invisible Cities*, Teresa de Lauretis, 'Semiotic Models, *Invisible Cities*', *Yale Studies* 2 (1978) 1, pp. 13–37.

12 Charles Taylor, *Modern Social Imaginaries* (Durham and London: Duke University Press, 2004).

13 Benedict Anderson, *Imagined Communities: Reflections on the Origin and Spread of Nationalism* (London: Verso, 1983).

14 Andreas Huyssen, ed., *Other Cities, Other Worlds: Urban Imaginaries in a Globalizing Age* (Durham and London: Duke University Press, 2008), p. 3.

15 Kenneth Burke (1897–1993) is an American literary critic who is known for his rhetorically based analyses of the nature of knowledge and for his views of literature as symbolic action where language and human agency combine. Among his books are: *Counter-Statement* (1931; rev. ed., 1968); *The Philosophy of Literary Form* (1941; 3rd ed., 1974); *Permanence and Change: An Anatomy of Purpose* (1935; rev. ed., 1959); *Attitudes Toward History*, 2 vols. (1937; rev. ed., 1959); *A Grammar of Motives* (1945); *A Rhetoric of Motives* (1950); and *Language as Symbolic Action* (1966). See: www.britannica.com/EBchecked/topic/85395/Kenneth-Burke (accessed 17 May 2015).

16 Kenneth Burke, *Language as Symbolic Action: Essays on Life, Literature, and Method* (Berkeley etc.: University of California Press, 1966), chapter 1, pp. 3–24.

17 Ibid., p. 5.

18 Ibid., p. 15.

19 Bruno Zeyringer, *Die Erfahrung der Fremde: Elias Canetti: Die Stimmen von Marrakesch, Italo Calvino, Le città invisibli (Die unsichtbaren Städte)* (Ludwigsburg: Neuphilologischen Fakultät der Universität Tübingen, 1995), pp. 180–84.

20 Huyssen, *Other Cities, Other Worlds*, p. 3.

21 Surrealism (OED): 20th-century avant-garde movement in art and literature which sought to release the creative potential of the unconscious mind, for example by the irrational juxtaposition of images.

22 Michael Sheringham, *Everyday Life: Theories and Practices from Surrealism to the Present* (Oxford: Oxford University Press, 2006), chapter 2.

23 See: www.comune.venezia.it/flex/cm/pages/ServeBLOB.php/L/EN/IDPagina/219 (accessed 17 May 2015).

24 Zeyringer, *Die Erfahrung der Fremde*.

25 See the game of chess in popular medieval texts such as *Le roman de la rose*, or in the second part of T.S Eliot's *The Waste Land* (1922). http://roseandchess.lib.uchicago.edu (accessed 17 May 2015).

26 Paolo Bartoloni, *Interstitial Writing: Calvino, Caproni, Sereni and Svevo*

(Market Haborough: Troubador Publishing LtD, 2003), p. 54.

27 Ibid., xvi.

28 Ibid., p. 2.

29 Maurice Blanchot, *The Space of Literature*, trans. Ann Smock (Lincoln and London: University of Nebraska Press 1982 [1955]). See: http://monoskop.org/images/9/94/Blanchot_Maurice_The_Space_of_Literature.pdf (accessed on 17 may 2015).

30 Saskia Sassen, 'The Global City: Introducing a Concept', *Brown Journal of World Affairs* XI (2005) 2, p. 28. See: www.saskiasassen.com/pdfs/publications/the-global-city-brown.pdf (accessed 17 May 2015).

31 Huyssen, *Other Cities, Other Worlds*.

32 Sassen, 'The Global City'.

33 After the fall of the Iron Curtain most workers emigrated from the new EU accession countries of the East to the West (mainly Great Britain, Spain and Ireland). Now, the direction has changed. The South is now again moving north, as it once did before between 1960 and 1970.

34 Zygmunt Bauman, 'From Pilgrim to Tourist', in *Questions of Cultural Identity*, ed. Stuart Hall and Paul du Gay (London: Sage Publications, 1996), pp. 18–36.

35 www.goethe.de/lhr/prj/daz/mag/mig/ang/en11307661.htm (accessed 17 May 2015).

36 www.goethe.de/lhr/prj/daz/mag/mig/ang/en11358249.htm (accessed 17 May 2015).

37 See: Migration and Integration. Goethe Institut: www.goethe.de/lhr/prj/daz/mag/mig/ang/en11358171.htm (accessed 17 May 2015).

38 www.goethe.de/lhr/prj/daz/mag/mig/ang/en11381443.htm (accessed 17 May 2015).

39 Derek Attridge points out what responding to a text involves: 'A literary work is not an object or a thesis', Attridge declares, 'literature *happens*'. (2004, xii) The *event* of the literary work can have powerful effects on its readers, and through them on the cultural and political environment. In doing justice to a literary work as an event, we encounter the 'singular demands of the other' (xii). This approach to literature seems to be a reaction against scholarly writing focusing on the text as such, and piling up theoretical work discussing the *ins and outs* of the texts of the canon. Attridge's plea, so to say, is to bring the text to the reader, to enhance the responsibility or ethics of reading, away from mummified theoretical discussions on the *werkimmanente Interpretationen* of the classics. Derek Attridge, *J.M. Coetzee and The Ethics of Reading* (Chicago and London: The University of Chicago Press, 2004).

40 Marjorie Garber, *The Use and Abuse of Literature* (New York: Pantheon Books, 2011).

41 Ibid., p. 167.

42 Zygmunt Bauman, *Wasted Lives, Modernity and its Outcasts* (Cambridge: Polity Press, 2004), p. 3.

43 Jan Nederveen Pieterse, *Globalization and Culture, Global Mélange* (Lanham: Rowman & Littlefield Publishers Inc., 2004); Suman Gupta, *Globalization and Literature* (Cambridge: Polity Press, 2009); Sassen, 'The Global City'; Huyssen, *Other Cities, Other Worlds*.

44 Elspeth Probyn, *Outside Belongings* (New York and London: Routledge, 1996), p. 19.

45 Cf. the stories on the website www.angekommen.com/iberer/index2.html (accessed 23 April 2014) told by guest workers arriving in Germany.

How to Dare, Interrupt, Intrude, Fictionalize and Scream for a Public

An Interview with Sarah Vanhee

Bojana Cvejić

The text below was distilled from a long conversation that took place in Brussels in November 2014. Several recurrent leitmotifs are interwoven in the account of four works by Sarah Vanhee in the words of the artist herself. Singling them out doesn't only point to the continuity of problems Vanhee persistently poses and tries to solve from project to project. More than this, they offer in this interview a performance score, which interrogates and explores a public in eclipse, and they resonate with me in the form of questions: Might fiction be a politicizing tool to exit one's privacy? Can art provide an efficient pretext to stir the consensus about art, diversity and common people? What does it mean to disturb the proceduralist democracy of experts with words dispossessed of a public political vernacular?

There is More Than One Fiction

Bojana Cvejić – Recently you realized four projects that, in various ways, decisively move out of the space of the theatre venue or any other art institution where your work has been hitherto presented. Thus *The Miraculous Life of Claire C* (2010) links the imaginary space of a novel with real physical encounters with strangers in the public space who have previously met through email correspondence; *Untitled* (2012, ongoing) involves visits to private houses whose tenants present their own choice of art works in their home; *I screamed and I screamed and I screamed* (2013) was developed with the inmates of a prison, and *Lecture For Every One* (2013, ongoing) interweaves a heterogeneous web of social gatherings behind the closed doors of various non-art-related places in a city. What prompted you to seek out and operate in another sort of publicness rather than that of the theatre or gallery?

Sarah Vanhee – One reason for choosing to operate outside the physical realm of art venues in these four works is that I experienced their limits, a sense of containment and controlling agency that I exercise under the roof of a theatre performance or an exhibition, together with their inherent, historically grown properties. I had the wish to admit foreign elements into my work, so that not everything would be in my hands and in the hands of the audience anymore. The work becomes porous, spills over, and alterity seeps through it in a way that I couldn't foresee. Another reason has to do with the relative homogeneity of the art audience, a tacit consensus in the worldview and fields of references, which risks neutralizing even the most so-called political work.

BC – The *Miraculous Life of Claire C*, or *The C-Project*, started with the unfinished novel by the Irish writer Guillaume McGuire, which you supposedly found in a stranger's belongings on a train. Not only is the novel unfinished, but its main character, caught up in an existential crisis, is also incomplete, or as you describe her: 'an unworldly, funny woman with an absurd mind and very thin-skinned', an insecure anti-heroine in search of her identity.

SV – Two questions were my point of departure here: How do fictional characters come into being and what status do they have? Since the novel was unfinished, what I asked next was what it would mean for the author to relinquish power. As the author loses dominance, the story itself and its characters take over. This also met my inquiry into how to position myself as artist and author of my own work. I decided not to follow the authorial track of completing an unfinished manuscript by writing it up, but to become the character, Claire C, which is literally, and figuratively, in her own personality, unfinished. Claire C would then come into being through the confrontation with the 'real world', as if, one could say, each life is a collection of stories.

BC – In the next step, Claire issues a call. I paraphrase: 'I am looking for the other characters that I meet in my book. Would you consider yourself as potentially being a character in a novel? Then please get in touch with me.' The letter, which you distributed through emails, Twitter, newspaper and supermarket ads as well as regular letterboxes in the neighbourhoods in Amsterdam, addresses strangers with the question of whether they recognize themselves as, for instance, 'a man who could be from another era' or 'an older woman with a good body who often wears dark blue, grey, brown and sometimes red', to quote two of the twelve characters of the quest. A somewhat 'odd', or as commented in the letter, 'out of the blue' invitation to imagine and cast oneself in the role of a fictional character, and solicit, by way of correspondence with an obscure Claire C, a real, that is, physical, encounter with Claire C on a bench in a park in Amsterdam.

SV – The found manuscript provided me with a framework to follow: a sequence of twelve chapters conceived as twelve phases in the life of Claire C (from *Être*, *Agir*, to *Voyager*, and so on), from which I partly derived information about the other characters.

The letter reached thousands of people, of whom two hundred contacted me. I was surprised by the amount of answers as well as the curiosity and openness of people. A selection of conversations is included in the book: the conversations also helped to construct the subjectivity of Claire. The correspondence that is included in the book attests to the process of an 'audition' for the character. Claire got in touch with many different people and finally chose to meet those who emerged as the most distinct or articulated among the two hundred that wrote to her. Although one could possibly find the link between Claire C and Sarah Vanhee if one searched far enough, most people I met didn't do this. I was amazed by their trust in my invitation's blind call to take part in something that wasn't clearly defined as fiction or reality.

BC – How did the encounter take place? And how could it be situated as a performance, a novel embodied and performed by anonymous strangers in the public space, without an audience?

SV – The first meeting I went to, obviously as Claire – I remember it was in Vondelpark – I was really afraid. But what I found immediately is that people had little reserve, and didn't come to 'play the game'. Perhaps it is difficult to convey it outside of these encounters, but Claire's character had a disarming effect. It may sound strange, but from the very first moment I went to the meetings, I *was*

Claire. I wasn't self-conscious or thinking about what motivated these strangers to participate in becoming a character in a novel. I was busy with an existential crisis of a person who doesn't know where to go and what to do with her life. So sitting there on a bench with an unknown person, casting them into a character of a story, was an empty sheet of paper.

BC – Characters in a novel don't have to apologize.

SV – No, they go to the essence of things, or else the books would be too long, having to describe every little practical detail. What I experienced strongly in these encounters is that people weren't acting. I believe that they were in a heightened state of performance, and maybe they would even coincide more with themselves more rather than less. Our encounter owes its intensity and our conversation its depth to the performative frame of the situation, a certain focus that doesn't exist in daily life, and it somehow affects the person. What operates in that moment is the awareness of being part of an art work which enables one to perform and fictionalize oneself. I don't mean it as a line of flight, an escape from this world into fantasy, but as a matter of lucidity.

BC – Nowadays the hunger for fiction is catered for by cinema or video images rather than by reading. Reading seems to be an obsolete, solitary practice in times when screen visuality dominates and generates desire as the motor of fantasy. How do you consider the social and political dimensions of the operation of a performance-novel? A private encounter between two individuals takes place in a public space, which will later be registered and transformed in a piece of writing. But after that, how do you account for the effect of the encounter spilling into the daily lives of those strangers? In other words, what could becoming a fictional character 'do' to them, once they exit the fiction?

SV – In *The C-Project*, the embodiment of fiction is at stake, thus replacing writing. Going to a park to meet a stranger with whom one is going to construct and perform – or rather, become a story, implies inscribing oneself into a narrative, which treads the border between reality and fiction. If I speak from the perspective of the one who goes to encounter Claire, I regard it as an act of transgression.

BC – Do you mean that the encounter enables them to transgress, as in crossing or infringing a certain border they are bound by in their daily lives?

SV – A performed embodiment makes the question of 'what is fiction' more urgent than would be the case in the situation of watching a screen or witnessing a spectacle where there is a border we won't cross. From the embodied and lived encounter ensues the question: if this is fiction, how many more fictions one could possibly live?

BC – Are you suggesting that the action of embodying a fictional character empowers the individuals to expand fiction into other aspects of their private and perhaps also public life? Does literary fiction specifically appear as a way to act upon reality in those places where it is blocked? A playful, ludic instrument to unhinge certain barriers?

SV – As a political tool, yes. Simon Critchley speaks of 'supreme fiction', a notion he borrows from Wallace Stevens: 'paradoxically, a supreme fiction is a fiction that we know to be a fiction – there being nothing else – but in which we nevertheless believe. ... A supreme fiction is one self-conscious of its radical contingency.'[1]

One could say that each life consists of several parallel fictions, personal and political. Let's say it is the dominant fiction of a capitalist, conservative society we are living in now. But it is important to consider it as a fiction that we created ourselves and yet happily believe in. Who says that it is more valid than whatever other fiction? The same goes for an individual life, and regarding it as fiction enhances one's power of imagination and creation.

BC – How does the awareness of this fiction, which I would call the contingency of a situation, help one substitute it with another one that won't yet be a self-delusion?

SV – There is nothing of delusion, fantasy or obscurity at hand. It is rather the opposite, that it comes with a certain lucidity of seeing different possibilities and trying to work out other ways of the meaning production than the ones we are familiar with or used to. It calls for taking an active position towards our own reality. I recourse to fiction in the sense of Jacques Rancière as well, 'not as a term that designates the imaginary as opposed to the real; it involves the re-framing of the "real", or the framing of a dissensus.'[2] Fiction as a way of changing existing modes of sensory presentations and forms of enunciation; of varying frames, scales and rhythms; and of building new relationships between reality and appearance, the individual and the collective.

BC – If we now turn to the public aspect of the operation, the encounters left traces in the form of plaques placed on the benches in the parks of Amsterdam, where Claire C met the characters of her novel. The plaques exhibit a quote from the conversation that took place on the inscribed date. Being more than a reminiscence, they also offer a Q&R code that gives access to the whole chapter of the novel online. A stranger who didn't participate in the creation of the novel can retrace and follow the road that Clare C. took in her miraculous life in Amsterdam.

SV – The plaques propose another way of weaving a history, bypassing the dominant discourse of winners. I am interested in the writing of history that did not make it into books. It potentially opens the thread of the history of a city through a fictional character, thus giving a platform to the so-called common people who live in the city, and not just the Multatulis and Anne Franks who are commemorated by public monuments in Amsterdam.

Commoning the Art World in its Shadows

BC – *Untitled* is another project that re-hallucinates the living fabric of a city based on the encounter of strangers at the intersection of private-public spheres. A presentation of art works chosen by the people living in the neighbourhood of an art venue takes place in private homes visited by individual visitors (or spectators) by appointment. What is the genealogy of this ongoing project?

SV – I was invited to an art biennial, and my first thoughts were about what it means for such an exhibition to temporarily land in a city, how it relates to the people living in its proximity on a day-to-day basis. Another cue was an interest in the relationship between the art object and art theory, which legitimates it as a work of art. The role theory plays in the art world nowadays contributes to the fact that contemporary art is judged as elitist by common people, especially in the recent upsurge of populist rhetoric in the Netherlands, where I was living at that time. I wanted to explore what art is to the so-called common people, how they speak about it, and whether I could conceive of their discourse in parallel to the function that theory has in the art world. So the point of departure would be an art venue as the centre of the dominant regime that prescribes what good art is. My concern was to unravel those places surrounding the art centre – houses in which people live – as a shadow or negative space of the museum.

BC – The topography of such places is relevant here, because nowadays, there are more and more contemporary art centres, or centres dedicated to experiment and research, which are geographically marginalized, that is, pushed into the poor immigrant areas of the city where the relationship with the local community is either weak or problematic. I am thinking here, for instance, of Les Laboratoires d'Aubervilliers, deliberately located outside of the centre of Paris. In which cities and places did *Untitled* happen so far?

SV – Indeed, it is not only the physical building, but also the location that plays a role in the project in the sense of cultural policy and urban planning. The first edition was at a festival, Artefact, at STUK in Louvain, a rather rich, bourgeois Flemish city. The second one was in the vicinity of Mousonturm, a theatre situated in a nowadays gentrified area in Frankfurt am Main, where some squatted places still remain. The third one took place around Campo, the Nieuwpoort Theater in Ghent, and the last one was around WIELS Contemporary Art Centre, located in Forest/Vorst in Brussels, a mixed neighbourhood of immigrant, poor, and white lower and upper middle-class households.

BC – How did you proceed in selecting the local hosts of the art works, and what was the question you approached them with?

SV – The process of encountering the strangers was once again pedestrian: strolling in the streets and giving letters to the people I met on the way. The question I posed to them was: Do you have something at your place which you would consider art, even if no one else would call it art, so regardless of what it would officially be considered, as art or not art? And would you like to talk about that?

One other criteria was whether or not these people were willing to receive strangers at their place, thereby letting them peek into their privacy. My preference was people who were mostly far removed from the contemporary art world as I know it, who didn't consider themselves artists, not even amateur artists (who would then probably want to show their own work). First and foremost, they would be spectators.

BC – The question goes beyond the division between art and non-art, as well as the distinction between conventional expertise and a layman's knowledge or passion. So what was there to discover in the items they chose to present; what kind of objects or things qualified as art for them? Was their function any different from the aesthetic autonomy ascribed to artworks in Western art museums?

SV – Definitely. The works they presented were inextricably connected with their own biographies and environments, their 'art' beautifully interwoven with their life. I was open to whatever they would deem to be a work of art. Everything would be okay for me, as long as it was art to them. An obvious choice were paintings. Quite a number to be found. But they would be made not only by professional or amateur artists, but also by children, or someone in the family. They were bought or lent, or travelled as inherited pieces in the history of the family. Sculptures were chosen as well, or it could also be an architectural element in the house. Sometimes, it would be a video, too. Or a piece of handicraft. One woman regarded her small child as a piece of art.

BC – Your question reflects the nominalism in the post-conceptual condition of contemporary art as in the speech act 'this is an art work if I say so', the only difference here being that the utterance isn't authorized by the art world. The same power applies to the 'common people', non-artists, to proclaim their works of art.

SV – Exactly. An important reference here was Arthur Danto and his thesis about the end of art, or in his own words, 'The end of the master narratives of art. And the fact that, as far as appearances were concerned, anything could be a work of art, and it meant that if you were going to find out what art was, you had to turn from sense experience to thought.'[3] Art can no longer be determined by just looking at it, but is instead the result of the discursive act of denomination. This was exactly what these people were doing. Through the act of nominating it as an art work and through their narrative account of why this is an art work, they were creating one. This raises questions similar to the ones *The C-Project* raises: Where is the art work? Where does it start – my art work, yours or their art work? For the spectator the same question applies: Whose art work is it? Where does it stop and end? What is the place of the art work presented in the larger framework of the art work called *Untitled*?

Moreover, the question does not only concern the work of art itself and its denominator; in parallel, it concerns art discourse: 'this is an art work because', and then a text not authorized by the art world but provided by common people in their terminology, with their references – singular and heterogeneous. There is not one voice.

BC – Visiting someone's private domestic space is an intense experience. I remember my visit to the two houses in Forest, one of a French middle-class, middle-aged woman with a family, and the other of a young man and a worker from Burkina Faso. I also recall the feeling just before entering these homes: you never know what you will find when you step into a stranger's house. There are smells and noises you cannot completely avoid. There is all this apprehension about seeing things you do not want to see. In order to indulge in such an encounter, the visitor has to be a bit of a voyeur and the hosting presenter an exhibitionist.

SV – I found it beautiful to see these works in the non-neutral domestic space, as opposed to the museum, which isolates and sterilizes. The works are immersed in the noise of everyday life. But I also noticed myself, as a visitor, and this experience was confirmed by others, that the role evokes the codes of behaviour of an exhibition-goer. I would focus on the object I was shown and feel it inappropriate to look around. Even in such a situation one reiterates the protocols of museum-going.

BC – I remember that the Burkinabé man shared several handicraft objects from various African traditions, and one was a kind of machete. He passed it to me, and I looked at it, holding it in my hands, and wanted to return it to him as soon as possible. It was uncanny, as you are on a territory where no security is guaranteed in that moment.

SV – Yes, your role is unclear. Your status as a spectator is troubled, complexified. You're not a participant in the strict sense either. Perhaps this uncanniness is amplified by the fact that the artist, the author of *Untitled*, isn't there, and as a visitor you are left alone with a map and instructions until you ring the doorbell of the house.

BC – Although you prepared the operation in which we participate, you are not there to survey it. Unlike museums, private homes are exempt from CCTV camera surveillance.

SV – Yes, there is something clandestine about the encounter and where it takes place, which somehow applies to all of my work.

BC – Speaking of the very encounter that takes place in *Untitled*, I would say that the visitors may belong to a more homogeneous profile filtered through the art venue. For instance, a predominantly white, middle-class, educated audience in the case of WIELS and Kunstenfestivaldesarts, compared to the ethnic and class diversity of the chosen hosts in Forest/Vorst, whose affiliation with the art venue might be very different.

SV – There is always already a gap between these two sides. In my collaboration with art venues, I sometimes had to deal with the agenda of the department for audience development, and with their request for social diversification. An art venue suggested to me that I should involve those people from the neighbourhood who are less 'represented' in their public. Well, the sixty-year-old collector of figurative paintings working in finances, born in Liège, seemed to me as 'underrepresented' in their public as the twenty-five-year-old shop assistant born in Ankara; they both had never visited the art venue in their neighbourhood as they both had no interest in contemporary art. My work is sometimes mistaken for the socially-engaged art that aims for social inclusion or representation. This is never my goal per se. In this case, I would work with anyone who would answer my question: 'What is art at your place, and can we have a conversation about that?' The diversity of answers came with the diversity of people – the outcome of an open question, not of a strategic plan.

BC – In my view, *Untitled* successfully critiques the hegemony of the art world by affirming another order of diversity, which needs no social or political representation under the paternalistic terms of art venues and their well-meaning, socially engaging policies.

SV – I believe that art institutions are wrong in their judgment of the lack of diversity. Their programmatic attempts to integrate differences are dangerous, as they annihilate a certain scope of heterogeneity. Thinking along the schemes of social and cultural stratification often means maintaining them and reducing a plurality of voices to a number count. I'm interested in art as a space for meeting, speaking, thinking, for potential dissensus.

Most of the participants would see the neighbouring art centre as one of many possibilities in their cultural life. What I found quite refreshing was when one of these people would tell me: I go to the spoken-word evenings, my friend has a band, my mother paints, and so on, and yes, sometimes we go to this contemporary art venue. Somehow they were able to unite all these into art, and their vision of art was very open, and not dogmatic.

BC – It confirms the thesis about the birth of the modern museum as an instrument not only to educate but also to instil public order, a device to monitor citizenship through aestheticizing behaviour, as Tony Bennett wrote.[4]

SV – Rather than being resentful, many people had an attitude of indifference toward the importance of art venues: 'Let the clan remain... I have my other, my own art experiences.' They can't be subordinated to the hegemony of the institutionalized art world. Maybe we should not be so surprised about the fact that not everyone wants to go see what the predominantly white, higher-educated, middle-class men have selected for us as art?

To come back to the idea of fiction, I think the art institution proposes one possible fiction – albeit a very important one, often a beacon or a point of reference or departure – but it is just one of many fictions about art.

Screams from Behind the Wall

BC – How did you come to work in the prison for *I screamed and I screamed and I screamed*, which was presented as a performance and an installation in the visual arts biennial Contour in Mechelen.

SV – Contour usually takes place in different places and at various sites in the city, as it also serves to market the symbolic capital of Mechelen. In 2013, the curator decided to focus on four places: the cathedral, the school, the prison and the exhibition venue. All of them shared the same disciplinary regime that operates on the division of authority between the dominating and subordinated forces. Usually I don't work by commission, but as for a long time I had had a wish to work with men in prison, this proved to be a good occasion.

BC – What were your initial thoughts about prison?

SV – First of all, it is one of the institutions as shaped by modernity about which I think, 'How is it possible that prisons still exist?' They have turned out to be ineffective, a consensus shared by both prisoners and prison directors. Two results of imprisonment attest to it: first, in prison, the main thing that prisoners learn is how to become better criminals, and when they exit, there is no way for them to be reintegrated into society. Prison doesn't serve the convicts; it isn't for 'them', but for 'us' as a guarantee of our own 'security'. Furthermore, one could also wonder if putting people behind the walls against their will is an act of violence in itself that also violates certain rights. This doesn't mean there are no people who are potentially violent toward society and who might be better locked up for a while so as to protect other people from them or protect them from harming themselves. But most people to be found behind bars do not fall in this category. They come from underprivileged backgrounds where there is a tradition, family history and practice of criminal behaviour as a way of life – people who never had a chance to go to school, for instance. This is something I would like to pursue further after this project: criminality not as a legal but as a legitimate, a viable way to live one's life.

Among other sources, one important reference was *Discipline and Punish* by Michel Foucault,[5] which traces the genealogy of penal systems in history, going from the early customs of public hanging and torture to the development of a disciplinary system as we know it today. What struck me while reading Foucault was how the body disappeared from view in the course of this transformation. The early practice of public torture featured a spectacle of the body with a participation of the audience based on a direct confrontation with the convict. I am not suggesting that this carnal spectacle was better than the penitentiary today. All I am saying is that the prisoner has become a legal matter, their body, and with it their personhood, has been evacuated from public attention. Prisoners are reduced to numbers. And my interest was to re-establish the connection from human to human, and let the subject who is behind these walls re-emerge. Revealing the face and the body seemed delicate, since it also discloses the identity, which the prisoners prefer to hide from public view. This is where I began to think about the voice, which, through the hearing and imagination it elicits, is some kind of raw matter, even more connected to the body than the visible body itself. In our visually dominated culture, we spend hours with our face, with which we present ourselves to the world, but very little attention is given to cultivating the voice in everyday life. The voice and its singularity as an identifying power are underexplored.

BC – Listening and hearing are underestimated in the current distribution of the sensible.

SV – Yes, and in my view, the voice is a richer source of information, or identity vehicle. I likened it to fingerprints. The prisoner must leave fingerprints as an index of his identity. The voice is also singular and could function like that: there are no two voices that are identical. Apart from certain exceptions, the voice has not been standardized yet, it does not fit measurements.

Apart from the perception of the voice, another element was the scream. Screaming is like breaking the law. It is something you don't do, it is not socially accepted.

BC – In several interviews you mentioned that screaming is a controversial gesture in some contexts. It is regarded as a breach of public order. In the simplest terms, it is read as a sign of pain or anger or intensity. You also evoke the muezzin's call – the invisible chant from a tower which is closed-off to nonbelievers.

SV – My initial idea was to make a choir of screaming men according to certain religious rituals, or as an appeal made by the human from the prison to the outside world. This was, among other sources, inspired by reading Alexander Solzhenitsyn's *Gulag Archipelago*, in which he describes how people arrested in broad daylight mostly didn't scream, and that there are different reasons for their being captivated in silence.[6] They would think it was a mistake, they still trusted the law, or it became such a strong bureaucratized action for which the first instinctive response was not to scream and alarm other people around you that you are being done an injustice.

The directors of the prison accepted my proposal without having understood the degree of engagement it entailed. I also understood that the prison in Mechelen was, in actual fact, a jail – a place in which the arrested are detained for an undetermined period. They are locked up in cells, with no plan, and they have no perspective about the duration of their imprisonment.

BC – Jails are places where law, or even perhaps society on the whole is suspended.

SV – The prisoners of a jail are the lowest citizens on the ladder. They don't know yet what the ordeal will be, how long they will have to stay there. It can be one week or three years.

I encountered many different obstacles in this project. First of all, screaming was not accepted by all inmates. It is by all means a provocative gesture toward a prison population, and it divided it into two camps: to scream or not to scream. Is it cool, or is it sissy, is it something that you do or don't do?

When I would meet them, we would of course have this dialogue. But very soon the conversation would diverge into what kept them busy most of the time: questions of justice. Not only in a legal sense, but in the sense of a moral feeling: they were constantly judging if they were treated with justice or not, whether they were just or unjust themselves. The men I met all tried to present their own goals in a comparison with others, trying to show to me, as an outsider, that they were a bit less bad than those other ones.

BC – There must have also been people who already felt too humiliated to want to cooperate.

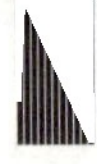

SV – There were also people who just wanted to stay in their cell and be left alone because they didn't trust the situation when an artist comes from the outside and wants to do something with them. How the project was communicated to them was unclear as well. It had to go through so many filters. So I explained it to them again and again. It was very transparent.

BC – When I think of resistance and obstacles you must have met on the way, then I imagine it as an endless series of locked doors that need to be opened.

SV – It is literally doors, and also functions embodied by people. But the harshest confrontation was with the bureaucratic kind of resistance from the staff who just wanted to do their job. It was another contemporary Western legal example of the banality of evil: the one who does his job does only that which he thinks he has to do as his job. There was only one person who helped us: the librarian, who was some kind of 'mama' for those inmates, who often came to confide in her, and she would semi-legally smuggle books, and so on. But she helped us not because she was convinced of the project ('could screaming be art?') but as a gesture of benevolence.

BC – Prison is, then, the place where there is the least good will to experiment, as if everybody operates as a mindless automaton. So to disrupt their routines is much more difficult. I can imagine that would be the same in a school, or in a hospital. What defines disciplinary institutions is a rigidity of rituals, protocols, rules, norms. And then you stumble upon a person who is willing to make it possible.

SV – That is almost a function in the dramaturgy of the preparation of my project: to find that little weak element or spot in a seemingly impenetrable environment that will say 'yes', 'I trust you', or 'I'll take the risk', 'you can enter'.

BC – How would you summarize the battle with the prison staff and inmates during the working process?

SV – Soon enough my original plan to train a choir of inmates over two months became a joke, a tragicomedy of errors. After the first session, already two people fell out, one because he was freed, which is something you can't be unhappy about. Because of the lack of communication within the prison, attendance was irregular – who would show up, and in what numbers. I figured out that it would not be possible to build a choir, so I adapted my way of working to shorter training sessions with a voice coach. We actually became experts in giving half-hour screaming sessions. As the training sessions were fruitful and intense, and people became quite collaborative in their approach, I began to think of other ways of evoking the scream. The idea of the choir became inadequate, because the inmates gathered together do not make up a group. They are just a bunch of individuals, and moreover, screaming is also individual. The quality of screaming is lost when voices are glued together. Hearing one voice at a time has a much stronger effect. Some people approached it technically, some worked from emotion, and others focused on language. Over time, a special bond was built with some of the inmates, who became experts in screaming and in encouraging the others to join. In general, art as a framing device helped once again: the moment a sound technician joined the rehearsals and brought out his equipment, the atmosphere changed and the inmates were more concentrated.

BC – The presence of the professional!

SV – And his equipment. Until then we asked them to scream towards the wall, but suddenly there was a microphone and they knew that the microphone would transmit their voice.

BC – After you undertook the process of a mission proven impossible in this jail, how did you decide to collect individual screams as 'donations' that would become part of the installation in the biennial?

SV – I still clung to the idea of transmitting the presence of the human beings in the legal role of inmates behind the prison walls. So instead of collecting their fingerprints, I collected their screams, of which some were exceptional. I knew from the outset that a live performance with the inmates screaming in a choir would not be possible. Still, I organized a live performance where I myself was screaming the text that recounts the project, while the collected and recorded screams were played back. We did it in front of the prison wall, knowing that behind these walls some of the inmates would be listening to the screams, and some of them would also scream along. The neighbours were watching sceptically from their balconies and the police came. There was an audience to attend our performance, and what I verified in this act of transmission was that some members of the audience reported that they too would like to scream. So in a way it transcends the image of the prisoner who screams toward a metaphor of 'we are all prisoners of a society regardless of whether we are standing in front or behind the wall.'

BC – Or as Foucault defined the shift from the disciplinary to the society of control, whose subjects internalize the disciplinary mechanisms of the prison, school, hospital et cetera. Speaking of the installation, how does it relate to the project and who does it address?

SV – The installation is a document representing the project: a twelve-hour long projection of the image of the prison wall, where the passage of time is visible only in the changes in light. A score of screams can be listened to through the headphones, and the text in which I explain the project in its process and all its difficulty is handed out.

But what really matters is the process and the performance. As with many of my projects, there is something semi-public and semi-private in this situation as a heterotopia. What happens remains among the people who took part in it, and there is no third party that could observe or mediate it to others. Invisibility can contribute to impact.

Words Dispossessed of a Public

BC – How did you conceive *Lecture for Every One* (*LFEO*)?

SV – I recall being discontented about the insularity of the intellectual and artistic community I am part of. There is no fundamental disagreement about politics, and it often feels like we are preaching to the converted. I had a wish to encounter another range of difference in views, ideas, and lives, and seriously engage with a heterogeneous kind of living together. What would it mean to confront my concerns with an outside that potentially disagrees or resists these questions. Another thought concerns language: how to speak to and be heard by those who are not usually part of my world? This is where the title suddenly cropped up: Lecture for Every One. What would it be like to make a lecture that could be understood by everyone? Everyone not in the sense of all, like a TED talk that you could just put online, but every individual one, gathered in an assembly.

BC – One definition of discursive community is a certain linguistic closure of those who share the same assumptions, concepts, rules and norms. But the reason why 'every one' is spelled here as two separate words emphasizes difference and equality, where singularities are addressed.

SV – Every one implies belonging to *the* multitude, each and every one addressed as being part of everyone. An assembly and encounter of different bodies.

BC – The performance of *LFEO* takes place at closed meetings. Why did you choose the social gathering as the stage for such a lecture?

SV – When I prepare *LFEO*, I observe the city in terms of how people move from one association or assembly to another get-together. I believe there is an incredible potential in all people gathering on a daily basis for various reasons or concerns. One can think that anything could happen whenever different people come together. Although these meetings are often strictly structured according to an agenda with time pressure, there is always the possibility of disturbing it, and taking the meeting elsewhere. As a stranger, I opt to intrude in those places – and my preference goes to those who could perhaps be most hostile and resistant to my words – where my presence can create an outside, make the inside of the meeting public.

BC – Until now, you have disturbed about three hundred meetings with the performance of *LFEO* in Brussels, Vienna, Berlin, Tallinn, Athens, and so on. What are the criteria by which you choose the range of assemblies?

SV – In every city we draw up a list of available meetings, which range from professional meetings in various disciplines to nonprofessional meetings based on education, leisure, cultural background, or religion, from governmental organizations to NGOs. The meetings vary on the level of the hierarchy of organization (from CEO meetings to those of employees of a lower position), but also topologically, whether they take place in the centre or the periphery of a city. Working with a network of agents who help us access the meetings, I and my collaborator seek to *read* the city through a selection of groups who potentially represent 'everyone'. A diversity of class, age, profession, ethnic and educational levels of citizens who currently assemble. Among the meetings that I or another performer disturbed were the air force of the Belgian military, a Congolese Mass, a sales meeting at IBM, a meeting of a lobby group of Nestle, a brass band rehearsal, an assembly of the entire sales team of a huge department store, a training of a basketball team, a board meeting of a mushroom collectors' club, a free masons' meeting, a meeting of taxi drivers, an elderly people's home, a fraction meeting in the EU parliament about transport in Europe, a meeting of the IT department of an elevator company, a Rotary club, et cetera.

BC – Could you describe the situation of the event and its protocol?

SV – There is usually one insider of the visited group who provides the entry into the meeting, but who doesn't know in advance the text of the lecture. For the other persons in the meeting, my appearance is totally unexpected. So *LFEO* is like an intruder: I enter the meeting, my contact person briefly introduces me, I say the text. The words are exactly the same for every meeting. The text that I speak is about fifteen minutes long, but it can also become longer if there is discussion or if people pose questions. Sometimes it lasts more than an hour. I'll answer them, but my aim isn't to have a conversation with them. Nor is it a monologue of an individual. I don't really present the words 'for them'. It's more like I spread them 'amongst us'. The words that I bring are like a porous object that resonates into the space, among the people. After having ended the text, I leave right away.

BC – The situation reminds me of a critical point that John Dewey made about the crisis of the public in representative democracy. Since it is based on representation and delegation, society is run by experts of whose knowledge the citizens are ignorant. Dewey was advocating the renewal of a 'great community' in the U.S. based on face-to-face dialogue.[7] Speaking and looking into the faces of those who are in the position of making decisions on behalf of others carries the weight of appealing to their responsibility.

SV – Indeed. The text criticizes this sort of top-down 'expertise'. And the 'experts' who happen to hear the text know that the 'non-experts' hear exactly the same words. As such, it addresses every one in their responsibility, without ever using that term though. As Roberto Esposito has it, community is nothing but the relation – the 'with' or the 'between' – that joins multiple subjects. The text speaks to the people present. My status as an outsider ignores all possible representation.

It isn't only the representative democracy that lacks this face-to-face dialogue, it is also the virtual internet culture in which bodies are missing. For instance, a lot of reunions take place via Skype, which wasn't the right mode for me to say the text. More than addressing faces – which are certainly very important, and I noticed how much I returned the kind of gaze I am looked at with when I am in those meetings – I address the different bodies present there by also naming them. The biopolitical dimension of democracy consists of the presence of bodies as vehicles of subjectivity. The liveness of the event and my own presence are crucial. Because not only am I interrupting their meeting; I can also be interrupted.

BC – What is it that you say in a lecture for every one? What is the common ground upon which every one can be addressed, since the text is repeated almost verbatim in every instance? And how does one speak to every one?

SV – Indeed it is '*a* lecture for every one', and not '*the* lecture for every one.' What was most difficult about *LFEO* was to write the text, choose the form of address (do I speak in the first person, do I address 'you', and, as I discuss it in the lecture itself, how do I conceive of 'we'). As the common denominator of myself as a stranger and the group in assembly, I opted for the way of speaking of a human to a human, as well as a citizen to a citizen. The common context is that we are citizens of Western liberal democracy in capitalism in Europe in 2013, 2014, 2015, and so forth. My preoccupation in the lecture is an inquiry into the state of the common in our societies. Part of that are the problems I implicitly invoke in the anecdotes I tell: living together (which is literally the Dutch word for 'society', *samenleving*), the crisis of representation in democracy, immigration, possessive individualism, fragmentation of social life, and so on.

At the beginning I ask the three questions that mirror the taxonomy used automatically in the West, a kind of tacit mutual levelling-out: 'Do you think you have more or less money than I have? Do you think you know more or less than I do? Do you think that you are stronger than I am?' It is a way of disarming oneself by saying let's just do it and be past that kind of measurement.

BC – At a certain point you also cast yourself as a contemporary subject, perhaps a citizen dispossessed of the public sphere. I quote: 'I am stupid, paranoid and powerless. I am over-rational and unreasonable. I am constantly under surveillance and I feel unsafe. I am ignorant about how to live with people who are not like me. About the future I am cynical. I think I am unique and original but I don't dare to stand out from other people.'

SV – It is indeed a description of a contemporary citizen, a certain diagnosis of the current state of affairs in Western public sphere. However, it isn't a personal confession, but rather a statement of someone, anyone.

BC – There are four notions you emphatically affirm: care, freedom, love and power. They connote humanist values that have become quite problematic.

SV – These words are comparable to what John Cage described as the sounds that wore off after WWII, and that it took him a while to use them again.[8] In the post-ironic times we are living in today, these words are similarly spent. I realized that I felt that I missed them. So I wondered about how I could reinsert them in the public space, in some way, rescue and re-appropriate them like one reclaims a public space one has been dispossessed of. So that's why I say 'let's try them out', although it is difficult. If I reclaim 'care', then I have to distinguish it from the consumerist and commercial sense of bodily care, and speak about caring about each other on an interpersonal level. At the same time, this doesn't exempt the government from its duty to care for its citizens through public services. Or when I affirm 'freedom', I try to disentangle it from its negative definition. We are taught about freedom by being reminded that we are 'unfree', and that we have to free ourselves from insecurity, diseases or problems, or that freedom is a matter of material acquisition and the logic of multiple choice. Freedom has nothing to do anymore with abundance or empowerment or imagination.

BC – You also link freedom to disobedience: freedom to refuse, to be angry and to disobey. What about love, which was most difficult for me to grasp?

SV – I deliberately avoid a precise definition. Instead, I consider love as a force against fear, or against closing oneself off to something perceived as a real or imaginary danger. Love becomes, as Critchley suggests, the willingness to be touched in the first place, as in an ethical reflex before judgment, a way of saying 'yes' that accepts the uncertainty of the consequences of the opening. It could be compared to those people who accept to let me present *LFEO* without knowing what I am going to say. Furthermore, love is something that you don't discuss with your colleagues or in any kind of professional meeting.

Finally, there is power, which I don't define. It is something I leave for the people assembled there, and it is the word with which I leave.

BC – Twice during the lecture, you interpellate your audience with the words: 'We've just created a moment together. this is a moment before. We are before.' Thus, you call for their awareness of their here-and-now presence together, as well as the interruption that your presence incurs: an interruption of the protocol of the meeting, the efficiency with which the agenda must be fulfilled, procedures implemented and decisions reached, roles played.

SV – This is a moment of suspension and caesura, of silence in situations where there is never silence. I literally seize the meeting by taking words to speak. It always de-configures the course of events that would usually take place. The atmosphere changes abruptly, the faces and the bodies become much more present not only to me, but also to each other. Our contact person, whom we call the day after, reports on the effects of the lecture. People start speaking to each other, or a discussion starts, even a dispute in some cases, or people fall silent or become emotional. In any case, in more than a half of the instances, it turns out that the meeting doesn't continue as planned. But I am never witness to this. The reason why I leave is not because I don't want to give them the opportunity to provide feedback. It's exactly because I want to leave them the space amongst themselves and not created by me. I don't own the moment.

BC – Your interruption isn't an abduction, or a colonization of the situation. You interrupt it and you leave.

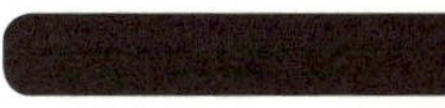

Notes

1 Simon Critchley, *The Faith of the Faithless: Experiments in Political Theology* (London: Verso, 2012), p. 91.
2 Jacques Rancière. *Dissensus: On Politics and Aesthetics*, trans. Steven Corcoran (London: Bloomsbury, 2010), p. 141.
3 Arthur C. Danto. *After the End of Art: Contemporary Art and the Pale of History* (Princeton, NJ: Princeton University Press, 1995), p. 13.
4 Tony Bennett. *The Birth of the Museum: History, Theory, Politics* (London and New York: Routledge, 1995).
5 Michel Foucault. *Discipline and Punish: The Birth of the Prison*, trans. Alan Sheridan (London: Vintage Books, 1995).
6 Aleksandr Solzhenitsyn, *The Gulag Archipelago*, trans. Thomas P. Whitney (London: Harvill Press, 2003), p. 13.
7 John Dewey. *The Public and Its Problems* (Athens, Ohio: Swallow Press, Ohio University Press, 1927), pp. 126–127.
8 John Cage. 'Lecture on Nothing'. *Silence* (Hanover, NH: Wesleyan University Press, 1961), p. 117.

ActionScape

Rennie Tang &
Sara Wookey

In the film *Social Life of Small Urban Spaces* (1980) American urbanist William Whyte observed that people moving about in public spaces naturally become part of an urban choreography. By closely watching the way people behave in public space he noticed that certain patterns begin to emerge, as if choreographed, that relate to natural human tendencies. He noticed every detail, from where people tend to gather, the proximity of two bodies in conversation and how people pass each other to minute social gestures of the hands and feet. His film also reveals how the design of a space – from its urban furniture to its architectural and urban context – drives human action. Our process for creating *ActionScape* began with one similar to that of William Whyte, which is the act of people watching. We studied daily human movement in relationship to the pathways and places of pause that make up our site, an urban park. These studies enabled us, as choreographer and architect in collaboration, to generate a palette of movement material and spatial configurations that are genuinely derived from the park itself.

ActionScape is a performance that illuminates everyday human action as an integral component of the landscape. The performance took place on December 3, 2013 in Grand Park, a civic park in downtown Los Angeles spanning three city blocks located between the City Hall and the Music Center. Led by choreographer Sara Wookey and architect Rennie Tang in collaboration with Olivia Booth, Katya Kahn and Corina Kinnear, the piece provoked subtle shifts in the everyday life of the park. Ramps, stairs, walkways, planters, seat walls, benches, terraces and plazas became co-creators of the piece upon which we traced a set of movement patterns that eventually turned into a graphic score. Choreographic techniques, developed by Wookey, such as repetition, accumulation and pause were incorporated into the score. We used the score to guide us as we transitioned back and forth between everyday movement and choreographed formation. Performers wore brightly coloured socks as a way to visually anchor the movements to the ground.

The performance calls attention to the physical landscape and urban context of Grand Park while revealing the inventory of the daily movement patterns present in the park such as sitting, strolling, pausing, leaning and lounging. Commencing at the top of the park near Grand Avenue, *ActionScape* weaves its way longitudinally across the park and traces its descending topography. It crosses Hill Street and North Broadway, terminating at the lower end of the

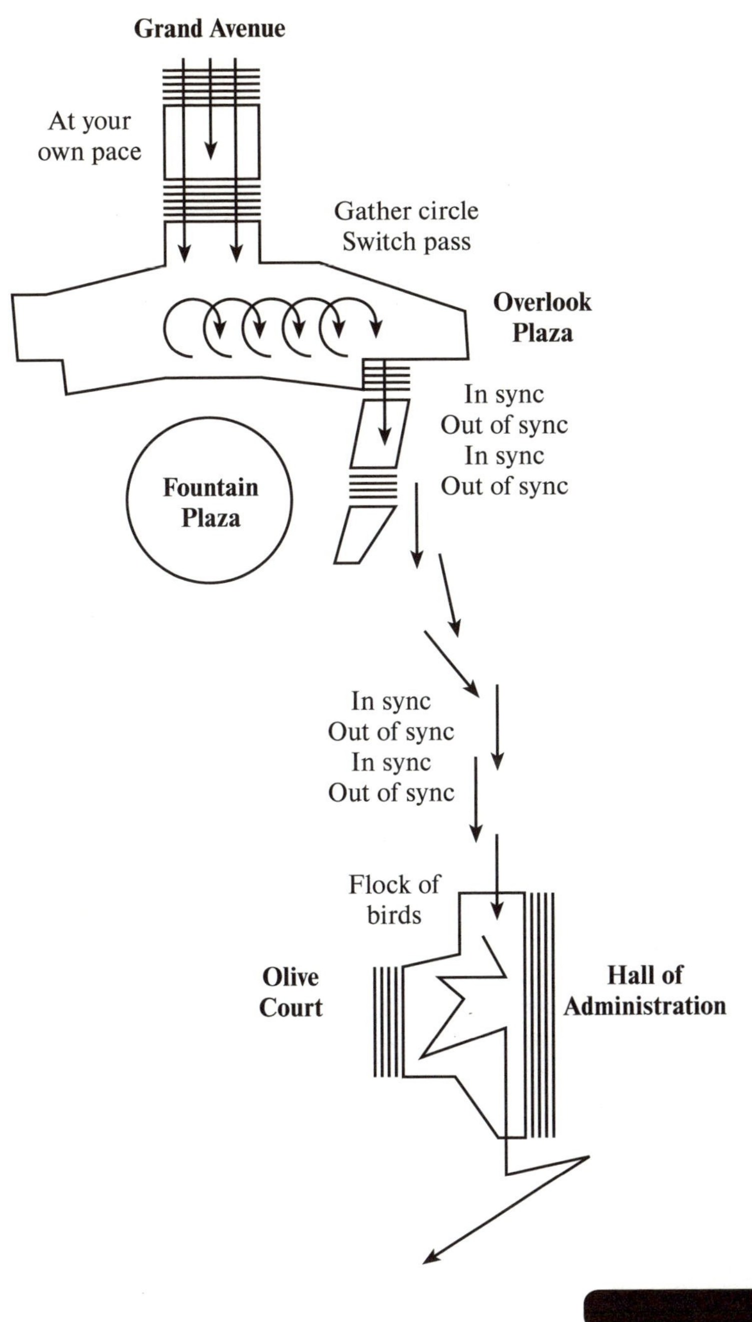

Grand Avenue
At your
own pace
Gather circle
Switch pass
Overlook
Plaza
In sync
Out of sync
In sync
Out of sync
Fountain
Plaza
In sync
Out of sync
In sync
Out of sync
Flock of
birds
Olive
Court
Hall of
Administration

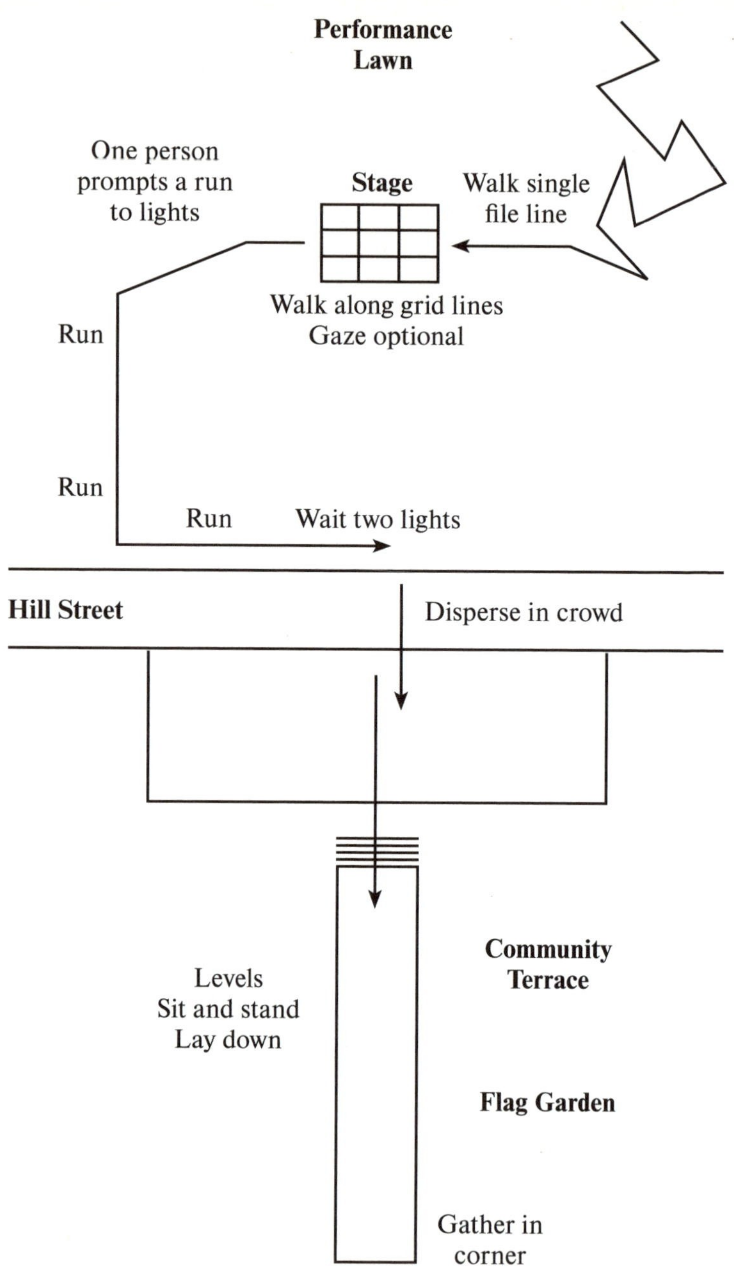
Performance Lawn
One person prompts a run to lights
Stage
Walk single file line
Walk along grid lines
Gaze optional
Run
Run
Run
Wait two lights
Hill Street
Disperse in crowd
Levels
Sit and stand
Lay down
Community Terrace
Flag Garden
Gather in corner

park in the open grass field along Spring Street. As the performance moves from one zone of the park to the next, movement sequences reinforce the qualities of each space. Beginning in an elevated plaza looking down upon a bubbling fountain, our opening sequence of square dance patterns reinforces the geometry of the space. Throughout the piece concrete pathways prompt us to walk slowly, quickly or in a delicately balanced single file line as if on a tight rope. Open spaces are encounters that invite us to follow given patterns on the ground or flock towards zones of attraction. Whether the space is intimate and quiet, vibrant and colourful or expansive and grandiose, each has a particular character for our actions to respond to. At times movements disappeared into the scenes of urban life, for example when the dancers blended with the pedestrians waiting for lights at the crosswalk.

Viewers of the performance are passers-by, office workers on their lunch break, people relaxing in the sun or quickly moving through the park to get to their destination. Some follow the performance for its full length, others passively engage from a distance, while some find themselves almost 'within' the performance and allow it to momentarily pass through their personal space. Performers and park-goers share the same space and at times their movements appear synced. Viewers might come away from the performance with a new spatial understanding of Grand Park or simply a curiosity about what they saw when they glanced up from their cell phone. The performance is intentionally subtle yet distinctly present, like a moving pattern that is momentarily absorbed into everyday life then released into structured performance.

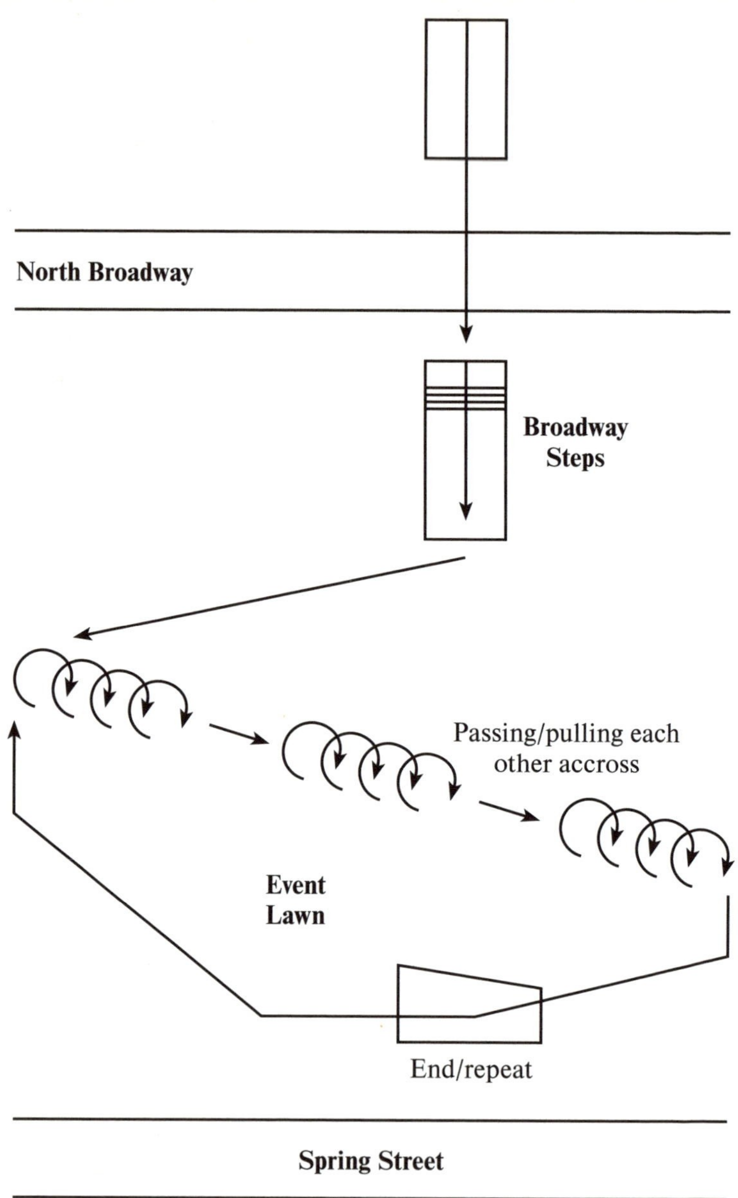
North Broadway
Broadway
Steps
Passing/pulling each
other accross
Event
Lawn
End/repeat
Spring Street
City Hall

Part 2

The City and Its Politics

Can We Tolerate It? Notes on the Public Sphere after the End of Liberalism

Bram Ieven

Introduction

Today, almost 55 percent of all human beings live in an urbanized environment. That number is expected to rise dramatically over the next couple of decades. More significantly, despite the fact that only half of the people living today reside in an urbanized environment, these urban environments use up to two thirds of the earth's resources. In short, the city, taken as a name for the urban centres as well as their sprawl, is one of the dominant social and political structure of contemporary society today, not only because of its gigantic production and use of resources, information and social interaction, but also because of the number of people it affects.

So what is a city and how does it define our public sphere? In this essay I will take a three-step approach to understanding the urban public sphere, its aesthetic and material make-up and the possibility to interrupt it or wrest it open for something new. The first part of my essay makes an attempt to define the city and its influence on producing and controlling the public sphere. What plays a pivotal part in my understanding of the contemporary city – and urban life in general – is that I call into question the liberal idea of the public sphere and the free individual that moves in it, freely engaging in political conversations. Instead, in this essay I want to draw attention to the complexity and structural diversity that characterizes contemporary city life to suggest that this complexity, rather than the philosophical premises of modern liberal political thought, should be taken as the starting point for understanding how the public sphere is constituted. The city is a dense environment – dense in spatial terms, rich in symbolic and semantic interaction, full of social encounters and exchanges, highly productive and bustling with life. As such, it serves as both the breeding ground for political ideas and for the political sphere as such. If the city is far too complex to be reduced to an historical concept, then surely the political sphere that it produces – that realm of everyday social interaction – is too contingent and too material to be elevated to something as generic as the 'public sphere' in which 'political subjects' are free to interact with one another.

To develop this argument, the second part of my essay engages with Herbert Marcuse's critique of liberal political theory. More in particular, in the early 1960s, Marcuse developed a critique of Western society, claiming that the Western political premise of 'individual liberty' had led to a repressive and restrictive political infrastructure. Within the context of industrialized society,

Marcuse argued, our political agency is rapidly deteriorating. This is so, not because of a restriction of freedom, not because social critique and political activism are banned, but precisely because they are tolerated and recuperated within the existing system. In other words, the society of affluence that Marcuse described in the early 1960s was also a society where critique and dissent no longer had a potent or significant role to play. But if we delve into Marcuse's argument, his social critique not only has some dire consequences for how he thinks of the public sphere; it also interferes with how he thinks about the city. Like many political philosophers, Marcuse is first and foremost interested in conceptualizing the premise of politics, its outcomes, and only in the last instance does he look at the material political infrastructures that this can lead to. But what if we start by looking at the infrastructures that have developed? What if we start by looking at the city and try to conceptualize the public sphere from the bottom up.

In short, thinking differently about the city may entail thinking differently about the constitution of the public sphere as well. So, in the third and final part of my essay, I take the example of the borough of Kanaleneiland (Utrecht, the Netherlands) to indicate that the city and the way it is planned hardly ever coincides with how it is used in practical daily situations.

Defining the Public Sphere: Market, Media and City

In my view, two elements are decisive for the public sphere. First, there is the classic element of the city and its spaces for encounter, congregation and discussion; this is the *polis* and, more specifically, the *agora* or marketplace where citizens encounter one another. Second, there is the complex media apparatus that connects citizens to one another, even in different cities or on different continents, and serves as the main distribution channel for political ideas, discussions and sentiments. In both cases, the city has an essential role to play. But what if we would rethink the very notion of the public sphere on the basis of the contemporary city? What happens in a city? There is no longer one marketplace or agora where the townspeople congregate to discuss public affairs; instead, we have a myriad of multifaceted moments and places for encounter and an extremely dense communication network.

On a purely practical level, the city is a congregation of resources: human labour force, instruments of production, different facilities, and so on. According to Ferdinand Braudel, an

economy always needs these hubs or centres of production: 'A world-economy always has an urban center of gravity. News, merchandise, capital, credit, people, instructions, correspondence all flow into and out of the city. Its powerful merchants lay down the law, sometimes becoming extraordinarily wealthy.'[1] But the city is more than just a convenient congregation of resources and capabilities. The strength of the city consists in the fact that the concentration of labour and resources reaches a critical threshold beyond which this concentration becomes more valuable because it becomes capable of generating and multiplying its own complexity and productivity. The city, at that point, becomes too complex to control by one merchant or by one political leader.

The city is both a spatial and temporal construction on a vast scale, a congregation of resources, activities, and productivity in which 'at every instant, there is more than the eye can see, more than the ear can hear, a setting or a view waiting to be explored. Nothing is experienced by itself, but always in relation to its surroundings, the sequences of events leading up to it, the memories of past experiences.'[2] Lynch's *The Image of the City* serves as a reminder that the city, even on an aesthetic or sensory level, is anything but an open and a-historical public sphere. Rather, it is a complex system that is based on what becomes visible and what remains invisible.

And yet the city, and more specifically the material and cognitive patterns that it weaves and that guide its inhabitants, serves as the material basis for the construction of a public sphere. It does so in two ways. First, the city is a complex aggregation of public facilities, which facilitate real life public encounters and gatherings in which the exchange of ideas takes place. But of course, just like Habermas connected the rise of the public not only to the rise of mercantile capitalism in early modernity but also to the rise of journals and newspapers that facilitated the exchange of ideas on a large scale, the city today also works as a node in a large, global communication network. The dense network of communication technologies that the city hosts, its technological infrastructure and know-how, allows the city's inhabitants as well as its private companies and public institutions to be connected to the other inhabitants, companies and institutions in the same city or in other cities all over the world. This conglomeration of technical facilities and know-how enables the city and its suburban sprawl to act as the social and technological foundation for a widened, global public sphere in which ideas, information and knowledge are exchanged at a rapid pace. This turns cities into complex hubs or nodes in an even more widespread and complex global communication network. This is the material element in the construction of the global public sphere; and instead of conceptualizing the public sphere and only afterwards looking at the city, our understanding of the public sphere should start from an analysis of the city as providing the material infrastructure for the social interactions in the city.

Because of the expanded communication infrastructures that allow cities all over the world to connect to each other, the Spanish-American sociologist and urbanist Manuel Castells has suggested that most cities today should be understood as global rather than local social hubs. The phenomenon of the global cities is moreover not restricted to the twenty-something large megacities around the globe. To the contrary, medium-sized cities are also global cities in the sense that they are connected to an urban network of other global cities all over the world. The global city phenomenon, he writes, 'is a process that connects advanced services, producer centers, and markets in a global network, with different intensity and at a different scale depending upon the relative importance of the activities located in each area *vis-à-vis* the global network.'[3] Castells' most powerful observation about global cities that are affected by the information technologies is that these cities are increasingly characterized by *spatial discontinuity* or *disconnection*. For Castells, who argues that 'space is not a reflection of society, but its expression', this means that discontinuity becomes the dominant phenomenon of the global city, on a geographical, social as well as physical level. So, he argues about megacities such as New York, Mexico or Jakarta, 'it is this distinctive feature of being globally connected and locally disconnected, physically and socially, that makes mega-cities a new urban form.'[4] In short, the impact of new communication technologies on the city is that they rearrange the public sphere, social interaction and political cooperation.

The pivotal characteristic of the global city, then, is its capacity to connect the city to other urban centres and therefore to other economic, cultural and social workflows. In the process it has the possibility to allow for an ongoing social, cultural and political exchange. New ideas and insights can spread more easily from one city to another. This public exchange of ideas in the global city is what makes it a complex, global public sphere. But what are the connections and how are they established? And do the global connections that are made possible through information technologies also imply that connections on a local level are lost? This may perhaps be true for the economic activity of a city, but how about everyday social interactions? I am not so sure.

Repressive Tolerance, the Public Sphere and the Functional City

There are two reasons why I wish to zoom in on the connections between on the one hand the global city and the global public sphere it is able to constitute through an elaborate communication network, and, on the other hand, the material and practical organization of the city and its neighbourhoods, which establishes a local public sphere. First, if we only focus on the informational flows that characterize the global city we risk observing only the 'dissipating forces' (as Castells has it) that push our understanding of city life away from actual streets, squares and real-life contingent encounters that take place in them. And yet, it is in this concrete manifestation of the city that political encounters between citizens take place. Secondly, by focusing on the technological revolution of the city over the last couple of decades, Castells has not yet addressed the way we think about the public sphere or how this might alter the constitution of the public sphere. This is, to be sure, not Castells intention. However, if we wish to understand how the global city generates a different take on the public sphere than has hitherto been developed, we need to take his argument one step further and look at how this new technological framework interlocks with concrete, everyday city life to constitute a new, deeply complex public sphere.

According to most liberal political theorists, the public sphere is 'a notable characteristic of liberal democratic societies'. The distinction between public and private is rather complex though. The distinction between the private and the public is complex, Margaret Thornton argues, because in between the private (family, intimate personal relations) and the public (government affairs) there is:

> the existence of two further significant areas of activity that are neither wholly public nor wholly private. These hybrid domains are the civil society and the market, both of which

are domains of freedom. Within civil society, or the social public, individuals are free to associate, litigate, travel, worship, and participate in education. Within the market, individuals are free to contact and engage in entrepreneurialism and private sector employment.[5]

The premise on which this understanding of the public sphere hinges, is that within it and because of it we achieve a certain amount of freedom, which at the same time constitutes the democratic potential of liberal society. Similarly, Craig Calhoun explains that

> the modern public sphere has two related meanings: it refers both to the open discussion among members of a collectivity about their common concerns and to the activities of the state that are central to defining that community.[6]

The question then becomes up to what extent the open discussion can take place. The idea of an open discussion presupposes the existence of an open space where the people can congregate and talk freely. But does such an open space exist?

To gain a better understanding of the problem we are facing with the city as a sphere of free public debate, it will be rewarding to take a look at Herbert Marcuse's critique of tolerance. What Marcuse is interested in when critiquing tolerance, is first and foremost exposing the liberal principles that lie at the core of this concept of tolerance. The concept of tolerance, which stems from a liberal tradition in Western political thought, is premised on a specific understanding of the role and capacity of the individual within society. In other words, at the heart of the tradition of tolerance lies a liberal understanding of the individual, which has been described in political philosophy by C.B. Macpherson as the theory of possessive individualism. The idea of possessive individualism, Macpherson maintains, 'regards the individual as human in his capacity as proprietor of his own person; the human essence is freedom from any but self-interested contractual relations with others.'[7] Marcuse's critique of tolerance is based on a similar critical analysis of possessive individualism. Like Macpherson, Marcuse argues that the premise of individualism is essentially false. Liberal tolerance, Marcuse writes,

> was ... based on the proposition that men were (potential) *individuals* who could learn to hear and see and feel by themselves, to develop their own thoughts, to grasp their true interests and rights and capabilities, also against established authority and opinion. This was the rationale of free speech and assembly.[8]

However, Marcuse suggests, this idea of the 'free individual' is deceptive. Individuals and their political and social behaviour are the result of the economic, political and social forces that are operative in the society in which they grow up. I would suggest that we think of these operative forces as including the governmental apparatuses, the economic system that the community is engaged in, the school system and more generally the way knowledge is transferred from one generation to the next, and the material and technological facilities it has available to achieve its aims (including mass media). The city is the locus where these forces are most densely layered, enmeshed and are working upon each other to create new, unpredictable situations. Indeed, precisely because of this density the city is an 'apparatus for living' that is very, very difficult to predict or control. The failed modernist projects in planning the city point in this direction, as do the cities of slums that dominate so much of the world's largest cities. Taking into regard these social and political forces, it becomes difficult to maintain that there can ever really exist such a thing as a free individual.

In short, the *principle* upon which tolerance is based, is false – that is to say, the principle of the free, self-determining individual is untenable.

However, it is only once this idea of a free, un-manipulated individual has been overcome that Marcuse takes the decisive step in his critique of tolerance. First, he presents us with the defence that a liberal political philosophy may have against the argument that the idea of a free individual is untenable. The argument runs as follows. Even if we accept that all political subjects are shaped by their political communities (i.e. by the economic, social, and technological forces that are operative in it) and by their historical and cultural situation, we could put forth the suggestion that there must exist an ideal combination of these influences that shapes human beings into responsible and free individuals. In other words, once we acknowledge that society shapes the individual we need not yet give up the liberal idea of society as an environment in which individuals act freely with each other on the bases of their own interests; rather, what we need to do is develop a just way in which these societal forces act upon the individual, so that the individual will become a free, entrepreneurial and engaged citizen within society. But Marcuse seems to have anticipated this argument and he is ready to undermine its premises:

> One might in theory construct a state in which a multitude of different pressures, interests, and authorities balance each other out and result in a truly general and rational interest. However, such a construction badly fits a society in which powers are and remain unequal and even increase their unequal weight when they run their own course. It fits even worse when the variety of pressures unifies and coagulates into an overwhelming whole, integrating the particular countervailing powers by virtue of an increasing standard of living and an increasing concentration of power.[9]

The key to understanding Marcuse's critique of tolerance – the key to understanding the potential but also the shortcoming of his social critique – is found in the thesis he develops in this passage, namely that the powers that organize society 'remain unequal and even increase their unequal weight when they run their own course'. Marcuse's critique starts from a simple observation: today, he argues, we live in a 'society in which powers are and remain unequal'. The liberal dream of an ideal equilibrium of social, economic and political pressures, interests and authorities may seem ideal in theory; and it may even be realized within the constraints of society as we know it today. However, such a well-balanced division of different social pressures does not lead to a free society. The point Marcuse makes is not that such an equilibrium of forces is unachievable – an argument which I will return to later on in this essay – but rather that even its completion does not lead to a free society.

Why would this be so? The answer is as simple as it is important: even if we can achieve such an evened-out, well-divided and balanced pressure of social forces, the 'free individual' that this interplay of social forces will produce will not at all be free: it lacks in *political imagination*, it is and will remain incapable of envisioning a different social system than the one it is living in today. More exactly, the free individual, because it is a product of the liberal set-up of society (evened-out and balanced pressure of different social forces) will become the sort of free individual that will *a priori* agree with the liberal political premises upon which society is based. Imagining a truly different society, or engaging in a political project that tries to overthrow existing society, thus becomes difficult.

It is this 'loss of difference' which, according to Marcuse, leads to the repressive tolerance that characterizes modern society. The different pressures that a society would need to truly guarantee and respect the constitution and circulation of different opinions and ideas, are under the sway of a more encompassing process of unification. This unification does not result from a disrespect for the fact that all of these forces and pressures that act upon citizens (economic, social, cultural, political) should 'run their own course'. Quite to the contrary, it is precisely the fact that they run their own course which leads to this process of unification Marcuse complains about.

What Marcuse is warning us for, is a loss of difference, not just a mismanagement of a variety of social and political forces. Such a recuperation of difference, carried out by a repressive (or even destructive) form of tolerance, Marcuse argues, can only succeed in an affluent democracy. Here is Marcuse's description of what such an affluent democracy looks like:

> Within the affluent democracy, the affluent discussion prevails, and within the established framework, it is tolerant to a large extent. All points of view can be heard: the Communist and the Fascist, the Left and the Right, the white and the Negro, the crusaders for armament and for disarmament. Moreover, in endlessly dragging debates over the media, the stupid opinion is treated with the same respect as the intelligent one, the misinformed may talk as long as the informed, and propaganda rides along with education, truth with falsehood. This pure toleration of sense and nonsense is justified by the democratic argument that nobody, neither group nor individual, is in possession of the truth and capable of defining what is right and wrong, good and bad. Therefore, all contesting opinions must be submitted to 'the people' for its deliberation and choice.[10]

This is the point where Marcuse's critique of tolerance leads him to a critical analysis of the public sphere. In as far as the public sphere tolerates both sense and nonsense to the same extent, it has become nothing but a mere semblance of political discussion, Marcuse argues. His critique of tolerance nourishes a distrust in the public sphere. But this distrust, I would argue, is ultimately based on the conviction that modern society leads to a liberal form of totalitarianism and control: an equilibrium of political forces will lead to a prototypical liberal individual, which will be able to express all of its free ideas but will lack the agency or imagination to really change society.

It is at this point that I want to take some distance from Marcuse's argument. My criticism of Marcuse's hinges on my conception of the city, which is different from his. Although Marcuse does not explicitly discusses his ideas on the city, I believe there are some indications that he underestimates the difference and complexity that characterize the city and that are also produced by the city. One might argue that the city, taken in its Greek original as the *polis*, is what lies at the heart of our idea of the political. This is certainly true for modern political thought, which has not only been developed in the urban centres (this was also the case for classical political thought), but has also seen the city becoming a bigger and bigger machine for living throughout modern times. But today we will also have to concede that the city has become so big and so complex that it makes little sense to argue that any political or economic regime would be able to single-handedly control its flow and production. The city is a complexity generating machine, and in that sense it has once again reached its destination as the prototype of what the *polis* is about.

When it comes to Marcuse, his conception of the city, or the *polis* if you will, seems in line with how modernist urban planning envisions the city. An influential group of modernist architects and urban planners such as the CIAM developed the idea of the functional city. It is this idea of the functional city that seems very much in line with affluent democracy. The ideal of the functional city, after all, was to divide the city into separate areas for work, leisure, and living. This would create a well-balanced, functional living space; 'a machine for living' (*machine à habituer*), as Le Corbusier, one of CIAM's most influential members, called it. The difference between Marcuse and the modernist vision of a functional city is that Marcuse saw this functionality, this guaranteed liberal freedom, as a problem rather than as a solution. In that sense, we could reverse the argument: I would argue that what becomes clear by confronting Marcuse's critique of affluent democracy is that urban design theories such as the functional city developed by the CIAM, are deeply indebted to a liberal, individualist conception of society. Like the more realistic version of political liberalism, modern urban planning focused on creating the ideal political environment; and like affluent democracy, as Marcuse had argued, the functional city essentially leads to a loss of difference, a dismantlement of political imagination and ultimately of political agency. The modern machine for living, then, becomes a machine for control.

City Dwelling: the Borough of Kanaleneiland

Both Marcuse and modernist urban planning may have underestimated the complexity generating machine that sits at the heart of today's society: the city. More generally, an underestimation of the city and the hyperdiversity it generates on all levels is something that was not sufficiently taken into account by most thinkers and urban planners during the first half of the twentieth century. The modernist legacy of the functional city has exerted a major influence on how one thought about the city and its political potential. But Marcuse was writing at the brink of a change in how one thought about urban planning and city design. Whereas in the modernist paradigm of the functional city urban planning was top-down, by the mid-1950s several leading architects and urban planners started to realize that taking into account the ideas from the people living in the neighbourhood was probably a much better way to plan an urban district. Marcuse's critique of tolerance and his ultimate scepticism of the public sphere affects both these views on city design. Marcuse's argument is not that the city or *polis* cannot be planned. It can be, and it seems as if Marcuse is under the impression that modern society is relatively successful in planning its cities.

But can the city really be planned? Does this not imply an underestimation of all the different forces and pressures that are actually at play in the city? And if it can be argued that the city is much more complex that both modernist urban planning and modern political thought has realized, then what does this imply for the public sphere that is constructed and maintained in the city?

In many ways the borough of Kanaleneiland [Canal Island] in the city of Utrecht, the Netherlands, serves as a prototypical example of the functional city. At the same time, it provides an excellent example of the impossibility of planning a city in this way. Practically speaking, the design for Kanaleneiland was largely inspired by the Pendrecht district in Rotterdam. In the immediate aftermath of the Second World War, the Dutch government saw itself beset with the task of rebuilding the larger cities of the country, which had been subject to bombing by both the German troops at the beginning of the war (in the case of Rotterdam, for example) and by the allied forces throughout the war. Although former city planner of Rotterdam and one-time collaborator of De Stijl J.J.P. Oud had eagerly tried to land the job of rebuilding the city of Rotterdam during the Nazi occupation, in 1942, the task of rebuilding was mostly postponed until after the war. It was at that time that the construction of the Pendrecht neighbourhood began. The project was put in the hands of the Bauhaus-educated architect Lotte Stam-Beese. The urban plan for the neighbourhood of Pendrecht would be of crucial significance for the development of post-war Dutch modernism. It set the tone and served as an example. For the CIAM, which in the early 1930s had come up with the plan of the functional city, 'Pendrecht became an international town planning prototype of the neighborhood idea: a residential district for urban man, who was less an individual than a member of a multifarious aggregation.'[11] The impact of this sort of neighbourhood on Dutch cities and the process of gentrification that they underwent – which in turn has created the material conditions for the existence of a public sphere – can hardly be overestimated. After all, what are we to think of an inhabitant who is 'less an individual' than part of a common crowd? What is already indicated in this characterization of the functional city, is that it leads to a loss of difference. Yet at the same time, such a process of unification – for that is what it really is – leads to 'an environment differentiated with regard to forms of living, which met the need for freely chosen, mostly fleeting contacts.'[12] Freely chosen contacts – that is, indeed, the ideal of liberal society and its conception of the individual. In as far as achieving this ideal requires that individuals now become less individual and more part of the crowd, the functional is a paradoxical political machine to say the least.

The way in which it becomes possible to illustrate why the planning of such a relatively functional living environment top-down, as the CIAM hoped to do, can never work, becomes particularly clear in the case of Kanaleneiland. The 1960s in the Netherlands not only saw the completion of major late modernist projects such as Pendrecht, the Bijlmer district, or Kanaleneiland, all still built within the immediate vicinity of the city centres of Rotterdam, Amsterdam and Utrecht, respectively. This was also the period in which the Dutch railways and other infrastructure were improved considerably. Consequently, more and more people began to make use of this infrastructure, with the number of commuters in the Netherlands going up. While more and more people were living in the western part of the country, what was significant is that more and more people chose to live outside of the inner city, often in the immediate vicinity of the city, and commute to work. The combination of these two trends was inevitably paradoxical: whereas the suburb of Kanaleneiland had been designed with the aim of attracting young city-dwellers who earned a medium income, these young families preferred to live outside of the city, which meant that the Canal Island area quickly turned into a neighbourhood populated by less wealthy, new inhabitants of the Netherlands – its migrant workers. Over the next three decades, Kanaleneiland transformed from a relatively prestigious borough built according to the state-of-the-art principles of the functional city, to a run-down neighbourhood where only the very poor citizens of Utrecht chose to live.

Conclusion

Architecture and urban planning are just two of the elements that constitute the city, but they are important ones. However, the reason why architecture today is important may have more to do with its failure to express the image of the city that it tried to convey than with its success. Or better yet, its success may be its failure: where modernist urban planning such as the districts of Pendrecht in the city of Rotterdam or the district of Kanaleneiland in the city of Utrecht succeeded in having the effect that they hoped for on the inhabitants of these districts (free-floating individuals, autonomous yet part of an egregious crowd) they also failed. They failed because what they could not foresee, was the unpredictable interplay between the different forces and elements of the city and of society: economic, political, and cultural. At the very moment when the late modernist urban project known as Kanaleneiland was completed, the more well-to-do citizens preferred to live outside of the city, an evolution made possible by the expansion of the roads, the possession of cars and the growth of the railway system in the Netherlands. Studying the city means studying a complex and unpredictable environment in which urban planning, coincidental encounters and economic transformations on micro- and macro-scale have their impact, but in which the *common* is ultimately created both by the citizens on a day-to-day basis – that is to say, on the basis of contingent everyday encounters within the larger historical genesis of their urban environment – and by the contingent interaction of different forces operative within society. Unlike what Marcuse and modernist urban planning maintained, these forces and the way they interact within the city are too complex to control. This is also where a new idea of what the public sphere consists of may be based upon on. Instead of thinking of the public sphere as an ideal of liberal political theory, we can think about the public sphere as generated by these sort of contingent interplay of forces.

Notes

1 Ferdinand Braudel, *The Structures of Everyday Life* (Berkeley and Los Angeles: University of California Press, 1982), p. 27.
2 Kevin Lynch, *The Image of the City* (Cambridge, MA: MIT Press, 1960), p. 1.
3 Manuel Castells, *The Rise of the Network Society* (Oxford: Blackwell, 2000, 1st ed. 1996), p. 411.
4 Ibid., p. 436.
5 Margaret Thornton, 'Public Sphere', in *The New Oxford Companion to Law*, ed. Peter Cane and Joanna Conaghan (Oxford: Oxford University Press, 2008), pp. 968–69, p. 968.
6 Craig Calhoun, 'Public Sphere', in *Dictionary of the Social Sciences*, ed. Craig Calhoun (Oxford: Oxford University Press, 2002), p. 392.
7 C.W. Macpherson, 'Revolution and ideology in the late twentieth century', in *Revolution*, ed. Carl J. Friedrich (New York: Transaction Publishers, 1966), p. 151.
8 Herbert Marcuse, 'Critique of Repressive Tolerance', in *A Critique of Pure Tolerance*, ed. R.P. Wolf et al. (Boston: Beacon Press, 1965), pp. 81–117, p. 90.
9 Ibid., p. 93.
10 Ibid., pp. 94–95.
11 Hans van der Cammen and Len de Klerk, *The Selfmade Land: Culture and Evolution of Urban and Regional Planning in the Netherlands* (Houten: Spectrum, 2012), p. 228.
12 Ibid., p. 228.

The Machinic-Dividual City

Gerald Raunig

The conceptual concatenation of 'public sphere' and 'city' is a highly modern notion, marked by centuries of discursive consolidation and, at the same time, of the political furtherance of ideologemes such as 'the public intellectual', the 'democratic function of the media', or 'public space' as an ideal object for theories of both consensus and conflict. Yet there is little left of these grand ideas from the nineteenth and twentieth century today. The transition to post-Fordist production, to the increasingly totalizing valorization of immaterial, communicative, cognitive and affective labour, in short: to the paradigm of machinic capitalism, has led to the complete erosion of the dialectic of the private and the public, in recent decades. The ludicrous 'interventions' of ever new New Philosophers only prove the total functionalization of the position of the 'public intellectual' as now only completely remote- and externally controlled media intellectuals. Today, the 'media public' exists, if at all, merely as spectacle. And even the radical (post)-avant-gardist versions of producing situations (as in the practice and theory of the early Situationist International) or of producing public spheres as a non-representationist practice as in the Reclaim the Streets parties of the 1990s up to the present,[1] promise no solutions at the pinnacle of the new paradigm.

Today 'interrupting the city' does not mean resistance, but gentrification, gating, and militarization[2] of the city, preventing the 'undercommons', suppressing the remainders and appearances of transversal sociality, introducing ever new logistical strategies of the neoliberal, modulating city. Gilles Deleuze already wrote about this in 1990 in his 'Postscript on the Societies of Control', in a passage that sounds more like a prophecy than a postscript:

> The conception of a control mechanism, living the position of any element within an open environment at any given instant (whether animal in a reserve or human in a corporation, as with an electronic collar), is not necessarily one of science fiction. Félix Guattari has imagined a city where one would be able to leave one's apartment, one's street, one's neighbourhood, thanks to one's (dividual) electronic card that raises a given barrier; but the card could just as easily be rejected on a given day or between certain hours; what counts is not the barrier but the computer that tracks each person's position – licit or illicit – and effects a universal modulation.[3]

Twenty-five years after these truly prophetic lines were written, the machinization of control has become part of our lives, as the machinization of technical apparatuses, as the machinization of our social relationships and desires in social media, as the dividualization of our bodies, our intellects, our data.[4] In machinic capitalism, 'city' and 'public' are no longer relevant categories, but merely vague memories and markers of a past era.

Becoming-Machine of the Technical Apparatuses

The concept of machinic capitalism,[5] which does not indicate a new phase of capitalism, but an increasing significance of the machinic in contemporary capitalism, does not imply a further version of the dichotomous preference given to objects (over subjects), animals (over humans), materialities (over the immaterial), realisms (over discourses). Rather, it concerns the flows passing through these dichotomies and through the single things – data flows, currents, wishes, becomings, middles, dancing relations, the in-between of dividual sociality.

Becoming-machine of the devices, apparatuses, equipment: When technical apparatuses come into play, they are never only technical apparatuses, but most of all components of machinic intercourse. To this extent, the notion of the machine invading the human being is already wrong: cardiac or brain pacemakers, for example, are more than technical apparatuses, non-human alien elements that turn the human being into a machine; an electronic tag is more than a substitute for prison walls; chips for locating animals are more than the dog leashes of the control society. Human enhancement is more than the improvement of human beings by technical artefacts, prostheses, implants, neural interfaces, operations, and substances. In all of these examples the machinic is not simply a means used by humans, but a specific relation, first of all a relation of appending.

In many situations it appears as though machines are not penetrating into human beings as much as humans are being drawn 'into the machine'. I am not only dependent on a 'machine' external to me, which surveys and subordinates me, but I also want to become part of the machine, append to it. In this sense, machinic servility is entirely different from subjugation to the machine. The pull of machines, their attraction, has undoubtedly led to new, very bodily desires, to relations of pending, streaking, and enveloping. Material size plays no role in this: regardless of whether it is a small mobile telephone or the extended facilities of the NSA – all that is relevant is appending to the networks, the clouds, the machines.

Pending to the machine also means being dependent on the machine. The desire to be online, for instance, has aspects of being permanently reachable, of Internet addiction, and of apparatus fetishism at the same time. Yet the latter is more than just a means of distinction, compulsion to consume, or simply the desire for the latest devices and gadgets. There is also an urge for increasingly strong haptic techniques of streaking, swiping, stroking. Swiping across screens, thus streaking screens, simultaneously de- and re-territorializing the screens, this is undoubtedly just as much a new cultural technique as the accelerated thumbs of the smartphone generation. Streaking/swiping the screens also has something of a haptic differentiation that goes far beyond identifying letters in text messages, in email or social media messages on the smartphone. Swiping across the screen not only means streaking the device, gently striating it, but also affectively approaching it, stroking it. To the extent that this ephemeral stroking carries out the same movement in the same place, it corresponds to a reterritorialization. To the extent that it does not stroke the same place twice, but instead scrolls over the surfaces of the virtual contents, streaking them, stroking over them, it is deterritorialization.

The more differentiated the development of appending to the machines is – the material relations of proximity – the more it appears as though human beings want to 'get into the machine'. Yet 'getting into the machine' is a notion that is just as false as that of the 'machine penetrating into the human'. Perhaps it is more of an endless convergence with the technical apparatuses, which endlessly differentiates both material and immaterial intercourse. It is a relatively small step from typing letters on keyboards to swiping across screens, which could be expanded in the future. Verbal control is a potential mode of this expanded assembling, or also using body parts other than fingers and hands. Feet could come into play, for example, as with a sewing machine, a drum, an organ, or a wah-wah pedal, or the whole body – like the sound assemblage of a one-man band, singing with a drum on the back and a tambourine under one foot.

Large desktop touchscreens take over from operating via keyboard, and yet notebooks, pads, and smartphones are still carried around as personal production means, fetishes, gadgets. Future machinic environments may perhaps be imagined more in the logic of enveloping than in that of appending or of physically touching. Whether we want it or not, whether we know it or not, most data is already largely in the clouds. All that is missing then is omnipresent access to the data-pumps that we can plug into anywhere without further mediation, or a step further: what is missing is a way of dealing with data clouds that tends to be not at all incorporeal, but indeed imperceptible. Touchscreens drive the development of apparatuses from visible appendage toward an increasingly invisible envelope. Machinic sensors do not necessarily have to work through touching the apparatuses. Gestures, hand signs, body language instead of Google Glass and data gloves. Perhaps the Theremin is the instrument of the future. No external, visible envelope that comprehensively envelops everything, but rather an endless (self-)enveloping of every single person, access, at the same time, to the machinic environment, to the extent that the control of the codes allows it.

Ghostly music, glissandi generated without touch, hands and arms gliding through the air, electromagnetic fields moved by the electric vibrations of the body. Gliding, flowing, floating, flying music. Just as Leon Theremin began to play his instrument nearly a hundred years ago, the people of today are beginning to play the technical instruments, the apparatuses, the equipment that surrounds, besieges, envelops them, the environments and surroundings, and they are played by them. There is something of virtuosity at work here on both sides. But as said before, this is not a matter of instrumental relations, of machines as tools and means of human beings or vice versa. We are not playing instruments, but rather playing with them, the way children play with other children, with things and machines.

In the 1970s some children played with remote-controlled cars, boats, and airplanes. These were wonderful tools for teaching especially boys to control machines at an early age. The overkill that was to be avoided in all cases was the removal of the boat/car/airplane from the range of the remote control. Fifty years later it will be a question of keeping all single things, not only apparatuses but also people, within the range of remote control, whether in gaming, in street traffic or in everyday life. Only the remote control is missing, and so is the person who operates it. Just as the auto-mobile does not really move itself, the self-driving car will not drive itself either. Where people once divested themselves of effort, now they are divesting themselves of control. Machinic self-conduct means a complex interplay of various components that assemble, assemble into an assemblage. Self-assembling and assembling the assemblage.

And not only the streets want to be machinically regulated, but airways increasingly also require machinic engagement. With regard to the acquisition of drones, while politics insists almost too conspicuously that drones are controlled by humans, with Stefano Harney and Fred Moten it can be said that 'drones are not un-manned to protect American pilots. They are un-manned because they think too fast for American pilots.'[6] The dystopic and pantopic fantasy of logistics aims to limit human beings as 'controlling agents' as far as possible, to liberate the flow of commodities and weapons from human time and human error. This does not mean that humans become superfluous: to the extent that they survive them, they will continue to have to explain the collateral damage of drones. It is inherent to their 'signature strikes' that they are not always completely free from errors. The drone brings death or it brings an order from Amazon, based on algorithmically produced risk or potentiality profiles. Most of all, it promises precision beyond human exactitude. Targeted, smart, reliable, damage-minimizing precision in a machinic environment. The drone is the machinic animal of the present and at some point it will also unfold itself, multiply itself.

The New Privacy of Facebook

'Facebook enables you to connect with the people in your life and share with them what matters to you.'[7]

> One has to be completely taken in by this internal ruse of confession in order to attribute a fundamental role to censorship, to taboos regarding speaking and thinking; one has to have an inverted image of power in order to believe that all these voices which have spoken so long in our civilization – repeating the formidable injunction to tell what one is and what one does, what one recollects and what one has forgotten, what one hides and what hides itself, what one is thinking and what one thinks he is not thinking – are speaking to us of freedom.[8]

Machinic assemblability and self-assembling, confessional communication and self-division. That is what Facebook also is: in addition to being a means for self-presentation, communication, and manically showing off one's life, in addition to being a hotspot of future social media bubbles, in addition to being a tool for Facebook and Twitter revolutions, in addition to being an indelible memory of millions, it is also a medium of confession, indeed a compulsion to confession, and in this sense it is a medium not just of com-munication, but also of self-division.

Facebook enables me to further optimize this machinic practice of division. The 'formidable injunction' of our civilization to 'tell what one is and what one does, what one recollects and what one has forgotten, what one hides and what hides itself, what one is thinking and what one thinks he is not thinking', is in good hands with Facebook. With one limitation: what does not apply, or only under certain conditions, is the external compulsion inherent to the word 'injunction'. Here everything revolves around machinic servility, the will to confess, the desire to communicate.

In the first volume of *The History of Sexuality*, using material on medical tests, psychiatric examinations, pedagogical reports, and family controls of sexuality in the eighteenth and nineteenth centuries, Foucault describes a new form of power, which is based most of all on various new forms of confession: 'it required an exchange of discourses, through questions that extorted admissions, and confidences that went beyond the questions that were asked.'[9] Counter to that which Foucault calls the repression hypothesis, he brings the intensity of the confession into play, the ineluctable relation of power and pleasure:

> Power operated as a mechanism of attraction; it drew out those peculiarities over which it kept watch. Pleasure spread to the power that harried it; power anchored the pleasure it uncovered.[10]

As pastoral power, Christian morality combines the compulsion to confess with the desire to admit. It can refer to a long genealogy of confession practices since the High Middle Ages. Since these medieval upheavals, power as a mechanism of attraction, a siren call to confession, has multiplied, enticing from all sides, spreading its sounds across all social strata. It not only entices me to relieve myself in confession, but also with the promise that I could decipher my most inner secrets just by making them public:

> The obligation to confess is now relayed through so many different points, is so deeply ingrained in us, that we no longer perceive it as the effect of a power that constrains us; on the contrary, it seems to us that truth lodged in our most secret nature, 'demands' only to surface ... .[11]

his is the central statement of Foucault's confession theory. The idea of a truth only waiting 'in our most secret nature' to surface, is also the basis for the ubiquitous propaganda of transparency today. Its primary procedure is to connect an identitarian self and its truth that *must* step out of the dark; if this does not succeed, then it can only be because transparency is shackled by a power, a force, a compulsion that it must liberate itself from. Reversal of the perspective to power: instead of seeing a manifold power at work, which operates by invoking confession and permanently producing desires to confess, every kind of power is regarded as a homogeneous block of the potential repression of confession. In contrast to this, confession has a liberating effect from this perspective, it helps to escape from silence, sets truth free. Here division primarily assumes the excessive form of confessional communication and publication. Truth deprived wants to surface, that which has been kept from the public, what is de-privatized.

Against the background of this appeal to make freedom of confession possible, the private increasingly ends up becoming defensive. Privacy appears as a concept in the limited meaning of data protection, at most: in the field of social networks, discourses focus on the illegitimate storage of personal data and the impending loss of privacy. Privacy is supposed to provide an answer to the question of how this data may be protected from access by others: protected, first of all, from state repression against single persons, but also from the valorization of the (accumulated) personal data by commercial actors. In light of the increasingly excessive state surveillance programs as well as the commercial misuse of personal data, these are problems that need to be taken seriously; at the same time, however, they are barely varied repetitions of the one-sided narratives of decline, which have lamented the decline either of the public or of the private sphere in ever new combinations. And these narratives often go below the level of even the old, surveillance society science fiction motives from *1984* or *Brave New World*.

Beyond the data protection discourses, or rather parallel to them, the 'internal ruse of confession' gains a new explosiveness. What does it mean when a desire spreads that does not lament the decline of the private sphere at all, but seems instead to flirt with voluntarily abandoning all privacy? What does it mean, when in social media people are not simply forced to sell their data for the economic purposes of others, but instead virtually develop a compulsion to de-privatization? Taking the example of Facebook: the problematic aspects of the business model of Facebook lie not only in the exploitation of unpaid labour, in the identification of users for advertising clients, or in the opacity of the privacy policy and the privacy settings of Facebook. The underexposed side of social networking is the desire to publicly communicate oneself, to divide one's data for sharing, to divide oneself.

This new desire for 'self-division' in the social media is based on the urge of the virtual sociality to surface, on an urgent necessity for visibility, which is connected with a new notion of privacy as deficiency. Of course, deficiency, lack, being deprived, has always been inherent to the concept of the private sphere; in antiquity it was a lack of office, a lack of publicity, a lack of the possibility of political agency. In the sociality of contemporary social media, however, privacy becomes more of a problem because it implies invisibility, the decoupling from the lifeblood of social networks. Felix Stalder describes this new fear of – now digital – disappearance as the reverse side of the promise of authentic communication in social networks:

> In order to create sociability in the space of flows people first have to make themselves visible, that is, they have to create their representation through expressive acts of communication. ... There are both negative and positive drivers to making oneself visible in such a way: there is the threat of being invisible, ignored and bypassed, on the one hand, and the promise of creating a social network really expressing one's own individuality, on the other.[12]

So rather than supposing the core of the authentic self in privacy and leaving it there, it is sought and produced in the expressive practice of confession in the social networks, in order to ward off the danger of disjunction from the life-sustaining social networks at the same time. The fully active maintenance of the machinic connection sustains the infrastructure for the manic practice of confession, and at the same time it protects against slipping into the dark fields of activities that are not or only barely visible and thus dangerous or simply not commodifiable, because they are not there for valorization.

It is no longer a small number of authority figures that are the addressees of machinic confession, those to whom one confesses in a decidedly personal relationship, but an increasingly larger, often incalculable number of 'friends'. However, this relationship is only rarely social in the traditional sense – if at all, sociality usually appears in the inverse form of the shit storm or other abuses on the Internet, as an asocial sociality. Machinic confession persists in the mode of conduct between the self-identifying self and its truth in front of the opaque wall of a social confessional, Facebook. Although Foucault did not know Facebook, he described the way it works very well:

> Its veracity is not guaranteed by the lofty authority of the magistery, nor by the tradition it transmits, but by the bond, the basic intimacy in discourse, between the one who speaks and what he is speaking about. On the other hand, the agency of domination does not reside in the one who speaks ..., but in the one who listens and says nothing; not in the one who knows and answers, but in the one who ... is not supposed to know.[13]

The unknowing, incalculable and silent majority of 'friends' dominates the scene. Their sharing, as invoked by the Facebook slogan, being as smooth as possible, 'smooth sharing', consists of pressing a button, of clicking on a link, the share-button. The effect of the truth discourse, however, is to be found among those who confess something or everything about themselves.

On Nietzsche's scale from compulsion through 'voluntary obedience' to 'instinct', the motion has so far gone some distance in the direction of what Nietzsche calls 'instinct' in *Human, All Too Human*, which he links, first of all, with habituation, in other words naturalization and normalization, and secondly with pleasure. These two aspects are directly coupled in Facebook's practice: the habituation to machinic appendage concatenates with the machinic desire for total sharing. 'Division' functions for Facebook not – or not only – in the sense of the illicit appropriation of personal data by state or economic actors, but in the desire of the data-producers for dividualization, in a kind of 'voluntarily obedient', 'voluntary' division, self-determined self-division. Facebook is based on invoking the liberating effect of confession, on the figure of privacy as a deficiency to be avoided, and on the presumption that the machinic confession is not compelled, but instead implies voluntariness, desire, pleasure, and – with Nietzsche – 'vanity'.

Post-Public Cities of Big Data

Nietzsche's view remains, even in the critique of what is all too human, a view of the human being, most of all the individual human being. His thesis of the self-division of man in morality remains stuck – essentially also like Foucault's ethics of confession – at the question of the compliance of individuals. Yet what social and media technologies like Facebook do cannot be explained solely with a view of human beings nor of individuals and their relationship to a collective, nor can it be explained with a subjugation of human or non-human individuals to machines. The machinic-dividual itself goes far beyond techno-media apparatuses and individual desires.

Nietzsche wrote: 'In morality man treats himself not as individuum but as dividuum.' Yet there is no dividuum. In the strong substantive sense, 'the dividuum' does not exist: as in the philological evidence, in which the Latin word occurs only rarely, and even then only as a weak, heteronomous substantive, it makes little sense to speak of 'a dividual' or 'dividuals'. Even 'in morality', individuals cannot become dividuals, but in and through dividualization they can indeed become conforming, compliant, obedient individuals. 'In morality' ever new forms of servitude, of conformity, of adaptation emerge, ever new 'compliant characters', yet this servitude, to the extent that it remains at the individual level, does not cover the dividual.

Over a hundred years after Nietzsche, Gilles Deleuze posits the transition from the disciplinary to the control regime with a similar formulation relating to the concept of the dividual. With this he takes up the ideas of his friend Michel Foucault, with whom he was co-responsible for the critical French edition of Nietzsche's complete works. According to Deleuze's explanations in the 'Postscript on the Societies of Control', the disciplinary regime has two poles, in which it is equally interested. It masses together and individualizes, constituting the mass as a body and modularizing its members as individuals – entirely in keeping with Nietzsche's notions of morality and the self-dividing individual, and entirely in keeping with Foucault's interpretation of the mode of governing of pastoral power: *omnes et singulatim*. Deleuze reformulates this equal interest of pastoral power in its two poles: the disciplinary society is marked at the individual pole by the signature, as unequivocal indication of the thus identifiable author, and at the mass pole by the number or administrative numeration [*numéro matricule*] that identifies the position of the individual in the mass. It is this relation, by no means oppositional, but rather mutual, between 'single-ones' and 'one-all', which is exemplarily attributed to the compositions of German Romanticism in *A Thousand Plateaus*, in which the groupings of power are fully diversified, but only as 'relations proper to the Universal'.[14] The romantic hero acts as a subjectified individual under the conditions of an orchestral whole. Always *omnes*, all as one, one-all, orchestra – *et*, and – *singulatim*, single-ones, single voices, related to the one-all.

A completely different regime is that in which the mass is individuated by group individuations and cannot be reduced to the individuality of the subjects and the universality of the whole – in *A Thousand Plateaus* Deleuze and Guattari describe this completely different relation of (now no longer one-all, but rather) dividual one-crowd and single-one with musical examples from Debussy, Mussorgsky, Bartók, and Berio. Here the mass is not individuated by persons, but by affects, and to this extent the single-one is not individual and related to the universal, but rather singular. Deleuze developed the downside of this new 'dividual scale'[15] a decade after *A Thousand Plateaus* in the 'Postscript on the Societies of Control' – and Nietzsche still seems to resonate through Deleuze's formulation: 'Individuals have become "dividuals", and masses [have become] samples, data, markets, or "banks".'[16] That which is dividual (unlike Nietzsche, Deleuze uses the adjective dividual) and the banks, though banks are meant less in the traditional sense, but more as databases: yet not only the bank as a place populated by counters, clerks, and payment forms seems oddly outmoded to today's ears, when describing dividual data flows in the societies of control. Even the image of the database still holds far too much of a territorium that can be clearly situated, a storage space that is administered, arranged and ruled by human beings. The reality of today's dividual data sets, enormous accumulations of data that can be divided, recomposed and valorized in endless ways, is one of worldwide streams, of deterritorialization and of machinic expansion, most succinctly expressed as Big Data. Facebook needs the self-division of individual users just as intelligence agencies still hold on to individual identities. Big Data, on the other hand, is less interested in individuals and just as little interested in a totalization of data, but all the more in data sets that are freely floating and as detailed as possible, which it can dividually traverse – as an open field of immanence with a potentially endless extension. These enormous multitudes of data want to form a horizon of knowledge that governs the entire past and present and is thus also able to capture the future.

The collection of data by economic and state actors, especially secret services, insurance and banking industries, has a long tradition, but it has gained a completely new quality with machine-readability and the machinic processing of the data material. This quality applies not only to credit rating agencies or intelligence agencies, but also to all areas of networked everyday life, all partial data of individual lives, for instance about children, divorces, debts, properties, consumption habits, communication behaviours, travelling habits, internet activities, movements in real space, whereabouts, health, fitness, eating habits, calorie consumption, dental care, credit card charges, cash machine use, to name only a few. Refrigerators, ovens, thermostats, smart-guide toothbrushes, intelligent toilet bowls, networked offices, networked kitchens, networked bedrooms, networked bathrooms, networked toilet facilities – all controllable via smartphone, all accessible via the cloud. This machinic data can potentially be combined, for instance for the logistics of individual thing-movements, and made accessible according to dividual logics.

In order to make it possible to traverse, divide and recombine these data, cooperation is needed from those previously called consumers. Participation means the most comprehensible free (especially in the sense of unpaid) data exchange possible, not only sharing existing data, but also producing new data. Data valorization plays out in the terrain of externalizing production processes and activating consumers, as this has been intensified since the 1990s in all economic areas. Crowds, multitudes, dispersed masses – their modes of existence and living are captured, stretched, appropriated and exploited beyond the realm of paid labour. Scoring, rating, ranking, profiling. Consumers who are activated and generate value with their activity do not have to be paid. The Open Source model of program development by the *crowd* has meanwhile become established as a business model and spread to all economic sectors. Free labour in free association, but to the advantage of the enterprises of the New Economy.

And instead of the added value thus produced being invested in higher wages, the 'free labour' of the freelance data brokers results in exactly the opposite consequences, namely a further devaluing and elimination of paid labour. The economy of partition and domination becomes a no less dominating economy of dividing/sharing, boosted by self-government. A sharing economy that lifts the minus of community from the Christian genealogy into contemporary machinic capitalism. Appeals to cut spending, de-growth compulsion, austerity by other means.

The economy of sharing/dividing data commodifies not only automatically accruing and occurring data, it also stimulates the production of data beyond all professional activity. Recently this can be easily followed in the realms of physical self-measurement and bookkeeping about body data. In my old-fashioned format of Kieser Training, this bookkeeping is still limited to an analogue procedure. The machines appear as relatively plain and at least not visibly networked apparatuses for bodily fitness, explained as rationally as possible in both their function and effect, and enabling concentrated individual training without disruption. Yet the machine is not only the mechanical equipment by which I am stretched, but most of all the board in which I stretch the table that I note my small steps of progress in. Whether it is a matter of progress or regress, it raises the tension, the pressure, the desire. In the desire of appending to, being stretched in the machines, it happens that I overheat. Self-division functions well here, but data-division not yet.

The concurrence of individuals measuring themselves on the one hand and producing dividual body data on the other remained reserved to the Quantified Self movement. Whereas the confession techniques of self-government in social media primarily produce discursive outputs, their quantitative representations consisting mostly in the number of likes, the permanent measuring of the self is to be commodified directly and simply as the production of quantitative data. First of all, Quantified Self implies observing oneself as continuously as possible. Together with confession literature and lifelogging, the machinic connection of physical and discursive self-techniques is probably even more relevant than that of the lineages that link single techniques with their historical genealogies: the Quantified Self with the old growth marks on the door frame, the charts of weight measurements from the family scale, and other classical body records, lifelogging with writing log books, diaries, travel journals, and other records. Yet a further combination drives the commodification to an extreme: feeding quantitative and qualitative data into the social networks, with the speed of their feedback adding aspects of sociality and social control to the individual privacy of body data and the discursive narratives.

A further zone of the expansion of dividual data is that of search engines. What is searched is perhaps not so interesting by itself, but the accumulation of search data determines both the individual and the dividual forms of data processing. Machinic search processes basically lead to the probable, to what is dominant for the majority, to what is normalized, and certainly to what is economically lucrative for the search engines. Google & Co tailor search results individually on the one hand (geographical position, language, individual search history, personal profile, et cetera), but on the other hand also in keeping with their commercial interests. Over time, all the individual profiles become increasingly valuable as part of Big Data. In principle, however, searching is still determined too much by humans and thus dangerously uncontrolled. This is why there is currently a massive transition to machinic industries of suggestion, which save the consumers the trouble of engaging in a relatively undetermined search process. Before users even start to think of searching, they can count on suggestions. These suggestions are not always presented to the customers by fully automatized systems: algorithms often collaborate with humans to develop fine gradations and endless combinations of possibilities based on the previous habits not only of the individual customers, but also of their social and territorial surroundings. The results are unrequested and yet suitable individualized suggestions for books and other purchases from Amazon, travel suggestions from Air Berlin, viewing suggestions from Netflix, and even these specializations are increasingly dissolving.

The compliant character is receptive to machinic suggestions. Machinic control is expanding as far as it can: everything is

suggested, wherever possible there are no more open, unmeasured search movements. Yet not even the boundary between the measurable and the immeasurable is stable. The measuring gauges seek to reach further and further into the immeasurable. Not only the measurable is to be measured, but also as much of the immeasurable as possible is to be shifted into the area of the measurable. That is the endless desire of the modulating mode of collecting data: to maintain control not only over the measured and measurable territories, but also to penetrate into uncontrolled realms not previously desired and to measure them as exactly and comprehensively as possible. White spots in real and virtual spaces, videos that have not interested anyone before, internet links that have never been clicked on.

The government of the number, the measuring gauge, the standard measure reaches its limitations, and in the regime of control the code therefore replaces the polar system of signature and number: whereas disciplinary regimes are distinguished, according to Deleuze, by the identification and counting of individual bodies and mass-bodies, the signature of the control society is the 'code of a "dividual" material to be controlled'.[17] In the story by Guattari cited in the beginning, where Deleuze does not interpret the plot as fiction, a city is imagined in which the dystopia of the gated community appears to have been overcome. The city is not divided by barriers, walls, blockades into licit and illicit zones, but is modulated by a machine that records the position of the single elements in an open milieu. Thanks to their dividual electronic cards, those who inhabit the city can leave their apartment, street, neighbourhood, but – and this is the catch: 'the card could just as easily be rejected on a given day or between certain hours'.[18] This is not something like a technical defect, the fragility of the electronic material. There are certain hours or even only seconds, during which certain territories may be entered. That the card is invalid may be due to the individual carrying the card, whose signature does not allow certain movements. Yet perhaps the problem of validity is not even due to the identity and number of the individual, but rather to conspicuous movements of single things and multitudes that cause the temporary closure of a territory. To this extent, the card itself is less dividual than the machinic assemblage, the codes of which control the openings and closings of relays, and which move through a large number of individual cards as 'dividual material to be controlled'.

In this setting, disrupting the assemblage of the public city means disrupting the logistics of the neoliberal city, disrupting its machinic flows in order to recompose them anew. Not returning to the paradigm between public and private, but rather in the middle of the dividual sociality, to the extent that it can subvert the privatization of the General Intellect below and above the radar of the public sphere. At the same time, the coming artistic and intellectual strategies must not lock themselves up in the old dichotomous notions of public and private, collectivity and individuality, virtual and real space. They must draw machinic-dividual lines at the height of the times athwart to these dichotomies, in order to newly invent the city as dividual.

Notes

1 Which is not to say that the streets should be left to radical right-wing groups like PEGIDA (*Patriotic Europeans Against the Islamization of the West*) in Germany or 'Golden Dawn' in Greece.

2 The method of militarization is also increasingly being used by non-dictatorial city governments; cf. for instance the militarization of Brazilian cities in the context of the football World Cup 2014. Not only mafias or paramilitary associations are suppressed in this way, but at the same time everything moving beyond the access and safeguarding of machinic capitalism.

3 Gilles Deleuze, 'Postscript on the Societies of Control', *October* 59 (Winter 1992), pp. 3–7.

4 For an extensive study on the concept of dividuum from its Latin origins to its Nietzschean connotation, from medieval scholastics to late twentieth century feminist social anthropology, from Novalis to Deleuze, see: Gerald Raunig, *DIVIDUUM: Maschinischer Kapitalismus und molekulare Revolution* (Vienna: transversal texts, 2015). (The English edition will be published by Semiotext(e) in the spring of 2016.) Dividuum today does not just mean the opposite of in-dividual, but a new paradigm of divisibility, not only of data and derivatives, but also of bodies and socialities. For tipping dividuality to its resistant flip side, one has to take into account not only its spatio-social quality, but also the temporal aspects. With its components of dispersion, singular subsistence and similarity/co-formity, dividuality is a central quality of machinic capitalism, but it also carries the potentiality of con-dividual, molecular revolutions. For the development of the Guattarian concept of machines as technical, body, and social machines toward the new concept of machinic capitalism, see ibid. and Gerald Raunig, *A Thousand Machines: A Concise Philosophy of the Machine as Social Movement*, trans. Aileen Derieg (Los Angeles: Semiotext(e), 2010).

5 I share the concept of machinic capitalism and its genealogical lines (Marx's machine fragment, its post-operaist development, and especially Félix Guattari's theory of the machinic) with Matteo Pasquinelli (cf. for instance, 'Machinic Capitalism and Network Surplus Value: Notes on the Political Economy of the Turing Machine': http://matteopasquinelli.com/docs/Pasquinelli_Machinic_Capitalism.pdf), but I do not want to place the concept in the context of the theoretical current of accelerationism. Mistaking the resistive affirmation of specific, indeterminate lines of flight in the field of immanence of contemporary forms of capitalism on the one hand with the naïve optimism of a generalized acceleration and overcoming of capitalism on the other is based not only on a misunderstanding in reference to the aforementioned theoretical foundations of the machinic, but also on simplifying notions of the linearity of history and the absolute deterritorialization of time. See also the critique by Franco 'Bifo' Berardi: 'L'accelerazionismo in questione dal punto di vista del corpo', in *Gli algoritmi del capitale. Accelerazionismo, macchine della conoscenza e autonomia del commune*, ed. Matteo Pasquinelli (Verona: ombre corte, 2014), pp. 39–43.

6 Stefano Harney and Fred Moten, *Undercommons: Fugitive Planning & Black Study* (Wivenhoe, NY: Minor Compositions, 2013), p. 88.

7 Original Facebook slogan, which is still present in the German translation: http://de-de.facebook.com/.

8 Michel Foucault, *The History of Sexuality, Volume I: An Introduction*, trans. Robert Hurley (New York: Pantheon Books, 1978), p. 60.

9 Ibid., p. 44.

10 Ibid., p. 45.

11 Ibid., p. 60.

12 Felix Stalder, 'Autonomy and Control in the Era of Post-Privacy', http://felix.openflows.com/node/143.

13 Foucault *The History of Sexuality*, p. 62.

14 Gilles Deleuze and Félix Guattari, *A Thousand Plateaus: Capitalism and Schizophreni*a, trans. Brian Massumi (Minneapolis: University of Minnesota Press, 1987), p. 341.

15 Ibid., p. 342.

16 Deleuze, 'Postscript on the Societies of Control', ('Les individus sont devenus des "dividuels", et les masses, des échantillons, des données, des marchés ou des "banques".')

17 Ibid.

18 Ibid.

The Political Art of Urban Insurgency

Erik Swyngedouw

> Today art can only be made from the starting point of that which, as far as Empire is concerned, doesn't exist. Through its abstraction, art renders this inexistence visible. This is what governs the formal principle of every art: the effort to render visible to everyone that which for Empire (and so by extension for everyone, though from a different point of view), doesn't exist.[1]

According to Alain Badiou, there are four domains in which a truth-event may occur and through which subjects that animate a truth procedure emerges: Art, Politics, Love and Science.[2] A truth procedure is the process through which an act or intervention becomes retroactively inaugurated as a truth-event, a rupture in the order of being that radically transforms the co-ordinates and matrix of being and opens up a truth procedure through the declaration of fidelity to the inaugural event. The truth-procedures associated with each of the four registers of truth differ fundamentally in terms of the count that declares the truth of the event. The truth of Love and of Science operates under the count of Two. The truth of Love resides in the affirmation of its truth by the one to whom it is declared: the event of Love. The truth of a scientific statement resides in the affirmation of its truth by another scientist. The truth of Art is singular; it resides in the declaration of the truth of Art by the One proclaiming its truth and declaring his or her fidelity to the truth of the event. The truth of politics, of course, resides in the multiple, the many, the militant fidelity of a universalizing multitude to an inaugural emancipatory event (like October 1917, the Paris Commune, or May '68). It is the affirmation of the truth perceptible in an inaugural political event, one that unfolds through the universalization of declarations of fidelity to an event, an interruption that retroactively can be designated as a political event.[3]

The relationship between art and politics, therefore, resides fundamentally in the articulation between two distinct truth procedures, establishing the relationship between the one and the multiple, the singular and universal. Let me illustrate this reasoning. When on 1 December 1955 in Montgomery, Alabama, Rosa Parks sat down on a whites-only bus seat to go home after work, Rosa could have declared it a work of Art, a gesture that would be reminiscent of Duchamp's urinal gesture. Rosa chose not to do so. As had happened many times before, the act was properly policed by the bio-political power of the state. Rosa was arrested. However, the retroactive declaration of Rosa's minimal intervention in the common-sense order of the day as political event – the symbolic inaugural event of what later would be named 'the Civil Rights Movement' – resided in the subsequent declaration of a multitude, with highly varied gender, ethnic, racial, or class inscriptions, of their fidelity to the truth of the emancipatory act performed by Rosa's minimal disturbance.[4] An emancipatory politicizing sequence, which would turn out to be highly performative, unfolded, one that would transform the co-ordinates of collective life and produce a new common sense that radically replaced and declared as utterly nonsensical the common sense that prevailed before the act (i.e. that it was perfectly sensible to exclude coloured or black people from certain urban places and functions).

On 3 November 2014, just a few days before the commemoration of the 25th anniversary of the fall of the Berlin Wall (an unparalleled urban artistic political intervention in itself), a group of activist artists removed seven crucifixes inscribed with the names of the East-Berliners that had died in their fateful attempt to cross the divide between East and West, and were located on the banks of the river Spree to bear witness to the perverse effects of walls and their separating functions. In their stead, a sign with the inscription 'There is no thinking going on here' was left. The seven crosses re-appeared on the outer steel and concrete borders of the European Union in Bulgaria, Greece and the Spanish enclaves in Northern Africa (Melilla and Cueta). Through this intervention, the artists re-inscribed the memory of the divided and walled city in the actually existing geo-exclusive politics and practices of a gated Europe. Here too, the *Zentrum für Politische Schönheit* as the artists call themselves, aspired to a de-aesthetization of contemporary post-democratic politics and its exclusionary common sense by means of re-articulating the semantic enchainment of Walls, Division, Separation, and Suffering to a new common sense, a new distribution of the perceptible, around the universalizing signifiers of equality, freedom, and inclusive humanity.[5]

The examples above illustrate how both Art and Politics dwell in the register of the Aesthetic understood in a Rancièrian mode as 'the distribution of the sensible', the partitioning of what can be heard, voiced, sensed, felt, registered, and through which a common sense becomes configured. Artistic and political interventions are interruptions in sense and sensibility; they signal in their performative staging the inegalitarian forms of the existing state of the situation, and through their interruptional performativity, address 'the wrong' of the inegalitarian condition while performing, voicing, rendering sensible, what 'equality' is all about. While the truth of Art remains singular, the truth of politics is a universalizing one.

Indeed, as Jacques Rancière keeps reminding us, Art and Politics revolve around similar aesthetic procedures. We are not referring here to the aestheticization of politics that Walter Benjamin identified with Fascism, or that can also be traced in contemporary forms of consensual and aestheticized post-political forms of technocratic management of the givens of the situation, but rather to the politics (and art) of the aesthetic. Both revolve around the registers of the perceptible. As Rancière notes:

> In the end everything in politics turns on the distribution of spaces. What are these places? How do they function? Why are they there? Who can occupy them? For me, political action always acts upon the social as the litigious distribution of places and roles. It is always a matter of knowing who is qualified to say what a particular place is and what is done to it.[6]

For Rancière, artistic practices, like political interruptions, are an integral part of the partition of the perceptible to the extent that they suspend the common sense of sensory experience and reframe the relationships between subjects and objects, the common and the singular, one place and another. With Alain Badiou's notion of the event and Jacques Rancière's conceptualization of art and politics as interruptions in the order of the sensible – a disruption of the police order – we may begin to discern precisely how urban art and emancipatory urban politics intertwine. Indeed, the articulations between Art and Politics find their expression precisely in the spatial, in the urban. As David Harvey keeps insisting, every political project is a spatial one, and every spatial project is a political one.[7] And the notion of 'the political' has to be taken in the precise meaning that Alain Badiou, Jacques Rancière or Chantal Mouffe,[8] albeit it in different ways, assign to 'the political' as an immanent moment of interruption, an intervention that destabilizes the order of being and aspires to an infinitely inclusive universalization, one that destabilizes 'politics' as the existing common-sense modalities of being-in-common. Such 'political' interventions stand indeed in stark contrast with the celebration of the relationship between (public) art and politics (the latter understood as the everyday choreography of diverse interests in formally codified or informally practiced routines of conflict-intermediation, collective decision-making and public management). The radical difference between a political urban intervention and an intervention that re-enforces the suffocating and often violent hold that politics/the police exerts over the potential emergence of a political event can be easily exemplified by two recent events that took place in Amsterdam. In an act of an urban guerrilla intervention, artist Arturo Di Modica placed his third (after New York in 1989 and Shanghai in 2010) *Charging Bull* (of Wall Street fame) on Amsterdam's Beursplein (Exchange Square) on 4 July 2012 (not co-incidentally U.S. Independence Day), just a little while after the site was cleared off a small coterie of Occupy activists, too small in numbers to even itch the powers that be or attract international attention. Is the *Charging Bull*'s presence – the triumphant symbol of a victorious capitalo-financial-parliamentary order – not one of the most tell-tale signs of the symbolic re-appropriation of urban space by the 1%, by those who resist change, who defend the prevailing common sense by all means available? While the square was cleared of its protesters, the unauthorized intrusion of the *Bull* was quickly legitimized and approved by the city administrators. It now takes pride of place as Amsterdam's elite made quite clear to all what the Beursplein and city politics stand for. It signals the mobilization of the aesthetics of guerrilla urban interventions to ensure that nothing really changes, to re-affirm that Art and Politics can seamlessly fuse together while suppressing the nurturing of urban interventions that seek to transform the state of the situation, that re-orders the common sense of everyday life, one that embryonically signals the desire for the inauguration of a new politics.

It is from this perspective that I wish to explore in this contribution the Political Art of Urban Insurgency, as manifested in the seemingly never ending proliferation of urban rebellions, unfolding against the backdrop of very different historical and geographical contexts, that – since the magically riotous year of 2011 – profoundly disturbed the apparently cosy neoliberal status-quo and disquieted various economic and political elites. There is indeed an uncanny choreographic affinity between the eruptions of discontent in cities as diverse as Istanbul, Cairo, Tunis, Athens, Madrid, Lyon, Lisbon, Rome, New York, Tel Aviv, Chicago, London, Berlin, Thessaloniki, Santiago, Stockholm, Barcelona, Montreal, Oakland, São Paulo, Bucharest, or Paris, among many others. A wave of profoundly urban interruptions is rolling through the world's cities, whereby those who do not count, 'the part of no-part', demand a new constituent process for producing space politically. Under the generic name of '*Real Democracy Now!*', the heterogeneous mix of gatherers are outraged by and expose the variegated 'wrongs' and spiralling inequalities of autocratic neo-liberalization and actually existing instituted democratic governance. A politicized and disruptive mobilization, animated by an eclectic mix of insurgent urban architects, is increasingly choreographing the contemporary theatre of urban politicized struggle and conflict.[9] From a radical urban political perspective, the central question that has opened up, after the wave of insurgencies of the past few years petered out, revolves centrally around what to do and what to think next. Is there further thought and practice possible after the squares are cleared, the tents broken up, the art destroyed, the energies dissipated, and everyday life resumes its routine practices?

The Spectral Return of the Political

For Jacques Rancière, democratizing the polis is inaugurated when those who do not count stage the count, perform the process of being counted and thereby initiate a rupture in the order of things, 'in the distribution of the sensible', such that things cannot go on as before.[10] From this perspective, democratization is a performative act that both stages and defines equality, exposes a *wrong*, and aspires to a transformation of the senses and of the sensible, to render common sense of what was non-sensible (and non-sensical) before. This is where Art and Politics as aesthetic procedures meet. Democratization, Rancière contends, is a disruptive affair whereby the *ochlos* (the rabble, the scum, the outcasts, 'the part of no part') stages to be part of the *demos* and, in doing so, inaugurates a new ordering of times and places, a process by which those who do not count, who do not exist as part of the polis become visible, sensible, and audible, stage the count and assert their egalitarian existence. Egalitarian politics is about

> the symbolic institution of the political in the form of the power of those who are not entitled to exercise power – a rupture in the order of legitimacy and domination. It is the paradoxical power of those who do not count: the count of the 'unaccounted for'.[11]

Egalitarian-democratic demands and practices, scandalous in the representational order of the police yet eminently realizable, are precisely those staged through mobilizations varying from the Paris and Shanghai communes to the Occupy, Indignados, and assorted other emerging urban political movements that express and nurture such processes of embryonic re-politicization. Occasionally, such interventions are spectacular, often they are mundane as in the case of the re-ordering of the spaces where state sovereignty is suspended (such as Churches, for example, in Brussels, Paris, or London) when undocumented migrants occupy such sacred spaces and turn them into sites of asylum and places for the performance of equality. Identitarian positions become, in the process, transfigured into a commonality, and a new common sense, and they can be thought and practiced irrespective of any substantive social theorization – it is the political in itself at work through the process of political subjectivation, of acting in common by those who do not count, who are excessive, surplus to the police.

There are many uncounted today. Alain Badiou refers to them as the 'inexistent', the masses of the people that have no say, 'decide absolutely nothing, have only a fictional voice in the matter of the decisions that decide their fate'.[12] These inexistent are the motley assortment of a-political consumers, frustrated democrats, precarious workers, insurgents architects and artists. undocumented migrants, and disenfranchised citizens. The scandal of actually existing, instituted (post-)democracy in a world choreographed by oppression, exploitation and extraordinary inequalities resides precisely in rendering masses of people inexistent, politically mute, without a recognized voice.

For Badiou, 'a change of world is real when an inexistent of the world starts to exist in the same world with maximum intensity'.[13] In doing so, the order of the sensible is shaken and the kernel for a new common sense, a new mode of being in common becomes present in the world, makes its presence sensible and perceptible. It is the appearance of another world in the world, and as such a profoundly aesthetic affair. What was considered normal, right and beautiful cannot any longer be perceived or lived as such; new registers of senses, voices, and semantic sequences emerge, something that Antonio Gramsci would consider a shift in hegemony, produced through the mobilizing force of universalizing, and thus spatializing, counter-discourses and -practices. Was it not precisely the sprawling urban insurgencies that ignited a new sensibility about the polis as a democratic and potentially democratizing space? This appearance of the inexistent, staging the count of the uncounted is, it seems to me, what the polis, the political city, is all about. Indeed, as Foucault reminds us, '[t]he people is those who, refusing to be the population, disrupt the system'.[14]

The notion of the democratizing polis introduced above is one that foregrounds intervention and rupture, and destabilizes the apparently cosy bio-political order, sustained by an axiomatic presupposition of equality. Democratization, then, is the act of the few who become the material and metaphorical stand-in for the many; they stand for the dictatorship of the democratic – direct and egalitarian – against the despotism of the instituted 'democracy' of the elites – representative and inegalitarian.[15] Is it not precisely these insurgent architects that brought to the fore the irreducible distance between the democratic as the immanence of the presupposition of equality and its performative spatialized staging on the one hand and democracy as an instituted form of regimented oligarchic techno-managerial governing on the other? Do the urban revolts of the past few years not foreground the abyss between 'the democratic' and 'democracy', the surplus and excess that escapes the suturing and de-politicizing practices of instituted governing? Is it not the re-emergence of the proto-political in the urban revolts that signals an urgent need to re-affirm the urban, the polis, as a political space, and not just as a space of bio-politically governed city life?

Of course, the social markers of the insurgencies are geographically highly differentiated, the quilting points around which the interruption becomes articulated are invariably particular, specific, and concrete: a threatened park and a few trees in Istanbul making place for the vernacular architecture of an

Ottoman mosque and shopping mall, a religious-authoritarian but nonetheless democratically elected regime in Egypt, massive austerity in Greece, Portugal and Spain, social and financial mayhem in the U.K. or the U.S., a rise in the price of public transport tickets in São Paulo, the further commodification of higher education in Montreal, large-scale gold-mining in Rumania. Yet, the urban insurgents quickly turned their particular, occasionally identitarian, grievances into a wholesale attack on the instituted order, on the unbridled commodification of urban life in the interests of the few, on the highly unequal socio-economic outcomes of actually existing representational *post-democracy-cum-capitalism*. The particular demands transformed quickly and seamlessly into a universalizing staging for something different, however diffuse and unarticulated this may presently be. The assembled groups ended up without particular demands addressed to the elites, to a Master. In their refusal to express specific grievances, they demanded everything, nothing less than the transformation of the instituted order. In their urban socio-spatial interruptive acting they staged new ways of practicing equality and democracy, experimented with innovative and creative ways of being together in the city, and prefigured, both in practice and in theory, new ways of distributing goods, accessing services, producing healthy environments, organizing debate, managing conflict, practicing ecologically saner life-styles, and negotiating urban space in an emancipatory manner. The dominant aesthetic and semantic registers of common sense were blown apart while others embryonically emerged and were experimented with.

These insurgencies are decidedly urban; they may be the manifestation of the immanence of a new urban commons,[16] one always potentially in the making, aspiring to produce a new urbanity through intense meetings and encounters of a multitude, one that aspires to spatialization, that is to universalization. Such universalization can never be totalizing as the demarcation lines are clearly drawn, lines that separate the us (as emancipatory multitude) from the them, i.e. those who mobilize all they can to make sure nothing really changes.

The democratizing minority stands here in strict opposition to the majoritarian rule of instituted democracy. As much as the proletarian, feminist or African American democratizing movements were (and often still are) also very much minoritarian in terms of politically acting subjects, they nonetheless stood and stand for the enactment of the democratic presumption of equality of each and all. The space of the political disturbs the socio-spatial ordering by re-arranging it with those who stand in for 'the people' or 'the community'.[17] It is a particular that stands for the whole of the community and aspires towards universalization. The rebels on Tahrir, Syntagma Square, or Taksim Square are not the Egyptian, Greek, or Turkish population; while being a sociological minority, they stand materially and metaphorically for the Egyptian, Greek, and Turkish People. The political emerges, Rancière attests, when the few claim the name of the many, to embody the community as a whole, and are recognized, sensed, as such. The emergence of political space is always specific, concrete, particular and minoritarian, but stands as the metaphorical condensation of the generic, the many, and the universal.

These attempts to produce a new commons offer perhaps a glimpse of the theoretical and practical agenda ahead. Does their acting not signal a clarion call to return the intellectual gaze to consider again what the polis has always been, namely the site for political encounter and place for enacting the new, the improbable, things often considered impossible by those who do not wish to see any change, the site for experimentation with, the staging and production of new radical imaginaries for what urban democratic being-in-common might be all about?

The Artistic Violence of Urban Insurrection

Indeed, the ultimate aim of urban interventions is to change the given socio-spatial ordering in a certain manner. Like any intervention, this is a violent act. It erases at least partly what is there in order to erect something new and different. Interruption is precisely predicated upon a voluntarist act of subjective violence, the will to place one's body, voice, practice in the circuits and flows of the given, and to expose oneself, to render oneself vulnerable to the violence of those who insist that life has to go on, that the flow and the circuits require uninhibited circulation and movement. In the face of attack or interruption, the key thing to do, the elites tells us, as George Bush Jr. reminded us after 9/11, is 'to keep on shopping'.

It is of central importance to recognize that politicizing acts are singular interventions that (aspire to) produce particular socio-spatial arrangements and urban milieus and, in doing so, foreclose (at least temporarily) the possibility of others to emerge. Any intervention enables or foreshadows the formation of certain socio-spatial matrices and closes down others. The subjective 'violence' inscribed in such choice has to be fully endorsed and its implications teased out.

The violence of urban insurrection and interruption is subjective; the result of a voluntarist decision to act, to stage the new, the different and, in the process, make visible the objective violence inscribed in, and often actively mobilized by, the instituted bio-political police order. While objective violence is precisely embodied and performative through the common-sense operation of the existing order that renders some more equal than others, that relegates some to the margins of life, that reduces some bodies to bare life, that assigns and allocates functions and places such that parts are distributed differentially, that some fall out of the count, become 'the part of no part'. Subjective violence, therefore, is the aesthetic practice of rendering visible, audible, and articulate that what the objective violence of the police order renders mute, invisible, inaudible, and inarticulate. Here too resides the impassable abyss between subjective violence of identitarian, and therefore exclusive, interruptions (like, for example, the unspeakably horrible brutal murdering of 13 journalists at *Charlie Hebdo*'s Parisian offices) and the subjective violence of democratizing and emancipatory urban interruptions. An egalitarian politics is radically inclusive; everybody is invited in, 'it is an inclusionary struggle'[18] that cuts through the socially segregating borders and boundaries of race, class, ethnicity, gender, location, or sub-alterity. Of course, the question then arises of how to confront those who remain on the outside, who will mobilize whatever dispositive to prevent the universalization of the inclusionary struggle. Against their symbolic and objective violence, it is vital to think about ways to protect and defend the universalizing process without descending into abyssal terror, about how to navigate the prospect of failure in the absence of effective defence as experienced by the Paris Commune or in the violence of political terror that marked so much of past emancipatory transformations.

Any political sequence is one that re-orders socio-spatial co-ordinates and patterns, reconfigures uneven socio-ecological relations (while foreclosing others), often with unforeseen or unforeseeable consequences. Consider, for example, how the historical struggle for political emancipation and equality was predicated upon sustained class and political struggle in the face of persistent and occasionally ruthless oppression and opposition. Such interventions that express a choice and take sides, invariably signal an autocratic moment and the temporary suspension of the democratic understood as the agonistic encounter of heterogeneous views under the aegis of an axiomatically presumed equality of all. The gap between the democratic as a political given, predicated upon the presumption of the equality, on the one hand and the autocratic moment of political intervention as the (temporary) suspension of the democratic on the other needs to be radically endorsed. While a pluralist democratic politics, founded on a presupposition of equality, insists on difference, disagreement, radical openness, and exploring multiple possible futures, concrete spatial-ecological intervention is necessarily about relative closure (for some), definitive choice, singular intervention and, thus, certain exclusion and occasionally even outright silencing. The tension expressed in the move from the political as interruption to the politics/the police as a new configuration of the sensible cannot be undone.

A political truth procedure or a political sequence, for Alain Badiou, unfolds when in the name of equality fidelity to an event is declared; a fidelity that, although always particular, aspires to become public, to universalize. It is a wager on the truth of the egalitarian political sequence.[19] Such a sequence can retroactively be traced through its process of de-localization from or spatialization of the originary site, encapsulated when, for example, the Indignados claimed 'We are here, but anyway it's global, and we're everywhere.' While aspiring to universalize, such spatializing movement can never be totalizing; while everyone is invited in, not all will accept the invitation. The repetition of the repertoires of action, the continuing identification with the originary Idea, and the moving-back-and-forth between insurrectional sites, may begin to tentatively open up new spatialities of transformation while pre-figuring experimental relations for new organizational forms. Such a process of spatialization renders concrete, gives content to the 'equality' expressed in the orginary event. In the process, equality becomes substantively embodied and expressed; and perhaps a new political name that captures the new imaginary and its associated new common sense may emerge with it.

While the political art of staging equality in public space is a vital moment, the process of transformation requires indeed the slow but unstoppable production of new forms of spatialization quilted around materializing the claims of equality, freedom and solidarity. In other words, what is required now and what needs to be thought through is if and how these proto-political localized events can turn into a spatialized political 'truth' procedure; a process that has to consider carefully the persistent obstacles and often violent strategies of resistance orchestrated by those who wish to hang on to the existing state of the situation. This procedure also raises the question of political subjectivation and organizational configurations, and requires perhaps forging a political name that captures the imaginary of a new egalitarian commons appropriate for twenty-first-century's planetary form of urbanization. While during the nineteenth and twentieth century, these names were closely associated with 'communism' or 'socialism' and centred on the key tropes of the party as adequate organizational form, the proletarian as privileged political subject and the state as the arena of struggle and site to occupy, the present situation requires a re-imagined socio-spatial configuration and a new set of strategies that nonetheless still revolve around the notions of equality. However, state, party and proletarian may not any longer be the key axes around which an emancipatory sequence becomes articulated. While the remarkable uprisings since 2011 signalled a desire for a different political configuration, there is a long way to go in terms of thinking through and acting upon the modalities that might unleash a transformative democratic political sequence. Considerable intellectual work needs to be done and experimentation is required in terms of thinking through and pre-figuring what organizational forms are appropriate and adequate to the task. What is the terrain of struggle, and what or who are the agents of its enactment?

The urgent tasks now to undertake for those who maintain fidelity to the political events choreographed in the new insurrectional spaces that demand a new constituent politics (that is a new mode of organizing everyday urban life) revolve centrally around inventing new modes and practices of collective and sustained political mobilization, organizing the concrete modalities of spatializing and universalizing the Idea provisionally materialized in these intense and contracted localized insurrectional events and the assembling of a wide range of new political subjects who are not afraid to stage an egalitarian being-in-common, imagine a different commons, demand the impossible, perform the new, and confront the violence that will inevitably intensify as those who insist on maintaining the present order realize that their days might be numbered. Such post-capitalist politics is not and cannot be based solely on class positions.

The aftermath of the insurgencies of the past few years saw a veritable explosion of new socio-spatial practices that are experimented with, from housing occupations and movements against dispossession in Spain to rapid proliferation of experimenting with new egalibertarian life-styles and forms of social and ecological organization in Greece, Spain and many other places, alongside more traditional forms of political organizing. Not all experimentations will succeed. Many will fail. In the face of inevitable setbacks – like the current catastrophe in Egypt – the fidelity to the democratizing process needs to be maintained and sharpened. An extraordinary experimentation with dispossessing the dispossessor, with reclaiming the commons and organizing access, transformation and distribution in more egalibertarian ways already marks the return to 'ordinary' life in the aftermath of the insurgencies. The incipient ideas expressed in the event are materialized in a variety of places and ways, and in the midst of painstaking efforts to build alliances, bridge sites, repeat the insurgencies, establish connectivities and, in the process, produce organization, symbolize its practices and generalize its desire. While the political art of staging equality in public squares is a vital moment in re-ordering 'the partition of the sensible', the process of transformation requires the slow but unstoppable production of new forms of spatialization quilted around materializing the claims of equality, freedom and solidarity. This is the promise of the return of the political embryonically manifested in the artistic violence of insurgent urban practices.

The second part of this chapter is based on Erik Swyngedouw, 'Insurgent Architects, Radical Cities and the Promise of the Political', in *The Post-Political and Its Discontents: Spaces of Depoliticization, Specters of Radical Politics*, ed. Japhy Wilson and Erik Swyngedouw (Edinburgh: Edinburgh University Press, 2014), pp. 169–88.

Notes

1 Alain Badiou, 'Fifteen Theses on Contemporary Art', The Drawing Centre, 4 December 2003, www.lacan.com/issue22.php (accessed 15 January 2015).
2 Alain Badiou, *Being and Event*, trans. Oliver Feltham (London: Continuum, 2005).
3 Alain Badiou, *Metapolitics*, trans. Jason Barker (London: Verso, 2006).
4 See Todd May, *The Political Thought of Jacques Rancière: Creating Equality* (Edinburgh: Edinburgh University Press, 2008).
5 See www.politicalbeauty.de/mauerfall.html (accessed 15 January 2015).
6 Jacques Rancière, 'Politics and Aesthetics: An Interview', *Angelaki* 8 (2003) 8, pp. 194–211, p. 201.
7 David Harvey, *Rebel Cities: From the Right to the City to the Urban Revolution* (New York and London: Verso, 2012).
8 Chantal Mouffe, *On The Political* (London: Routledge, 2005). For a review, see Japhy Wilson and Erik Swyngedouw, eds., *The Post-Political and its Discontents: Spaces of Depoliticization, Specters of Radical Politics* (Edinburgh: Edinburgh University Press, 2014).
9 Erik Swyngedouw, 'Where is the Political? Insurgent Mobilizations and the Incipient "Return of the Political"', *Space and Polity* 18 (2013) 2, pp. 122–36.
10 Jacques Rancière, *Disagreement* (Minneapolis: University of Minnesota Press, 1998).
11 Jacques Rancière, *Le Partage du Sensible: Esthétique et Politique* (Paris: La Fabrique, 2000).
12 Alain Badiou, *The Rebirth of History: Times of Riots and Uprisings* (London: Verso, 2012), p. 56.
13 Ibid., p. 56.
14 Michel Foucault, *Security, Territory, Population: Lectures at the Collège de France 1977-1978*, trans. Graham Burchell (London: Palgrave Macmillan, 2007), pp. 43–44.
15 Badiou *The Rebirth of History,* p. 59.
16 See Melissa García Lamarca, 'Insurgent Practices and Housing in Spain: Making Urban Commons?', paper presented at symposium on 'Urban Commons: Moving beyond State and Market', George Simmel Centre for Metropolitan Research, Humboldt University, Berlin, 27–8 September 2013.
17 Jacques Rancière, 'Ten Theses on Politics', *Theory & Event* 5 (2001) 3.
18 Slavoj Žižek, *Demanding the Impossible*, ed. Yong-june Park, (Cambridge: Polity, 2013), p. 126.
19 Alain Badiou, *The Meaning of Sarkozy*, trans. David Fernbach (Verso: London, 2008).

Part 3

Struggle with the City

Poet Interrupted

Bart Moeyaert as Antwerp's Poet Laureate (2006-2007)

Vanessa Joosen

Most contributions in this book shed light on how artistic practices intervene in and transform the public domain. In this chapter, I reverse that perspective, in order to shed light on how the city can affect the artist who becomes involved in transforming it. As a case study, I will explore the work of the Belgian author Bart Moeyaert, who was the third poet laureate of the city of Antwerp, from 2006 to 2007. During this period, several issues came up that invited explicit reflection on the public responsibilities associated with this office: how can artists function as public intellectuals? To what extent can and should a poet laureate be put at the service of the community that has appointed him? What does that 'artistic service' comprise? What are his rights and obligations, both ethically and artistically, and how does he balance his creative and personal needs and desires with the demands of the city? I will discuss these questions in relationship to Moeyaert's time as the poet laureate of Antwerp and highlight the choices that he made and the reactions that he received in the media. In the second part of this chapter, I will show how the debate around Moeyaert's public responsibilities as Antwerp's poet laureate affected his work in progress, more specifically the poetry he produced in this function, a novel he was writing at the time and a Faustian story in which he comes to terms with his public and artistic struggles in 2006.

The concept of the poet laureate goes back to Greek and Roman antiquity. It was reintroduced in 1341, during the Renaissance period, when Petrarca was appointed Rome's poet laureate, and, in more recent times, it is best known from the tradition in Great Britain, where the position of national poet laureate was held by such renowned authors as William Wordsworth, Alfred Tennyson and Ted Hughes. While at one time the poet laureate was required to write poetry for festive occasions and/or comment upon important national events, the British poet laureate nowadays has considerable freedom in what he or she chooses to write about.[1] The same liberty was granted to the Antwerp *stadsdichter* (poet laureate or 'city poet'). Antwerpen Boekenstad (Antwerp Book City – ABC), the organization responsible for the cultural activities when Antwerp was the Book Capital in 2004, installed the city's first poet laureate, Tom Lanoye, in 2003. Antwerpen Boekenstad is a cultural organization that is financially supported by the city of Antwerp and pays the city poet an annual fee. That does not imply, however, that the city poet needs to act as a spokesperson of the authorities. As Odile Heynders states about the Dutch poet laureate: 'The poet can make his point without taken the representativeness as such as too restrictive.' That being said, Heynders does point out that the poet laureate is expected to 'represent the *vox populi*, the voice of the people, and to reflect the *communis opinio*'.[2]

If we compare the function of the Antwerp city poet to the more traditional office of poet laureate, a few differences emerge. Whereas the traditional poet laureate endorsed the country's glory, the city poet seems equally invested in highlighting its weak spots. More than anything else, the city poet promotes the value of poetry itself as a powerful discourse to comment on life in the city and achieve an aesthetic effect. Many of the initiatives taken by Antwerpen Boekenstad served to bring poetry to a larger audience that it usually reaches in the twenty-first century. Moreover, in its promotion campaign, Antwerpen Boekenstad highlighted the interaction between literature and architecture in transforming the cityscape – sometimes temporarily, sometimes more permanently. As the website for the Antwerp poet laureate proclaims: 'The city itself became a carrier of literature.'[3] Lanoye, for instance, had part of a poem printed on a long banner that was hung from the Boerentoren. In the poem, the tower addresses the cathedral, which it faces. Lanoye was succeeded by the poet Ramsey Nasr, whose poetry still decorates, among other places, the Mechelseplein and a building at the University of Antwerp, and then by Moeyaert.[4]

The organization Antwerpen Boekenstad left open whether or not the poet laureate was also to engage in public debate. ABC director Michaël Vandebril stated that the poet was to comment on topical issues related to the city, and mentioned as examples the reconversion of the so-called Leien (big boulevards that run through the city) and the elections.[5] The choice for the first poet laureate, however, implicitly did mark the position as a political one. Once the *enfant terrible* of Flemish literature, Lanoye was known for his provocative lashes against the establishment and his leftist political views. Although critics, such as Yves T'Sjoen, questioned the utilitarian approach to poetry that the concept of a poet laureate fosters, the idea proved to be highly successful.[6] Lanoye managed to attract a lot of attention and appreciation for his work and – by extension – for the power of poetry.

The council of Antwerp maintained the office of city poet/poet laureate after its year as Book Capital was over, and does so to this date. In the rest of this article, I will use city poet and poet laureate as interchangeable synonyms.

Both Lanoye and his successor Nasr had acted as prominent public figures when they held the position of poet laureate, participating in performances, using their poetry to transform the cityscape and take a stand in public debates that moved the city and its inhabitants. With 'Mijn moeilijk lief' [My difficult lover] (see also below), Lanoye's first poem, he set the tone for his critical views on the city.[7] The poem described Antwerp as a difficult lover, and dealt with the so-called VISA affair, a corruption scandal stirred by the right-wing party Het Vlaams Blok, as a result of which the city's council was forced to resign. 'Vervloekt heb ik u, meer dan Beerschot ooit/ verloor,' reads the telling first line of the first city poem: 'Cursed I have you, more than Beerschot [Antwerp's football team] has ever lost.' The poem highlights the city's defeat, first in sports and then in politics and morals, while at the same time underlining the poet's love for Antwerp, despite its misgivings. Nasr chose a more comical tone for his criticism, opening his first poem 'Stadsplant' [City Plant] with a scene of himself walking on the Leien, Antwerp's boulevards, and falling into a large hole. Nasr seems to have taken Temmerman's hint, because the poem is a reference to the extended road works on the Leien. These were repeatedly delayed, also because of archeological findings (Nasr's poem mentions an encounter with a mammoth bone), and the consequent diversions and traffic jams irritated many of Antwerp's visitors and citizens.

With these two extravert, assertive predecessors, Bart Moeyaert felt some hesitation when he was invited to be Antwerp's third urban poet.[8] Yet, once reassured by the organizers that he would be able to make his own kind of mark, Moeyaert was intrigued, and did not want to let the opportunity pass to 'de-acidify' the city, as he calls it, to let his poetry embellish and interact with the public sphere, and to let himself be inspired by the city in which he had been residing for almost twenty years. That inspiration set in immediately, as ideas started popping up: door hangers and beer mats with poetry, the projection of poetry on the water of the River Scheldt, and so forth. Moeyaert thus envisaged creative ideas and opportunities to reach a broad audience that he had never had before, either as a children's author or as a poet.

What is striking, is that Moeyaert imagined the physical form of these poems as much more minimal and ephemeral than Lanoye's and Nasr's. This is a significant clue to understanding the careful statements that Moeyaert wanted to make.

Up to that point, Moeyaert had mainly worked as a children's author. He was highly influenced by Aidan Chambers, who (with reference to Milan Kundera) distinguishes between so-called 'writers', who produce texts to the meet the needs of their readers, and 'authors', who create a more purposeless form of literature – in its most extreme form, art for art's sake.[9] The first was a category Moeyaert did not want to fall into, and he had been happy creating literature within the four walls of his study, without reflecting on the possible effects of his work on readers.[10] Although Moeyaert stresses his own artistic perspective in his acceptance of the office of city poet, his intention to de-acidify the city does imply that he considered the effect on his readership and that he did have an ideological program. His first poem illustrates that he was not just writing art for art's sake. 'Nieuwstad 14' refers to Moeyaert's first address in Antwerp and his experience as a newcomer who finds it hard to be accepted. It was printed on door hangers in six languages and 30,000 copies were spread over the entire city, so that people would find it when they left or entered their houses. On the one hand, the autobiographical poem is an invitation to other migrants to reflect on their experiences when they first arrived in the city and on the extent that they felt accepted after living there for a certain period; on the other hand, it asks the autochthonic locals to adopt the newcomer's perspective and cast a critical glance on mild forms of xenophobia, which they themselves may have practiced. The personal operates on a public level in this poem – which can be read as an ideological, and even political statement. But its form is significant too. Moeyaert is making a plea for understanding a newcomer's plight without taking a controversial stand. Moreover, the fact that the poem was spread on door hangers is no coincidence if we compare it to how Moeyaert's take on being a city poet developed. Although it is a public office, with the door hangers Moeyaert asked people to take his poetry into their private sphere as it were, into their homes, and contemplate it with the patience to read between the lines and to marvel at the variety of languages that migrants bring to the city.

Moeyaert's idea that he could continue to work the way he was used to, as a hermit in his study, soon proved to be an illusion. In May 2006, a few months after Moeyaert's appointment as the city's poet laureate, 18-year-old Hans Van Themsche shot three people in the centre of Antwerp: 2-year-old Luna Drowart and her au pair Oulematou Niangadou from Mali did not survive the shooting; the Turkish lady Songül Koç did, but was severely wounded. Van Themsche's attack was motivated by racism and it violently confronted the city of Antwerp with a xenophobic undercurrent that had already become tangible with the rise of the extreme right Vlaams Blok party in the 1980s and 1990s.

Also, Moeyaert had a personal connection to the victims of Van Themsche. Little Luna's grandmother had bought a copy of Moeyaert's *Luna van de boom* [Luna from the Tree] at the Antwerp book fair that autumn, and he had signed a copy for the girl. With this tragic course of events, Moeyaert could not remain in his literary retreat:

> In the course of a news item the four safe walls of my study were torn down. The outside world seized my fortress. I had no idea whether I would find the right words, but I had to translate this horror into poetry.[11]

He wrote 'Vrouw en Kind' [Woman and Child] for Luna and Oulematou, and read it aloud at Luna's funeral. 'It does not take a second/ and the city has changed,' part of the poem reads.[12] But it was not only the city that had changed.

Based on his experiences as a writer of children's books as a form of literature that does not often get the respect it deserves, Moeyaert had always considered the social impact of his works as being rather limited. His performance at Luna's funeral, however, made him realize that he had been wrong:

> Halfway the poem I enter the racist's head and use his language. When I started reading those lines in church, people crossed their arms. They cast dawn their glances, they imagined me gone. From one moment to the next I transformed from being present into being undesired, not because *I* had changed, but because the shades of grey in my words had changed into mere black. My memory of the sudden cold silence in the church is that of a sledgehammer

blow. The total aversion of a large mass of people made it clear to me in a disconcerting physical way, for once and for all, that I had to face the consequences of my words, hard as I may find that to be: when you have chosen, as a person and a writer, 'to be there,' then you cannot possibly maintain that words have little power.[13]

In the beginning of his office as Antwerp's poet laureate Moeyaert had attempted to carry on writing the way he was used to, secluded in his room, oblivious to the effect of his works and with complete self-control. He realized that being a city poet would not only change the city, but also himself. This was the start of a battle that he would wage not only with his critics, but also with himself. Moeyaert dedicated 'Brug' [Bridge], the poem that immediately followed his tribute to Oulematou and Luna in August 2006, to the 'temporary' cast-iron bridge that spanned the Antwerp Rooseveldt square for more than three decades and that the Antwerp citizens both appreciated (for its practicality) and detested (for its ugliness). The poem opens as follows:

Especially at night I wonder whether I matter. Am I of use. What do I contribute.	Vooral dan 's nachts vraag ik me af of ik er iets toe doe. Ben ik van nut. Wat draag ik bij.[14]

The lyrical self can be understood to be both the bridge and the poet himself. The poem is the second one that Moeyaert wrote in the first person, after 'Nieuwstraat 14'. It was also the first to be displayed on a large scale, on a banner by the bridge. With it, and as told by the bridge, Moeyaert shares his doubts about the nature of his contribution to the city. After Luna's funeral, the issue of social impact had become crucial to Moeyaert's writing and self-image. He could no longer deny that his work affected his readers and that he had a role to play as a public intellectual. The numerous reactions after his public performance had touched him – and the fact that he was working and living in the city that was the very subject of his writing, intensified his internal struggle. Now more a public figure than ever before, people addressed him in the street to tell him about the effect of his poems. He was confronted over and over again with the fact that literature in the public sphere does not only have an aesthetic but also a social effect. This realization not only gave him satisfaction, but also insecurity. Because if, contrary to what he had always experienced, poetry does matter, then a huge responsibility rests on the shoulders of the poet. Moeyaert felt pressure that he needed to present a strong personality as Antwerp's poet laureate, and he forced himself to keep smiling in the process, even though he was often moved and angered by what he witnessed and experienced in the city. When questioned once again about the impact of his poetry during a so-called 'white march' (a peaceful demonstration) in 2006, Moeyaert again caught himself downplaying that impact in order to protect himself from the inner conflicts that he felt as he had become a public figure of a kind he had not been prepared to be.

During the summer of 2006, that kind of self-protection was no longer possible. A civil movement for tolerance was organizing the so-called 0110 festival, 0110 being short for the first of October, the date when it was to take place. Local elections were to be held on 8 October and the political implications of the festival were clear from the outset: 0110 was a plea for more tolerance, to put a stop to the extreme-right ideology (and parties) that had permeated the city and culminated in the tragedy of May that year. The festival was organized by Belgian rock musicians such as Tom Barman and Arno, and popular bands such as Clouseau joined in.

Moeyaert had decided that he wanted to be part of the crowd rather than perform on stage. He considered this to be a crucial aspect of his role as Antwerp's poet: sensing what mattered in the city, among the people who lived in the city. Yet, what had started as a musical happening for tolerance, developed into a broader festival, with a small literary event in the Antwerp theatre De Monty. Moeyaert had been invited to participate, but had declined. While he considered it possible to attract people who felt hostile about Antwerp's multicultural diversity to a pop concert, he thought it was rather improbable that those people could also be motivated to attend a literary festival. The latter was more likely to attract those who already felt strongly about the values proclaimed by 0110, such as tolerance and multiculturalism.

Moeyaert's decision not to take part caused quite a stir. 'Stadsdichter Moeyaert past "om strategische redenen" voor 0110' [City poet Bart Moeyaert declines invitation for 0110 'for strategic reasons'] the Flemish newspaper *De Morgen* headlined. The article cited Max Temmerman, who spoke on behalf of Antwerpen Boekenstad, which had continued to organize the election and activities of the city's poet laureate. Temmerman stated: 'The *city poet* is paid by the city. In a sense he is a city civil servant. To perform in this office on such an event is asking for trouble.'[15] The discussion brought to the fore the tension between the city poet's link with the establishment (with Temmerman suggesting that a neutral stance would be preferable) and his artistic and personal independence. As Odile Heynders observes about public intellectuals:

> The 'intellectual' element emphasizes the writer having (a certain amount of) authority, often rooted in an academic education or on the prestige of his oeuvre, and being able to judge things from a wider perspective. The 'public' element refers to the author performing a role as a social critic and mediator, both from the sideline and from the centre of a public sphere.[16]

Moreover, public intellectuals often draw their authority from being strong, outspoken personalities. Interesting in the debate around Moeyaert's absence at 0110, is that the institution responsible for his office argued that he should not enter the public debate, while several other public intellectuals scolded him for not making a public statement. Moeyaert himself was not just intellectually, but physically absent: he was on honeymoon. He was only able to explain his views in hindsight, when various opinions about his duties had already been voiced. While former city poet Tom Lanoye spoke in Moeyaert's defence, stating that the poet laureate does not need to perform at a festival to show his commitment, others, such as author Dimitri Verhulst, criticized Moeyaert for his lack of participation:

> If this decision is strategic, then I think it's a dumb strategy. As a *city poet* you stand out more at such an event by being absent than by being present. It may well be that [the right-wing party Vlaams Belang] *het Belang* might cause some controversy because of it, but since when have writers shied away from controversy?[17]

The same point was made more provocatively by author and blogger Marc Reugebrink, who under the title 'Triomf der lafheid' [Cowardice Triumphs] scolded Moeyaert for allowing himself to be muzzled by the Antwerp Mayor – a rumour that was later proven to be false.[18]

Moeyaert responded with a poem. The title 'Kies' refers both to the choice that a poet has to make ('choose') and to the upcoming elections. 'Bestaan kan iedereen', it opens [Everyone can exist], to continue: 'Er zijn vraagt moed' [To be there requires courage]. The poem can be read as Moeyaert's manifesto in which he demands to be the city poet he wants to be: not being put under time pressure (expressed in the poem as being led by alarm clocks) or public pressure, not to 'als een hond onthouden/ dat hij kan slapen tot/ het rinkelt naast zijn oor' [like a dog to remember/ that he can sleep until/ something rings besides his ear]. He refuses to reproduce the bold opinions that he hears voiced by others, but pleads instead that his personality should be respected and his desire for nuance be appreciated. The poet, he argues,

> is best placed
> to say something about
> the eraser, because he
> knows like no other
> how empty it is when he
> turns the page, how quick
> the mistake, but also how small
> and how paralyzed
> a hand with fear.
> And that is exactly why he keeps
> thinking in pencil,
> because that is according to him
> the essence of being there.

> is het best geplaatst
> om iets over de gum
> te zeggen, omdat hij
> als geen ander weet
> hoe leeg het is als hij
> het blad omslaat, hoe snel
> de fout, maar ook hoe klein
> en hoe verlamd
> een hand van angst.
> En daarom juist blijft hij
> in potlood denken,
> want dat is volgens hem
> het wezen van er zijn.[19]

The message that Moeyaert expresses with this poem is reminiscent of the paradox of the public intellectual that Odile Heynders describes, with reference to Pierre Bourdieu:

> While the defining characteristic of intellectuals is that they take a stand and deliver critique from a universal

> point of view, *public intellectuals* by the very fact of their having to present their ideas to the general audience are also forced to *popularize* their ideas and to fulfil the practice of debater and opinion maker.[20]

A comparable paradox arises for poets who are required to act as public intellectuals. As Heynders notes, '*public intellectuals* by the very fact of their having to present their ideas to the general public and performing a role in the media, are forced to *popularize* their ideas ... They find themselves in the middle of a public sphere that they also consciously have to detach themselves from, in order to be active as artists'.[21] In the case of writers, there is a further ambiguity. The aesthetic means of expression that are lauded in their literature – suggestion, open-endedness, personal imagery – may clash with the opinions they are expected to express.

At least, in Moeyaert's case they did. In 'Kies' he argues against black-and-white thinking and provocative statements, but writes a plea for nuance and doubt. Heynders argues that public intellectuals 'find themselves in the middle of a public sphere that they also once in a while consciously have to detach themselves from' to maintain their integrity. Moeyaert's poem makes explicit that detachment and he explains why he chooses not to appear where his presence is required according to some.

At the same time, that detachment was hard to sustain by someone who also wanted to be part of the city that had appointed him as poet laureate, to feel and be influenced by the issues that lived in the city. 'After those two years I was worn out,' he explains. 'I had empathized too much with the city and that took its toll.'[22] He had started developing physical complaints and a cynical tone. The very acidification that he had wanted to counter with his poetry when he accepted the position, had affected the poet himself.

Moeyaert the author and poet was 'interrupted' in the artistic course that he was trying to take. As shown above, the poetry that he was required to produce during his term, addressed some of the issues he was struggling with as a writer in the public sphere. But its influence extended beyond the work directly related to that office. Before his appointment as poet laureate, Moeyaert had started writing a book that would later be published as *De melkweg* [The Milky Way].[23] Tired of being called such a subtle and suggestive author time and again, he had initially envisaged *De melkweg* to be a cheerful, uncomplicated story that breathed the atmosphere of the summer holidays and was to start with three children sitting on a wall, being bored. He had already written the opening passages for *De melkweg* in 2005, but did not find the time to develop the story further during the two years that he was in office as Antwerp's city poet.

When he picked up the book again after his term, he found that he could not re-enter the uncomplicated, cheerful world he had wished to create. The atmosphere of the novel changed, and the book acquired an abrasive feel and a sharp edge. The cynicism that was the result of his time as Antwerp's city poet entered the novel in the form of a bet between the three children, who see an old lady and her dog walking by. They wager which of the two is going to die first: the old lady or the dog? *De melkweg* turned out to be a rather bleak book, to which miscommunication is central and in which the characters hurt the people they love the most. It evokes the loneliness that Moeyaert felt when he was the centre of public attention.[24]

Moeyaert sees the influence of his struggles as poet laureate also in the glow-in-the-dark picture book that he published in 2007. *De baas van alles* [The Boss of Everything] is an animal tale that starts with a cat who cannot understand a dog who is patiently waiting for orders from his boss.[25] In the rest of the story, the cat constantly tries to convince other animals that he is right, but ultimately obeys the girl who calls him inside. It is a story about power and different ways of dealing with it. While Moeyaert states that he would not like to be like the slavish dog and cannot be as independent as the cat, he ultimately identifies with the butterfly: 'the cabbage white butterfly that does not follow the straight line from A to B, but flaps about, and sits down here and there, because it likes too, but I also realize that a butterfly is very vulnerable'.[26]

Moeyaert finally seemed to come to terms with his time as a poet laureate with *Iemands lief* [Somebody's Love],[27] an adaptation of the Faustian story of *L'Histoire du Soldat*. The booklet tells the story of a soldier who returns from the war, anxious that he will have been abandoned by his loved one. On his way home, he gambles with the devil, and when he finally comes home, he finds that many years have passed and that he has long been assumed dead. 'Because of my time as poet laureate I still have the feeling that I have lived so much for a city and its people that I forgot myself. Sold my soul even', Moeyaert declares with regard to this book.[28]

Just like the soldier in the story cannot undo the pact that he has made with the devil and restore his old life, Moeyaert found that his term as Antwerp's poet laureate had an impact on his life and oeuvre that cannot be undone:

> It is an awful finding, but I can never become the person again that I was in 2005, when I could approach people much more openly, and was much more receptive. I would prefer to swipe those two years under the carpet, but apparently I need to come back to it over and again. They have been a caesura in my life.[29]

An intertextual link can been drawn between *Iemands lief* and the very first poem that an Antwerp poet laureate ever produced and that was briefly introduced above: 'Mijn moeilijk lief' by Tom Lanoye (Someone's love for Moeyaert/My difficult lover for Lanoye).[30] Moeyaert's novel tells the story of someone who hopes to be loved and be part of a community, but never succeeds in doing so. He makes a bad bet and becomes estranged both from the people he loves and from himself. Lanoye's poem shows an awareness that a city is a most capricious lover. It can be read retrospectively as a warning for any city poet that letting yourself be involved with such a beautiful, yet difficult lover can leave no one unaffected, unless you view it with irony and even cynicism – something that Moeyaert was not prepared to do. Moeyaert's poem 'Kies' is a strong counterpart to Lanoye's 'Mijn moeilijk lief'. It makes clear that a poet laureate as a public intellectual only makes sense if the very quality of poetry – its ambivalence and potential open-endedness in particular – are allowed and valued.

Notes

1 See its description on the web page of the British government. www.royal.gov.uk/TheRoyalHousehold/OfficialRoyalposts/PoetLaureate.aspx.

2 Odile Heynders. 'The Vox Populi in Poems: Ramsey Nasr as Poet Laureate and Public Intellectual', *The Journal of The Kenneth Burke Society* 10 (Summer 2014) 1, www.kbjournal.org/heynders_ramsey_nasr.

3 All translations in this article are my own. Original text: 'De stad werd zelf een drager van literatuur', www.antwerpenboekenstad.be/stadsdichters/5/tom-lanoye.

4 Moeyaert was succeeded by Joke van Leeuwen, Peter Holvoet-Hansen, Bernard Dewulf and Stijn Vranken.

5 Anon., 'Hugo Claus gevraagd als Antwerps Stadsdichter', *De Morgen*, 31 October 2002.

6 Yves T'Sjoen, 'Poëzie voor het volk' *De Standaard*, 30 January 2003.

7 Tom Lanoye, 'Mijn moeilijk lief', www.antwerpenboekenstad.be/stadsdichters/5/tom-lanoye/gedichten/8/1-mijn-moeilijk-lief.

8 Unreferenced assertions by Moeyaert, like this one, are borrowed from a personal interview that I conducted with him on 31 July 2014.

9 Aidan Chambers, *Reading Talk* (Stroud: Thimble Press, 2001), pp. 13-17.

10 Bart Moeyaert, 'Bestaan kan iedereen: Kellendonklezing 2012', p. 21, www.bartmoeyaert.com/database/beeldmateriaal_database/kellendonklezing_moeyaert.pdf.

11 'In de tijd van een nieuwsbericht werden de vier veilige muren van mijn werkkamer tot op de grond gesloopt. De buitenwereld nam mijn burcht in. Ik had geen idee of ik er de woorden voor zou vinden, maar deze gruwel moest ik vertalen in poëzie.' Moeyaert, 'Bestaan kan iedereen', p. 25, www.bartmoeyaert.com/database/beeldmateriaal_database/kellendonklezing_moeyaert.pdf.

12 'Het duurt geen tel/en de stad is veranderd'. Bart Moeyaert, 'Vrouw en kind', 2006, www.antwerpenboekenstad.be/stadsdichters/3/bart-moeyaert/gedichten/73/3-vrouw-en-kind.

13 'Halverwege het gedicht kruip ik in de kop van de racist en gebruik zijn taal. Toen ik in de kerk aan die regels begon, kruisten de mensen hun armen. Ze sloegen hun ogen neer, ze dachten mij weg. Van het ene op het andere moment veranderde ik van aanwezig in ongewenst, niet omdat ík veranderd was, maar omdat de tinten grijs van mijn woorden in alleen maar gitzwart veranderd waren. Mijn herinnering aan die plotse koude stilte in de kerk is de herinnering aan een mokerslag. De totale aversie van een grote massa mensen maakte me op een ontstellend fysieke manier voor eens en voor altijd duidelijk dat ik de gevolgen van mijn woorden moest dragen, hoe moeilijk ik dat ook vond: wanneer je als mens en dus ook als schrijver voor 'er zijn' hebt gekozen, dan kun je onmogelijk volhouden dat woorden weinig macht hebben.' Moeyaert, 'Bestaan kan iedereen', pp. 26-27.

14 Bart Moeyaert, 'Brug', 2006, www.antwerpenboekenstad.be/stadsdichters/3/bart-moeyaert/gedichten/72/4-brug.

15 'De stadsdichter wordt betaald door de stad. In zekere zin is hij een stadsambtenaar. In zo'n functie optreden op een dergelijke manifestatie is vragen om moeilijkheden.' Jeroen de Preter, 'Stadsdichter Moeyaert past "om strategische redenen" voor 0110', *De Morgen*, 9 September 2006.

16 Heynders, 'The Vox Populi in Poems'.

17 'Als deze beslissing strategisch is, dan vind ik het een domme strategie. Als stadsdichter val je op zo'n evenement veel meer op door je afwezigheid dan door je aanwezigheid. Kan best zijn dat het Belang er een controverse rond zou maken, maar sinds wanneer zijn schrijvers bang van controverse?' Verhulst cited in De Preter, 'Stadsdichter Moeyaert past "om strategische redenen" voor 0110'.

18 http://reugebrink.skynetblogs.be/archive/2006/09/09/triomf-der-lafheid.html and http://reugebrink.skynetblogs.be/archive/2006/09/13/scheepstoeter.html#more.

19 Bart Moeyaert, 'Kies', 2006, www.antwerpenboekenstad.be/stadsdichters/3/bart-moeyaert/gedichten/69/7-kies.

20 Odile Heynders, 'Individual and Collective Identity: Dutch Public Intellectual Bas Heijne.' *Journal of Dutch Literature* 4 (2013) 1, pp. 43-61, p. 46, https://www.google.nl/?gws_rd=ssl#q=17+Odile+Heynders%2C+%E2%80%98Individual+and+Collective+Identity:+Dutch+Public+Intellectual+Bas+Heijne-.%E2%80%99+Journal+of+Dutch+Literature+4+(2013)+1%2C+pp.+43-61%2C+.

21 Ibid.

22 'Na die twee jaar was ik op. Ik had teveel met de stad meegeleefd en dat heeft zijn tol geëist.' 'Bart Moeyaert', *Gazet van Antwerpen*, 22 June 2013.

23 Bart Moeyaert, *De melkweg* (Amsterdam: Querido, 2011).

24 Moeyaert in an interview with Sofie Mulders: Sofie Mulders, 'De wereld komt te hard binnen', *De Morgen*, 20 March 2013, p. 29.

25 Bart Moeyaert, De baas van alles (Antwerpen: Manteau, 2007).

26 '... het koolwitje dat niet de rechte lijn volgt van A naar B, maar fladdert, en hier en daar gaat zitten, omdat het dat zelf zo wil, maar ik besef ook wel dat een vlinder erg kwetsbaar is.' 'Het codewoord is weer plezier', *Gazet van Antwerpen*, 8 September 2007, p. 6.

27 Bart Moeyaert, *Iemands lief* (Amsterdam: Querido, 2013).

28 'Door het stadsdichterschap heb ik nog steeds het gevoel dat ik zó hard heb geleefd voor een stad en haar mensen dat ik mezelf toen ben vergeten. Mijn ziel verkocht heb zelfs.' Moeyaert cited by Mulders, 'De wereld komt te hard binnen'.

29 'Het is een verschrikkelijke vaststelling, maar ik kan nooit meer de persoon worden die ik in 2005 was, toen ik mensen veel opener kon benaderen, en veel ontvankelijker was. Ik zou die twee jaren het liefst onder de mat vegen, maar ik moet er blijkbaar over bezig blijven. Ze zijn een breuk geweest in mijn leven. Voor andere schrijvers is dat een echtscheiding, voor mij was dat het stadsdichterschap.' Ibidem.

30 Lanoye, 'Mijn moeilijk lief'.

Embodying the Possibilities of Public Space – Circus Amok
An Interview with Jennifer Miller

Tessa Overbeek

Is your house on fire? Does your mother love you? Has your lover left you? Ladies and gentlemen, boys and girls... and the rest of us! These problems are small, because today is the day that the circus comes to town!

As the American scholar Janet M. Davis describes in her fascinating socio-historical analysis of circus and society a century ago, circus has a history of disrupting regular daily life with its arrival to a town or city.[1] In the early twentieth century, banks would close, factories would shut down, fields would be left untended and schools would cancel classes just for the occasion. As a provider of transient sights and experiences that were not often available any other way, the circus was not to be missed and would draw audiences from all ages, genders and layers of society.

Everyone was anxious to feast their eyes on the highly-skilled performers, the exotic animals, the freaky sideshow performers and strangers from far-off places, not to mention the remarkable phenomenon of a traveling circus itself, functioning like a well-oiled machine, brimming with activity, there and gone in a matter of days or even hours. Fleeting as it was, it would nevertheless leave a strong impression on those who saw it. Davis convincingly argues that the touring big tops were partly responsible for a whole host of deeper societal effects, changing perceptions of issues such as labour organization, gender, nationhood and race, among others. It is unlikely that this was the primary goal of these often large-scale, profit-driven entertainment enterprises, but it makes one wonder about the possible impact of a circus that would use its inherent disruptive potential in a more focused way, in order to consciously affect certain changes in society. Could a traveling circus be even more than a temporary escape from the daily grind, into a weird world of magic and wonder, where many of the usual rules don't apply?

As its name suggests, Circus Amok aims for a more radical intervention in social reality. The quote above, taken from the standard opening to all of its shows, rightly suggests that like more traditional circuses, it involves a certain dose of diversion. Upon closer inspection however, it draws the attention away from certain daily struggles and worries and onto itself, only to redirect it to larger, often more pressing social issues that normally have a tendency to be overlooked, or to provide new perspectives on things that will usually be perceived as too unchangeable to consider.

Circus Amok was founded in 1989 by Jennifer Miller, who has over the years been a street juggler, clown, stilt walker, fire eater, dancer, playwright, director, and teacher of performance courses at the Pratt Institute in Brooklyn. She has performed in many different contexts, from circus tents to theatres and churches, but also in a modern day sideshow at Coney Island, where she used her own unusual appearance to explain the difference between a bearded lady and a lady with a beard, infusing a traditional form with contemporary social awareness.

She has done the same with Circus Amok, which performed indoors for the first five years of its existence, primarily at PS122, a renowned venue for experimental theatre in New York City, where the circus resides. The small-scale, politically engaged, queer circus group started touring the city's parks, squares and other public spaces in 1994. They perform without a tent, in the open air, and are freely accessible. Miller, daughter of two professors, was raised in a liberal, politically active environment and sees the performances she makes as an opportunity to raise issues about social justice. She believes the impact can be greatest when performing in a public space, for varied audiences, and addressing issues that are directly related to city life. This makes Circus Amok's history an interesting chronicle of the sometimes changing but often recurring issues in New York, regarding public housing, immigration, gentrification and privatization, police presence in the public space, city bureaucracy, unequal rights for minorities, public transportation campaigns, public health care and education policies. The events of 9/11 and the resulting changes in legislation, such as the Patriot Act, fear mongering by the government and the War on Terror were addressed several years in a row, while police brutality (especially towards people of colour) sadly continues to recur as an urgent topic to this day.

Like traditional circus shows, Circus Amok's performances are made up of separate numbers, which can include anything from dancing on stilts to acrobatics, but also juggling and clowning, sometimes combined with text, something rarely heard in the circus. Both clubs and statements about topics such as racial profiling or radical feminism may fly back and forth between jugglers. The numbers can also involve song and dance, theatrical monologues or dialogs and satirical skits with parodies of famous politicians and other public figures. Sometimes the numbers are part of an overarching storyline, such as in 'At the Crossroads', an absurd tale about a 'desperate circus performer and former operatic contralto' who is informed about climate change, and presented with a dystopic image of the world in the future. Although he has the opportunity to prevent this catastrophe, he is preoccupied with his desire to go on a date with Matt Damon.

Two weather goddesses, played by Miller and Ashley Brockington, oversee and comment on the state of the world. Fully covered except for their faces in large, striking glittery puppet costumes with bulging eyes and enormous hands, they embody respectively an 'aging, raging, menopausal' goddess and a somewhat younger and more optimistic one, who reminds her counterpart that things aren't all bad, because 'they are lynching only one black man a week these days',[2] and besides, New York has a 'black lesbian mayor now!'[3] These kinds of quips are characteristic of Circus Amok's shows, which sometimes really test the limits of the different kinds of activity and information that can be combined in a performance. One can be alternately or even simultaneously attracted to the physical skills and the fantastic live brass band, amused and confused by the clever, funny and critical text and wowed by the beautiful costumes, props and set pieces, hand-made with low-budget materials such as cardboard and tin foil. In a sense, this interesting mixture mirrors the vivacity and occasional harshness of the city itself. It is loud, colourful and surprising – an attack on the senses and the mind alike. Yet instead of making people want to shield themselves against it, it seemed to make the roughly 350 audience members, children and adults alike, sit up and listen, and maybe even open up.

In this interview, conducted the following day, founder, director and performer Jennifer Miller talks about Circus Amok's history, influences, practices and the many developments that have affected public space over the years, from the themes addressed in the shows to the rise of virtual spaces, the fear felt in embodied public spaces and the obstacles people face when they want to raise their voices in these spaces. It is developments such as these that Amok tries to counter with its over-the-top, multi-layered extravaganzas, playfully reminding people that public space is filled with possibilities.

Taking the Show on the Road

Tessa Overbeek – You've been performing in the parks of New York for 20 years now, but the first few years Amok performed inside. Can you explain the difference?

Jennifer Miller – Performing indoors is great: people can hear you, you can be much more minimal, it is easier, you don't have to build up the set and put it in a truck every day, you can just leave it inside. I love working indoors craftwise, but I also love the exuberance of touring park to park: different lighting design from the weather goddesses, different soundtrack from the neighbourhood around, and different audiences.

TO – How do the audiences you would draw indoors differ from those you meet in the park?

JM – They are a much smaller slice of the pie of the ones that we meet outside. When performing inside, for these five or six years, we were just seeing the same few hundred people over and over again. It is one community, not many different communities. The public is made up of various different publics, that is what we find as we travel around New York. Each has a different personality. We also see is how neighbourhoods have changed. Harlem is not a mostly black audience any more. Brooklyn used to be a much more racially diverse audience, as was Williamsburg. Basically two-thirds of the parks that we used to play that were much more racially diverse are not now. People with money are filling up all of these different neighbourhoods and people without money – who are more people of colour, because of the racist culture we live in – are getting pushed out. So we see New York City spreading out from the centre into all of the Burroughs, becoming more moneyed and wider.

TO – Does that mean that you will travel further to the peripheries, to continue to reach diverse audiences?

JM – Well, there is the question of the future of the circus. I am at a point which people will tell you I've been at for a while, saying: I can't do it anymore! But if we were to do another circus, I would definitely do that, it's just a question of looking at the map and going to some new neighbourhoods. It's hard because there are fewer and fewer, and we have really liked coming back to the same parks, because we do develop relationships, informally. Kids come every year. Some of them have their own kids now. They'll say: I first saw you when I was eight! But yes, I would definitely move out if we were to do it again. We've learned a lot about choosing our sites over the years. Sometimes in smaller parks out in the Burroughs, there aren't big fields, so we play on a basketball court. That can be good if it doesn't get used that often. But once or twice we had got a permit for a basketball court, and it turned out there were kids that played there every Saturday afternoon, so we were infringing on their public space. We try to be careful not to do that.

Problems and Perks of Performing in Public Space

TO – How does performing in the parks affect the themes you pick for your performances?

JM – It helps to be dealing with local issues that a lot of people are concerned about. All power to the people that want to do Shakespeare in the park, or a more abstract dance piece, I've done that too, but I really want to appeal to the public that is there. We're finding that if we are dealing with material concerns of our audiences, it's a much stronger and faster connection than if we are dealing with national concerns. The Iraq war is a harder topic to take on when we are traveling from park to park, than school budgets. Everybody in our audience is concerned with those, or police brutality, or environmental racism, or gentrification. Affordable housing has been an issue in New York since we hit the streets, certainly since the early 1990s. I've witnessed the gentrification of several neighbourhoods over the years and it has just sky-rocketed under the Bloomberg and the Giuliani administrations. It is still an issue.

TO – Since you have been doing this for so many years, it is interesting to see the transformation in the themes you pick, as they reflect local politics and social developments.

JM – This was an interesting year, because we haven't had a democratic mayor in years. We had the Bloomberg years and the Giuliani years, actually since we have been outdoors. Bloomberg came in on this education mandate, and he totally failed that, so in his first year we took on education. We looked at what they were up to, we enacted radical educators we loved, and addressed the notion of 'teaching to the test', that they were pushing. We've run through the basics of issues that concern city life, such as housing and immigration, and two years ago we addressed this over-policing behaviour called 'stop and frisk'. This year I was at a bit of a crossroads, as was the title of the show, about how to pick a theme. De Blasio just got in and we are like: 'Ha! He is not the enemy!'. We need to think about how to take a moment and breathe. I was musing about that and the fact that this big People's Climate March was going to be during our tour. The organizers reached out to us, which has never happened before, and they were encouraging people to make work around it. So I thought: All right, climate change. We like to do local issues, but one of the reasons that I'll pick a theme is that it will be part of a larger network of politically engaged activities on a certain issue. I thought there would be a lot of organizing around climate change and we wouldn't really have to make the argument. We could just bring it up, so we did that.

TO – When you perform in Prospect Park, or when you go to an area that is more diverse, can you feel a different energy coming from the audience? Yesterday, many people were getting all the references and jokes easily...

JM – In other places they would not. But with a circus, even if they don't get all of those references, they are getting other things, they are getting the energy. Like the clown acts that we do. In 2012, it was a street scene, with keystone cops, the hot-dog salesman, the lady walking by... It was all slapstick, but there was stop and frisk: you see one white guy doing drugs in the corner, but it was the black guy doing nothing that got stopped and frisked. So kids see clown, adults see clown with content. From park to park, people will get the references or they will just see the movement or the dance. Everyone will get pieces of it on a different level. Now we're going out on a limb, even though we've always been queer, queer, queer. To say 'black lesbian mayor', I am not sure how that's going to go over in some of the other parks.

TO – I read about one show about police brutality that got varying reactions in different parks, can you explain that?

JM – It was called *The Quality of Life II.* It was scary and sombre, it described a lot of shootings. In many parks we went to, people said to us: 'I knew that guy!' or: 'That was in our neighbourhood'. They expressed that they were seeing their experience represented, which is never represented on stage. We played one really rich, white park, where that stuff didn't happen, where they didn't want their kids to see that, so they were trying to shield them. That was an example of very different experiences in different parks.

TO – Do you just want people to think about these topics, or do you hope that it affects their voting behaviour, or that they do something themselves to help people?

JM – Sometimes we just want to raise questions that we feel aren't being raised in the mainstream, sometimes we really want people to vote or call on a specific thing, and sometimes it's just a question of steering consciousness. Often our work is made around legislation that is actually happening, so with 'stop and frisk', they were talking in the city council about legislation to limit the behaviour of the cops, and we wanted people to weigh in on it. During one show we asked the audience: 'Take out your cell phone, wave it in the air', and then we actually called the mayor and made a demand for mandatory inclusionary zoning, which means that when a developer builds a new building, it's mandated that they have to have a certain percentage of apartments that are affordable, whatever that might be. De Blasio is doing it now. Often we lean towards informing, for instance about the number of Iraqi that were getting killed in the war. We weren't getting any statistics about that. With this one about climate change I didn't want to go for any kind of solution or analysis. I wanted this to be part of what I felt was going to be a broader social fabric happening in the city. And I thought: we'll have a midway there, and they are going to talk about these specific things.[4] But I also wanted to make this show about struggling with hope and humanity. All of my concerns and frustrations about that are embodied in my opening statements about being an aging, raging, menopausal goddess who has lost all faith in humanity. When you are working in social justice, sometimes you look around and want to give up.

TO – Do you think performing in the parks has become more difficult for Amok?

JM – It's more difficult for me because I am older and more tired. And life in the city is harder for artists. People are much more worn out in general because you don't have cheap rent and you can't just have a shitty day job and make it work. You are not able to stay in the field, because the day job takes too much time and energy. We pay performers when we are on tour, and we only just started paying for rehearsals. In the past, people would come out of their commitment and would not get paid for rehearsals. You just can't do that anymore. It's harder for the individuals and it's harder for the fund-raising. It's not a city that supports creative, non-success-oriented, radical theatre making. I've been very lucky – I had a loft in South-Williamsburg. I always had really low overhead and we used to rehearse there. We don't fit there anymore, but we had a lot of storage there. That's one of the ways we were able to keep going for so long: this low rent was the secret subsidy of the whole thing. I still have it, because we were fighting in court for it for thirty years.

TO – Do you have any examples of legislation or societal developments that changed the public space and influenced how you can perform there?

JM – There hasn't really been any legislation that has inhibited our performances. It's mostly been city bureaucracy, gentrification, red tape, nay-sayers... If they are people who welcome community gathering then it's a little easier. So it's more the culture of the bureaucrats than the legislation that has been the problem. There are different obstacles in different parks; some parks are having more and more events, and their bureaucracy is getting thicker. Since we've been in the parks, they have gotten de-funded and then refunded then de-funded. Some parks in more moneyed neighbourhoods are now connected to conservancies, because in the Giuliani years, city money was pulled out of parks and they became more trashed and destitute. Private money and public money are working together more, but the private money controls the parks in a different way. People get together and say: We want to support our park, we will give our money to upgrading the rose garden, but we don't want those people running around doing their theatre in here. So all of a sudden they have more control because they are giving money. In order to play in a park, you have to get a permit. Some of our predecessors were opposed to having to get a permit. You have the stories of the San Francisco Mime Troupe claiming public space. We decided early on: Doing the show, the content, the spirit and the artistry of it are more important than the act of not asking for a permit. But it does enable the management to say no. They've been pretty good, but we do encounter blocks. For example, when we used to play Prospect Park, it cost us 25 dollars, and the last time we tried to go, the cost went up exorbitantly there. They wanted to have an architect's stamp on our set, they wanted us to rent a porta-potty, and so on. I got around that now, but they were charging 350 dollars to let us drive the truck in – for an escort in. We were very broke at the beginning of the season. Early on we thought we were going to do a much smaller, light show. Then it grew, and I couldn't get them to let the truck in, even when I offered them the money later. In the end we had to ask the audience to help strike the show.

TO – Was that a first?

JM – Yes. Usually volunteers will help, but this, having to ask... We have always been able to park the truck right by the show, then we can handle it. This neighbourhood really gentrified, and they have a lot more rules and regulations. It affected us in that way. There are so many things that have affected our relationship to public space and how we use and experience it. 9/11 was a real marker of the way public space was looked at. It began to be surveiled more, and stigmatized as a place where terrible things could happen, when meeting in public, with crowds gathering. I think some of that stigma has dispersed or lessened, but that was one big change.

TO – How do you think putting up a show in the park influences the way people experience their surroundings, maybe also after you've already gone?

JM – I think they will remember that event and that day with community, but they will also see it as a place where things can get made. Amok is a very low-tech enterprise with gorgeous things made out of papier-mâché on almost no budget and I think that the audience can see that too. Hopefully there's a sense of: One can make and do things in public space, it can be inhabited and not just controlled. So I think it leaves a little magical footprint in the city, and it also keeps prying open the notion that these spaces are ours and they are there to be used.

Politics and Circus, Concern and Celebration

TO – Can you say a bit more about why you chose to combine political concern with circus?

JM – Circus works incredibly well with issues of social justice. It's a popular form in the old-school sense, and it is a celebratory form. It is enticing, it is available, it has a blasting band, it is joyful and it is free. The fact that it is celebratory is a particular nugget, because people don't often combine a sense of celebration with a sense of concern in the way that Amok does. For activists and people who are toiling away out there, it's incredibly refreshing to have these moments where you can actually be concerned, be in the struggle, and yet feel a sense of joy that you don't often see. But when you do, it is often when we gather: in a demonstration, or a march, where there might be frustration and anger, but often joy too – if you get some song or dance going. Plus it tours the parks, it sees audiences that don't choose to come to see it, so you are not preaching to the converted. It reaches people across class and race. You are not just talking to a specific group of concerned citizens. Those characteristics are inherent in the form of touring and being outside. The circus skills draw people in. I think that sense of mastery or mystery in juggling or doing a high jump on the stilts also brings some sense of that possibility that we want to have in our lives, in our art, and in some vision of a possibly slightly better future.

TO – Yet the combination of circus and politics is not very common...

JM – It doesn't have a history of dealing with content or political themes. Its mythology is in a different place. I came to it through street performers, who were accessible, not through circus. When I was in high school I saw incredible Commedia dell'Arte performers at Renaissance fairs. As a young gymnast and juggler I was interested in circus skills, but the Commedia and the big physical clowning really helped. The San Francisco Mime Troupe had a bit of juggling before their shows in the early days, and their shows were very political. And Bread and Puppet theatre performs the Bread and Puppet Circus annually. So I was able to witness a few examples of it, but there just aren't that many. Even though it makes such perfect sense. Clowning is historically a political act. Not in the contemporary American circus, but...

TO – Do you mean the status issues in it? The role reversals?

JM – The status issues, and the truth-telling fool. If it's the court jester, maybe he's a safety relief valve, but at the same time he is challenging authority, just like comics such as Stephen Colbert or John Stewart, or these Russian clowns that Joel Schechter writes about in *Durov's Pig*. He addresses political clowning, and the clown's position historically as someone who stands up to authority. There are lineages.

TO – Do you think there is a tradition of not wanting to be political in circus?

JM – I think not that many people are drawn to both of those things. It's hard to find performers who have circus skills, who are political, who are willing to load and unload the truck. It's a small group. There are a lot of circus people in New York, but they are not necessarily ensemble players, who can pull off a good political irony, who want to get involved with dialog about one black man being killed every week. There are some, but then I am also looking for people of colour, so it's not easy. We've always done our gender-queer representation. We've always shown men waltzing with men, we had a lesbian couple in one show, but we haven't really talked about that. It is not easy to find people who, whether they are queer or not, want to be part of that image making.

Circus communities or companies always embody mystery: are they really a family, are they really from far-off exotic places? That draws people in, that alternate universe. It presents a lot of possibilities of ways to be and things to think about. The abundant theatricality, the glitter and the grandeur, is something I've also always loved about circus. There's something beautiful about the existential clown, or the beautiful trapeze artist, but we have a little bit more sarcasm and irony, and camp. We always want to see things a bit more dressed up and flamboyant.

TO – Are you never afraid that it distracts from the politically concerned part of the performances?

JM – No. I think that it allows people to take in anything. Laughter opens up the spirit: to think, to be concerned, to see, to have energy moving from one to the other... I think that sometimes there is a certain authority and wisdom in expressing something through comedy or camp: 'I've been there, I've done that, I know what I am talking about.' When police brutality came up this year, right before we were about to open, I couldn't believe this was happening in the streets. I thought about bringing up this old act, a very serious, beautiful and touching act that we did years ago, when Amadou Diallo was shot [1999, *The Quality of Life II,* mentioned before], and there were lots of uprisings in the streets. We were reading from the Amnesty International report about NYC police shootings, historically, and a big body was coming apart. It was very moving, and I thought: Do I want to bring that piece back? I started researching the text. But it didn't quite fit in the show and I was missing part of the puppet, so I just couldn't make it happen. Then Ashley and I were working on the two goddesses' lines and she said: Oh, things are better, they are only lynching one black man a week now! I thought: OK, great. It's a deep cut line that will take care of it for me in this piece. That's not camp, it's serious, but it was sarcastic, and yet true. I find that that end of the spectrum works really well. You can be reverent, and irreverent, a politically concerned person who has a sense of humanity and can exist with play and seriousness at the same time. I think they support each other.

Physical Presence and the Beginner's Mind

TO – Do people often come up to you to talk, after the show?

JM – They do. In smaller parks we will talk to kids and people and it is all easy going. People talk to us about the spectrum of things that come up. There will be a lot of questions from children about gender and sexuality: Is he gay? Are you a man or a woman? The parents come with, but they don't ask those questions. We know that the children ask the parents at home. That forces parents to think it through themselves and to think about ways that they want to teach.

TO – Do you think that maybe the adults start to feel like children again in some way too?

JM – Well, that's the traditional Ringling Brothers circus line: Children of all ages!

TO – That's an interesting combination then, with the concern, if it brings an openness and a receptiveness that children have.

JM – I don't think of us as really using that tagline, but it does make the adults feel lighter. I think that is a circus thing, that surreal, fantasy universe. Going back to the discussion of whether circus, or bringing comedy or lightheartedness, takes away from the seriousness of the issue, I think it might also bring beginner's mind, for a moment. This more open mind, this Zen sense of: 'Oh yeah! I can think about this!' It's an interesting mix of authority and innocence.

TO – Maybe also because we were helping you take down the set, I really did feel some sense of community. Carrying things through the park together, when they are heavy you feel inclined to offer help... It worked! Maybe you should do it all the time.

JM – People do want to help! I heard that a lot of people wanted to have their picture taken with their prop. I loved that people were getting to hold all the stuff, an old, wooden, classic piece of ring curb, seeing what a mask looks like... I don't think I would do it again intentionally because it was stressful. It's of growing importance to meet in public, embodied public. We think of the virtual public space as the ever growing and ever more important public space. So much research money is going there. Academic programmes are all about the on-line presence. To be together in a park seems to just be ever more bubbly and exciting because it is so rare. I'm finding that we need to put more energy in the embodied publics as we all get drawn into the disembodied publics.

TO – I felt having to get up and wave our arms at one point, reminded us as audience members of our physicality and presence in the space.

JM – The first time we did the audience movement was in a 'know your rights' song in the show about stop and frisk. It was about standing up, and about embodying things you really need to know if you get stopped by the police, real tools, and I think there are a lot of other interesting layers there as well. People get up and remember that they are in a body, and afterwards they are in a really pleasant place. They are not in between seats in the theatre. People really linger, talk to each other and find old friends. The whole community energy and the ambiance is allowed to exist much longer, in concrete terms, in an embodied way in that space.

TO – I think the playful, light, communal experience of the show in the park formed a nice contrast to other feelings you get in public spaces, especially as a foreigner in New York. The sense of dread when you arrive at the airport and the atmosphere at customs, when you board a ferry or go on a subway and see all these signs saying that they might search your bag, and urging you to help spot terrorists, saying: If you see something, say something!

JM – It's so normal for us... We got used to it.

TO – Well to be sitting there in a park, which is also part of people's daily lives, feels like you are blending in, being part of the same experience together, but in a positive way.

JM – I think that's important, and I do forget, but it does continue to work against all of the fear that the government is trying to instil in us. In the opening to the show this year we said: Is your house on fire, does your mother love you, do you know your zone? That's something that not everyone gets: 'do you know your zone'. It's a new thing about knowing where to go in a hurricane.[5] It's supposed to help you know what to do, but really it's an instilling of fear. We not only have the terrorism fear, but we've got the weather fear now. It's really hard to just relax in public.

TO – It's a common criticism I think, against yourgovernment, the instilling of fear, that I suppose still hasn't changed.

JM – It's just getting worse.

TO – Why do you think that is?

JM – Trying to keep people in check. These are the ways that governments that are not dictators or fascists control their population. One way is capitalism, another is through all kinds of fears. Fears of imagined enemies, through racism, or stigmas about non-normative behaviour. So we are also working around that. We are feeling safe and comfortable outside, being things that are usually stigmatized, whether it's being queer, or black, or bearded. And I think us being ourselves in some of those performative positions that one should feel vulnerable in, presenting ourselves as we are out in the parks, helps everybody relax.

The Possibilities of Public Space

TO – You also teach at the Pratt Institute. Do you think there is a young generation that wants to make this kind of work as well?

JM – There are some. Right now the Pratt Institute doesn't have a theatre programme, so I am teaching a minor in the humanities. We will start a Master's programme in two years in performance/performance studies, but right now I don't have that many students that are geared that way. But I think, like many professors, you get one or two every year that stick with you, that become an intern for the next show, or do design. I have one student who is off in Egypt doing political street puppetry now, so they are coming up.

TO – I could imagine that at a certain point, as a counter movement to the developments in disembodied public spaces, there could be an increase in this kind of work again.

JM – I think we are in a moment where we are seeing everyone kind of reel and stumble and consider what's going on. How is the brain changing, how is our attention changing, what can we do? What kind of software programs can you put on your Facebook hours? So I think that there will be a movement of real bodies meeting in real spaces to counter or be in discussion with all of this virtual time we are spending. A few years ago, students thought: Oh, live performance, that's so crazy, who sees that, compared to what happens on-line? But I think now they are beginning to understand that there is a thirst for being with real people in public. There have been a couple of documentaries about Circus Amok's work over the years. There's one called *Un Cirque à New York,* about the *Quality of Life II* show and events in New York that paralleled it. I showed it to some students recently. One of the things they were amazed about was how many issues were still the same. They think gentrification is new, but these were the early days of gentrification. Now we are three waves later. It's the same with police brutality. We have been battling these things for so long... The city was so different then, the looks of the parks and the neighbourhoods. It was not as slick or clean a city: there was graffiti, there were mechanics working on the street, but there was an urgency and a sense of possibility.

TO – Can anybody who wants to, as long as they pay the 25 dollars for the permit, do a performance in a park?

JM – I don't know. As I said, sometimes they say no to us if the community has an influence in a park's management. But I think so. I was at a conference a while ago and there was a lot of talk of 'them' not letting us perform in public, and I had to raise my hand and say: Actually, I'm a pretty political queer circus company, and you just have to apply for the permit. It's not that prohibitive. Because of all of the fear, the dressings and the security, and the way the state makes us feel, there is a sense that they won't let us. But actually more people could be doing free shows in the parks.

TO – The question is if people would come and watch...

JM – I know. People think we just throw up wild and crazy shows, but it's a craft to look like a madhouse, but to actually hold the attention that long.

TO – I was also thinking about Hyde Park, where you have Speaker's Corner, where anybody can stand up and shout out their views about the world.

JM – You can go somewhere, stand on a soap box and start talking. We see a lot of religious people doing it. It's fucking hard. Part of the reason people don't do it is other people, it's not just the state. You gotta get up there and yell your opinion. I don't know if this is me getting more conservative, but we tend to want to blame the state. I think there are many opportunities for us to express ourselves in public space and on the street, that just feel too scary. You gotta bring a circus with ya...

Notes

1 Janet M. Davis, *The Circus Age: Culture & Society under the American Big Top* (Chapel Hill and London: The University of North Carolina Press, 2002).
2 Referring to a recent wave of police brutality where black men were shot, such as in Ferguson, Missouri.
3 Actually referring to mayor De Blasio's wife, who had relationships with women before she married him.
4 On certain occasions, such as the show MOO from 2012, Circus Amok collaborated with other organizations, who would provide a midway, consisting of tables where people could get additional information about some of the issues that were raised, or where children could play games. This year it turned out to be too difficult to arrange a midway.
5 Introduced after Hurricane Sandy hit the city in 2012.

Mysteries of the Creative Class Or, I Have Seen The Enemy and They Is Us

Gregory Sholette

Artists and other 'creative' professionals are increasingly willing pawns in the State-backed gentrification games of developers and corporations. But can those that wish to challenge the underlying brutalities of 'culture-led regeneration' turn their creative powers against it? The New York artists' collective REPOhistory fights to re-write the story of urban renewal in Manhattan.

A painting of a smartly clad, long-necked and sophisticated trio of young white people conversing over a glass of wine fills a full page of *The Sunday New York Times*. Done in a 1930s Art Deco style, the advertisement is captioned 'An Oasis In Times Square'. This, the copy explains, is a place where the traveller, weary from business, can discover tranquillity amidst energy and 'A new level of self-indulgence'. It was the year 1999 when, with retrograde panache, the Hong Leong Group launched its flagship hotel in New York, the Millennium Premier. Even then I sensed the arrival of something new, a shift in tactics in the decade-old 'upclassing' of the city. I also knew something troubling about the hotel's recent past that made my hunch even more compelling. A veteran of anti-gentrification activism on the city's Lower East Side some 20 years earlier, I still recall the clumsy call for 'pioneers' to brave the city's harsh urban frontiers.

However, by the late 1990s this type of gambit had largely played itself out, at least in Manhattan. Already most of the island was well on its way to full-blown gentrification and what was left of the poor and working class largely scattered by force or rising rents in the wake of reverse white flight that began in the 1980s. However, this late 1990s wave of gentry wanted nothing to do with leaking pipes or chasing away crack-heads from street corners, and under no circumstances would they wear overalls. Yet the hotel's curiously retro illustration also avoided references to the fevered, techno-giddiness of those blissful, pre-crash 1990s. Instead, the unknown artist lovingly invoked the modernist conceit of the machine age some 60 years prior. Nor was it camp, for the irony was too far adrift from any rhetorical moorings to signal 'spoof'. Instead, like an arcane plot out of a Philip K. Dick novel, the very visage of the city I knew was being transmuted from lead to gold. The more I looked, the more I saw. Quaint Cafés replaced actual coffee shops. Futuristic bars and art galleries took over food processing and light industrial shops. An ersatz cosmopolitanism was everywhere and the Millennium was a part of this larger whole that involved wiping clean not merely the physical traces of the past, but its memories. What filled up the ensuing breach were artful surrogates and clever replicas of a city that no one had ever lived in but that nevertheless looked strangely familiar. Certainly it is easier to see this in retrospect, but the Millennium campaign signalled the start of an entirely new era in the administration of free market urban renewal. More abstract, more inspired, more creative. The question I wanted to answer most, then and now, is whose minds the hotel chain's marketers hoped to, well, gentrify, and what ghosts they sought to keep at bay?

It was the artists' collective known as REPOhistory that provided the key to unlocking this mystery, but its startling solution, like Poe's purloined letter, turns out to have been right in front of me all along.

Demolition in Hell's Kitchen by William Menking for REPOhistory circa 1999

Located on West 44th Street, the Millennium Premier Hotel stands in a once largely Irish and working class neighbourhood formerly known as Hell's Kitchen but re-christened with the sanitary sounding moniker 'Clinton' by real estate speculators in the 1980s. The Times Square from whose implied stresses it claims to offer an 'oasis' is no longer the porn playground of the fiscal crisis 1970s. It has been rehabilitated: safe for families, safe for business, efficiently emptied of homeless people and sundry other uninvited. In May of 1998, however, a metal street sign appeared outside the Millennium. The sign was flagged off of a lamppost, meters away from the hotel's tastefully subdued, black marble façade. Mounted low enough for passers-by to read, its text began portentously:

> What is now the Millennium Broadway Hotel used to be the site of 4 buildings including an SRO hotel that provided badly needed housing for poor New Yorkers...

Artist and architect William Menking designed the plaque to look like a busy montage of newspaper clippings. The story of the Hotel's less than tranquil past continues in bold type:

> In 1984, New York City passed a moratorium on the alteration of hotels for the poor. Hours before the moratorium

was to go into effect, developer Henry Macklowe had the 4 buildings demolished without obtaining demolition permits, and without turning off water and gas lines into the buildings. NYC officials declared, 'It is only a matter of sheer luck that there was no gas explosion.' Attempts to bring criminal charges against Macklowe for these actions were not successful. Macklowe built a luxury hotel on the site, then lost it to the current owners. The demolition of hotels for the poor during the 1970s and 1980s added to the city's growing homeless population. While streets of the 'new' Times Square seem paved with gold – for many they have literally become a home.

Like the materialization of an army of Dickensian apparitions, the Millennium/Macklowe sign was one of 20 temporary historical markers specifically sited around New York that made up the public art project 'Civil Disturbances: Battles for Justice in New York City'. Sponsored by New York Lawyers for the Public Interest (NYLPI) and produced by the art and activist group REPOhistory, its aim was to publicly landmark legal cases in which civil rights were extended to disenfranchised peoples. The content of the signs ranged from the famous Brown Vs the Board of Education desegregation case to the first woman firefighter sworn into service in NYC. Others, however, pointed to occasions when the law had failed to protect as promised and Menking's sign was in this category. Initially, for a time the city tried to stop REPOhistory from installing 'Civil Disturbances'. After weeks of legal manoeuvres, however, the signs went up from spring of 1998 to late winter of 1999. Nevertheless, right from the start several signs vanished after installation. Menking's was among them.

Responding to an inquiry, the Millennium freely admitted having its staff confiscate the legally permitted art work. They even returned it to the group. However, along with the returned sign came a letter threatening legal action if any attempt was made to reinstall it. The grounds? REPOhistory was damaging hotel business. It seems the return of an inopportune past can prove a powerful trigger revealing hidden ideological tendencies in what appears otherwise to be a purely market-driven process of privatization and gentrification. After considerable debate that internally split REPOhistory roughly along lines of activists versus artists, Menking's sign was reinstalled, but now at a greater distance from the hotel. And despite further threats the sign stayed in place, the project's permit ran its course, and neither side took legal action. It is five years on. Aside from this text and other scattered citations, Macklow's 'midnight demolition' is forgotten along with those he cruelly displaced. At the tranquil oasis in old Hell's Kitchen stylish guests still sip wine, discuss art, and continue to manufacture content for the information economy.

Winners and Losers

All of this is familiar now. The 1990s affection for the 1920s and pre-crash 1930s, its weird merger of avant-garde aesthetics, high fashion, and post-Fordist management theory all dolled-up in a neo-modernist longing for limitless progress. So what if the occasional act of terror was and remains indispensable to make it all seem real? Why dwell on conflict? If the creative class has supplanted the traditional labouring class in many places it has done so by greeting capital as potential equal, not as adversary. Winners are admired. Losers on the other hand are truly abject, lacking the aptitude to become exploiters themselves. Asserting a collective disarray, an enduring a-historicity, and a belief they have transcended labour/management antagonisms, creative workers think they can even avoid being exploited in the long run because their big, table-turning breakthrough is always just around the corner, always about to make that longed for reservation at the swanky Millennium tower a reality.

Anyway, it's 2004, and billionaires abound. According to Forbes' recent survey they number a record 587. Still, it's difficult not to notice a connection between this fact and the new economy with its deregulated markets, rampant privatization, decaying worker protection and widening gap between rich and poor. Nor are the super-rich all petroleum refiners and armament producers. Many belong to the so-called creative class. Among those joining the ten-figure income bracket include the rags to riches writer of Harry Potter stories, J.K. Rowling; Google creators Sergey Brin and Larry Page; and Gap clothing designer Michael Ying. So why am I still surprised when I walk down formerly forbidding streets to see such upscale consumption? Designer outlets, smart eateries, bars radiant with youthful crowds, and taxis shuttling celebrants to and fro. Block after block the scene resembles a single, unending cocktail party strung like carnival lights up and down the avenue. Between these cheerful stations other men and women, mostly in their forties and fifties, haunt the shadows gathering glass and metal recyclables from public waste bins. Certainly losers can't harm you. But what about ghosts?

I enter bar 'X'. Its ambiance probably not much different from bars in the Millennium New York, or Millennium Shanghai, or Millennium London. I shout for a dry, gin Martini over the mechanized music. (A cartoon thought-bubble appears, 'Am I the only person in here with a beard?' 'The only one over 40?') My mind returns to REPOhistory and its altruistic necromancy some six years earlier. 'If the enemy wins, not even the dead will be safe', Walter Benjamin once declared. Not safe from whom? Perhaps it was the noise and the alcohol, but a surprising correlation asserts itself. REPOhistory was part of the creative class. While its objectives were different, REPOhistory, like RTMark, the Yes Men, and similar artistic agitators made use of available technologies and rhetorical forms to reach the same erudite consumer-citizens this swanky bar hoped to attract. The Millennium had been correct all along: we were the competition. With a little toning down of its righteous antagonism, REPOhistory could have even taken its place amongst the web designers, dressmakers, MTV producers and other content providers of the new, immaterial economy. And come to think of it, right before the group folded it was increasingly being asked to travel outside to this or that city or town and install public markers about the quaint olden times; the local barber shop, the saloon, the red-light district and parade grounds. I had indeed found the enemy: it was me.

Like forgotten letters in some dimly lit archive, those not immediately part of the radical shift in the means of production remain out of sight, out of mind, fleeing from demolitions, downsizings and sometimes rummaging for cans. Not that this zone of dark matter was not always present and surrounding the upwardly mobile types such as the Millennium crowd. What is new, however, is the way this far larger realm of unrealized potential can gain access to most of the means of expression deployed by the burgeoning consciousness industry – that ubiquitous spectacle essential to the maintenance of global capitalism. By the same token, the so called 'insiders' might, if circumstances permit, decide to cast their collective lot in with the losers and the ghosts. REPOhistory et al. proves it can happen. Because even the new creative class with its 80-hour work week and multiple jobs has a fantasy, one half-remembered perhaps and a bit mad, yet still evident in times of stress and economic uncertainty. It goes like this: the bar tenders and the brass polishers and cooks, the laundresses and bell hops throw down their aprons and spatulas to join in mutinous celebration with artists, web designers and musicians. Raiding the wine cellar, they open up all 33 executive style conference rooms, set up a free health clinic in the lobby, transform the hotel into an autonomous broadcasting tower and party in a universe of creative dark matter.

I finish my drink and return home to wrap-up the essay.

First published in *MUTE* #29, The Precarious Issue (February 2005), www.metamute.org/editorial/articles/mysteries-creative-class-or-i-have-seen-enemy-and-they-us

Further Reading

More about the controversy surrounding Civil Disturbances see:

Gonzalez, David. 'Lampposts As a Forum For Opinion.' *The New York Times*, 20 May 1998, (Metro) p. B1.

Cohen, Billie. 'Guerrilla Tactics Around Town.' *Time Out New York*, 23–30 July 1998, p. 65.

Kolker, Robert. 'See You in Court.' *Time Out New York*, 28 May–4 June 1998, p. 45.

Sholette, Gregory. 'Authenticity2: REPOhistory: Anatomy of an Urban Art Project.' *New Art Examiner*, November 1999.

Sholette, Gregory. 'REPOhistory's Civil Disturbances NYC: Chronology of a Public Art Project.' *CHAIN* #11 (September 2004), pp. 278–84.

For an introduction to Sholette's concept of creative dark matter see:

'Heart of Darkness: A Journey into the Dark Matter of the Art World.' *Visual Worlds*, edited by John R. Hall, Blake Stimson and Lisa Tamris Becker, pp. 116–38. New York and London: Routledge, 2005.

Part 4

Common Public Space

Of Cities Roaring

Geertjan de Vugt

1

The tradition of political philosophy in the Occident began as a philosophy of the ideal *politeia*, i.e. the ideal constitution of the *city*.[1] Thus, political philosophy is, at its very origins, a philosophy of the city.[2] Before Aristotle incisively defined man as a *zoon logikon,* an animal gifted with language and, more importantly, as a *zoon politikon*, as a social or political being by nature, one finds a different political theory in Plato's *Politeia*. In the ten books of political discussion, Plato tries to formulate the best, that is to say 'justified', order of the city. This just order is not based on the fact that man is the animal gifted with language – this Aristotelian idea that continues to cast its shadow over political theory, as if politics is only a matter of rational deliberation. In what has become one of the first and most influential books of political theory (true, itself an excellent example of dialogue or deliberation, although like other dialogues of Plato often taking place outside of the city walls[3]) Plato comes to a formulation of the ideal order, based upon a specific logic.

At the very heart of the *Politeia* one finds a quarrel that informs every single line of the dialogue's reasoning. Readers have often been drawn to the quarrel between philosophy and poetry, as found in Book X. This, so it seems, is a dispute about the role of truth and the necessary insufficiency of representation. Without a doubt, the poet's banishment from the city appeals to the imagination of the literary critic, but it only turns up fairly late in the discussion, long after Socrates has expounded his views on the best order. Yet, a persistent myth would have it that Plato banned poets – the most playful figures of all citizens imaginable – from his ideal city because their works brought lies into the community. Certainly, one must concede that there is some truth to this myth. If one accepts Plato's line of reasoning, one must also admit that the artistic representation of, for example, a chair is necessarily insufficient compared with the artisanal fabrication of a chair, or, even further away, the Idea of a chair.

Be that as it may, readers of the *Politeia* often tend to take Plato's critique of mimesis, or representation, as the key to understanding his political philosophy as a whole. In all its simplicity, however, this representation of that characteristic gesture of Plato's political philosophy is so persistent that one would easily forget that the Greek philosopher might have had other reasons to do so. Those reasons may have less to do with his critique of mimesis than with a more fundamental logic that supports the construction of this city-state. As one recent commentator has shown, there is a much more fundamental quarrel informing the theory of the ideal city. It is not truth, Max Stankiewicz claims in his careful close reading of the book, but *akribeia*, 'exactness' or 'rigour' that is at stake in the *Politeia.* Already in the first two books, Plato sets up the terms of the debate, which, in the words of Stakiewicz, 'will extend through the entire Republic and beyond, until the last dialogues of Plato's career (*Timaeus*, *Critias*, and the *Laws*), namely, the debate between the rigour of philosophical and political distinctions and the play of mimesis'.[4] This, then, would be the fundamental opposition that informs every statement on the politics of the city in the *Politeia*: *akribeia* versus *paidia*, rigour versus play.

2

It is not difficult to see how this opposition affects the formulation of the ideal order. In the first two books, the city that Socrates takes as the ideal starting point for his argument is a 'city of necessity'.[5] Like Aristotle's theory, Plato's ideal *politeia* is based upon a definition of man's nature, but unlike Aristotle's it is not a general definition – such as the shared capacity to speak – applicable to all members of the city. In fact, this nature may differ with each and every single citizen. Now Socrates imagines an ideal distribution of citizens based on their capabilities. It is a distribution that is based on a rule that is perplexing in all its simplicity: one man, one task. For each activity there is a specialist. It would be quite inconvenient for a farmer to divide his time between the fields and other tasks, such as repairing clothes or the house. It would be better, if we follow Socrates, if a citizen were to perform only one task, to which he is assigned according to his mental and physical nature: 'More things are produced, and better and more easily, when one man performs only one task according to his nature, at the right moment, and is excused from all other occupations.'[6]

It is worth noting that Plato leaves no room for leisure. Instead, the needs of the citizens seem infinite. Hence, there is no time for other activities than the one to which a citizen is allocated. The practice of shoemaking does not leave time for anything else. In the words taken from the *Politeia*: 'no one could become an expert player of draughts or dice who did not practice the game exclusively from childhood but played it only as a pastime.'[7] Here we find Plato's rigour at full force. Play needs specialization too, and preferably in a most rigorous sense. However, the comparison between the artisan and the player is somewhat confounding, because in the city's ideal constitution there is no room for any activity other than the one that satisfies the needs of the fellow citizens. And play does not seems be such an activity.

Let us be clear: in Plato's ideal city there is no room for play. Yet, there is reason for Socrates' use of this comparison. Jacques Rancière has shown how the figure of the dice player functions as 'a child of superfluity',[8] a dangerous supplement that is. It is only through the negative example that the employment of each artisan, of each citizen in fact, is given its full meaning. And the negative example of the dice player also helped Socrates to reformulate the egalitarian distribution of occupations into a hierarchy of natures, which ultimately led to the well-known division between artisans, warriors, and philosophers.

If the citizens of Plato's city stick to the role and partition that they are assigned to according to their nature, the community, as Rancière observes, will function perfectly, that is, in harmony. It becomes, so to speak, a 'choreographic community'[9] in which the citizens dance to the rhythm and harmony that they themselves produce. It is important to note that this rhythm, this distribution, prevents the city from 'noise', from possible superfluity. In this sense, Rancière also notes, Plato's city becomes a 'nonpolitical city'[10] in which there is no need for deliberation and no time for power struggles. The logic of rigour and play that underpins the ideal constitution of the city allows no room for doubt, and its spokesman, Socrates, did everything he could to warn against the superfluity of play in favour of socio-political rigour.

Thus, the tradition of Western philosophy – or to be more precise: the tradition of Western political philosophy – commences with a curious gesture. In Plato's theorization of the ideal *politeia*, of the ideal city that is, there seems little room for play. This, at least, is true with regard to the role of adults in the fabrication of that city-state. The exclusion of the *homo ludens* from the ideal city was, as such, perhaps not explicitly formulated. However, the player functioned as a dangerous supplement. Nevertheless, it seems that the exclusion of the playful figure follows as a necessary consequence from Plato's rigorous distribution of bodies and roles that make up the ideal community. And thus political theory begins with an imagination of the ideal city that leaves no room for – indeed excludes – the *homo ludens*.

3

The rigour of Plato's socio-political logic demands him to exclude the *homo ludens*. But play did not disappear. In fact, it returns over and again in his *Politeia*, as well as in other books of his, albeit relegated to a realm with a specific task.[11] In his important review of Johan Huizinga's *Homo Ludens*, published in *The Journal of Politics*, Eric Voegelin even writes:

> The source of the theory of play as the element in which culture originates is Plato. In his last work, in the *Laws*, Plato has developed his theory of the connection between *paidia* and *paideia*, between the play of children and their education or formation to the full stature of man.[12]

Plato as the very source of the theory of play; Voegelin couldn't have been more explicit. At the same time he was quick to add that the form of play with which Plato is concerned, was a very specific sort of play. Play, in Plato, is child's play.

Following Voegelin's remark, it appears that Socrates is not blind to the value of play (*paidia*) and that he recognizes that play is of fundamental importance for the education (*paideia*) of children.[13] Voegelin emphasizes that in Plato play always functions in the upbringing and education of children. Play, we learn, has a specific aim, and is never conceived as a 'free activity' as Huizinga later would have it. When Plato writes about play in the ideal city, one must undoubtedly understand this – and Huizinga has observed this perfectly well – in terms of music.[14] Through musical play, children learned about rhythm and melody. That is to say, play was a means to create a sense for and understanding of order in the growing children. That is why Voegelin could write that play in Plato's city functions as 'the choric education of children' from which children not only learn about the order of the community, but of its aesthetics as well: 'on which is grafted, in due course, the content of communal culture – from the proper participation in the choric rituals of the community to the insight into the aesthetic, moral and religious values which they embody.'[15] *Paideia*, as a form of education through play, leads the child throughout his development towards an adult personality. It is a form of 'character building through habit-formation'.[16] Eventually it enables the grown-up child to enact its role in the 'serious play' of a community, as Voegelin calls it. But that is not a phrase one finds in

Plato's own writings. With the aim of installing a sense of order, the education of children in Plato's city-state is, to borrow a term of Lacoue-Labarthe, 'typographical' education.[17] That is to say, social types are literally inscribed in the young human beings through an act of mimetic play.

But is that form of play that has a specific aim still a form of play? Voegelin, having read both Kant and Huizinga, underlines that play is an act of free activity, without purpose. And yet he refrains from critically scrutinizing the Platonist idea of *paidia/paideia*. Moreover, if he really had studied Huizinga's book carefully, he would have known that the Dutch historian, in his acute discussion of Greek semantics, had dismissed *paidia* as a form of play. From this discussion we learn that in Greek

> the word for play – παιδιά – is always, on account of its etymology, fraught with the sense of child's play, the infantile, the nugatory. Hence παιδιά could hardly serve to denote the higher forms of play, it was too reminiscent of the child.[18]

What is more, in being too much attached to the realm of the child and its upbringing, *paidia* lacks precisely that what is characteristic of play: freedom. In his eagerness to read Plato's philosophy of the city as the source for the theory of play, Voegelin has unfortunately omitted the specificity of the Greek *paidia*. In Plato's ideal city there is, to be sure, room for child's play. But however ludic the child's upbringing and education in Plato's imagined city may be, play as a free, adult activity is dismissed – for the simple reason that the playful figure interrupts the rigorous distribution of bodies and tasks, while there is little or perhaps even no time to lose.

4

Voegelin offers his readers a Platonist interpretation of Huizinga's *Homo Ludens*. His review of Huizinga's book is a remarkable attempt to highlight something at the very origins of the Western tradition of political thought, which otherwise has been neglected for too long: namely, that play should form an essential part of any political theory of the city. One may, however, also read this attempt in a somewhat different way. As Voegelin highlights the importance of play in the emergence of political philosophy he also situates Huizinga in that very same tradition of political thought. It is an interesting gesture, and to give it the attention that it deserves one must scrutinize Voegelin's interest in another topos in the work of Plato.

Voegelin reserves a considerable part of his review for a discussion of the cosmological metaphorology that the ancients employed in their discussions of the ideal community. According to him, archaic communities, and, to be sure, the Hellenic city as well, conceived the polity in 'cosmological symbols', harmony perhaps being the most important of these. The German-American philosopher argues that

> [t]he order of the community can be conceived as a cosmic analogue because the cosmos is more than the field of time-, space- and mass-relations which enters into the equations of physics; it also contains the superabundans of meaningful order, form and rhythm which enters into the symbolization of human life in community.[19]

It is a curious observation, especially when one takes into consideration that for the ancients the cosmos offered a 'conception of the world as a finite, closed, and hierarchically ordered whole'.[20] A finite, closed whole does not seem to leave any room for anything superabundant. But Voegelin is aiming at a different sort of superabundans. Precisely as a finite and well-ordered closed whole, the cosmos attains a meaning that is more than the sum of its parts: the well-ordered whole is a beautiful and just whole. It is the idea of the Good, which then in all sovereignty reigns over physical reality.[21] The fact that there is a difference between the brute fact of existence and the content – be it spiritual or intellectual – of what he calls the 'cultural world' of the city, allows for a transposition of the well-ordered, Good cosmos onto the microscale model of the city. The aim of Plato's theory of the ideal city then is to provide a model in which the sum is also more than simply the total of its citizens. The ideal politeia is the very enactment of the Good. And thus Voegelin writes that the affinity of meaning between the superabundans on the cosmic and human levels enables Plato, in *The Laws* as well as in other works of his, 'to conceive the polity as a ritual play in which the order of the cosmos is re-enacted in the order of the community'.[22]

As is well known, Plato conceived this polity in terms of harmony – one of those cosmological metaphors that Voegelin hinted at. Voegelin, with all his stress on cosmological metaphors, however does not provide his readers with examples of specific terms. Order, rhythm, consonance, attunement, harmony, the political philosopher could have named them as examples of how Plato described the ideal constitution of the city. But instead he goes on to criticize Huizinga for the fact that his theory of play, based as it is on a 'scientistic interpretation of nature', could not 'adequately' cover 'the problem of cosmological symbolism'.[23] Huizinga's theory of play, so Voegelin seems to suggest, has the potential of a political theory, but it fails to explain the continuity that must exist between the inorganic world and the human, cultural world. If one follows Voegelin one must conclude that Huizinga's theory is unable to explain the relationship between the structure of the cosmos and the structure of the polis. While Voegelin himself sees play (*paidia*) everywhere in Plato, the Dutch historian was perhaps not enough of a Platonist in his study of the play element of culture. That is to say, in the end Huizinga's Platonism is a failed Platonism.

5

In his review of the *Homo Ludens* as well as in the volumes of his great project on *History and Order*, Voegelin discusses Huizinga's indebtedness to Plato. But it seems that he is not doing full justice to the work of his Dutch colleague. Trained as a linguist, Huizinga was very sensitive when it came to his choice of words. If Voegelin criticizes Huizinga for not being able to incorporate 'the problem of cosmological symbolism', he unfortunately fails to note the specificity of Huizinga's discourse. Thus one must return to the work of the Dutch historian itself. Two things will become apparent upon a careful reading of Huizinga: first, Huizinga points out that *paidia* is anything but the kind of play that he has in mind; and, second, Huizinga's theory of play does pay attention to 'cosmological symbolism' and is, in fact, drenched with a semantics similar to Plato's theory of the ideal city. Especially when he writes that play continuously confirms 'the supra-logical nature of our situation in the cosmos'.[24] At the same time, however, a reading of *Homo Ludens* will show that the Dutch historian is very pessimistic when it comes to the role of play in the modern city. In fact, his treatise on play offers the reader a narrative on modernity that has become quite a standard narrative. It is a narrative that can also be found in the work of other scholars of modernity, Walter Benjamin perhaps being the most important of these.

But the solution offered by the German philosopher is a completely different, much more positive one. Before discussing Benjamin's remedy to Huizinga's cultural pessimism, it is, however, necessary to first dwell upon Huizinga's theory of play and its decline in modernity.

Huizinga's main thesis in *Homo Ludens* is that Western civilizations arise in, out, and as a form of play. Play, he writes, is not only the driving force behind cultural formations, it also precedes human civilization. That is to say, animals play too. But for Huizinga play is not simply a physiological activity. Human beings reach a higher order in the activity of play. In his definition of play, Huizinga presents a series of formal characteristics of play, such as: (1) It is a free activity, which (2) takes place outside of ordinary life; (3) It absorbs the player intensely and (4) play is disinterested, there is no material benefit to be gained from it; (5) It takes place in a clearly demarcated time and space; (6) It creates order, and (7) it creates a community of players, it promotes the formation of social groupings, and (8) this all happens in the realm of a 'magic circle'. And, without a doubt, this list can be extended. In addition to the definition and a description of the formal characteristics of play, he offers a taxonomy of play forms in which those characteristics can be found: law, war, poetry, philosophy, and many other social domains may be understood as forms of play. What is even more important, however, is that his careful analysis of play forms allows him to present a critical diagnosis of his own time: since the nineteenth century, Huizinga declares in a somewhat pessimistic mood, Western societies witness a decline of play. To grasp what is really at stake in this decline, I would like to single out one specific characteristic of play, which Huizinga-scholars in their readings of *Homo Ludens* have seldom remarked upon. But it is a crucial aspect of play, and Huizinga's concern with this aspect runs actually from the very beginning of his scholarly career – that is, from his cancelled dissertation-project – up to *Homo Ludens* and beyond. This crucial aspect may be simply phrased as: play creates *stemming*, a certain (play-)mood, or to use that beautiful German untranslatable,[25] *Stimmung*.[26]

It would not be difficult to trace the route that this concept has taken in the work of Huizinga. In almost all of his work remnants of the cancelled dissertation-project can be found. For instance, his *In the Shadow of Tomorrow* – a book that has received much praise from writers and thinkers ranging from Fritz Saxl[27] to Italo

Calvino[28] – opens with a chapter titled '*Ondergangsstemmingen*', translated as 'Apprehension of doom', but which may also be rendered as 'moods of decline', or, in the excellent German translation by Annette Wunschel: *Untergangsstimmungen*.[29] In the English translation one reads that 'all was not well with our vaunted modern civilization'.[30] But Huizinga uses a different word here and if we take him literally, he seems to argue that modern society is no longer 'in order',[31] a key-word in the *Homo Ludens* as we will will see in a moment. As he goes on, he observes that 'the *key tone* of our general cultural mood' – it is difficult not to hear the musical semantics in this formulation – has changed. And this crisis of the Western world is first felt through 'sentient bodies'.

In the Shadow of Tomorrow was published in 1935, but its diagnosis *and* its semantics run directly over into *Homo Ludens*, where on numerous occasions Huizinga speaks about '*spelstemmingen*' – 'play-moods'. What must strike any reader of Huizinga's book is that it is drenched with musical semantics. He does not refrain from repeatedly underlining the musical nature of play – a theme that, as we have seen, goes back to Plato's theory of the ideal city in the *Politeia*. In fact, music, more than any other form of art, is one of the highest, if not the highest manifestation of play. Already in the opening pages of the book Huizinga announces that his main object of inquiry are higher forms of play, which are always 'social forms of play', and, moreover, 'saturated with rhythm and harmony'.[32] One finds, almost always, 'repetition', 'alternation', and '*refrain*'[33] in social play. Furthermore, 'it becomes', as Huizinga argues

> ... the *accompaniment*, the complement, in fact, an integral part of life in general. It adorns life, *amplifies* it and is to that extent a necessity both for the individual – as a life function – and for society by reason of the meaning/sense it contains, its significance, its expressive value, its spiritual and social connections, in short, as a culture function.[34]

Simply put, the function of play is to make social order, while at the same time being an *expression* of that very order. In short, play 'creates order, *is* order'.[35] There seems to be no preceding stage of disorder. Rather, as Huizinga keeps on emphasizing, first there is play, and only then disorder may arise.

6

Huizinga's analysis of play in *Homo Ludens* furnishes its readers with a taxonomy of different forms of play: law, war, philosophy, art, poetry, music, can all be seen as a different manifestations driven by the same principle. Those different manifestations of the main thesis, namely that every form of culture develops in, out, and as a form of play, may themselves be scrutinized along no less than three different lines. In the first chapter of the book, Huizinga writes that 'Genuine play possesses besides its formal characteristics and its joyful mood [*stemming van blijheid*], at least one further very essential feature.' This third feature he describes as 'the consciousness, however latent, of "only pretending"'.[36] From this passage we could easily grasp the three possible lines of inquiry. First of all one could scrutinize different forms of play according to formal characteristics, such as: 'free activity', 'without material interest', and its fixation in time and space. Secondly, one could inquire into the consciousness of the ones participating in play. According to Huizinga it must be possible to discern something such as a 'play-consciousness'. It is worth noting that he thus clearly distinguishes a rational, or cognitive aspect of play from a non-rational, non-conscious one. And, so we must emphasize, it is this non-, or supra-rational, sometimes also phrased as 'sacred' dimension of play that interests him most.

Nowhere does he get closer to that sacred dimension than on the third and final line of inquiry that one could follow, namely that of the *Stimmung* of the play. And although here phrased as 'joyful', a few pages earlier Huizinga was more careful in his description of this play-mood. 'The *Stimmung* of play', he writes,

> has both of its poles in resignation and exaltation. It is no coincidence that both words imply a state of 'being outside of'. Perhaps, one might say that the play-mood is always *in major*. Yet, this would bring us to psychological questions, which we precisely would like to avoid.[37]

To the passage cited above, Huizinga immediately added that

> The play-mood is *labile* in its very nature. At any moment 'ordinary life' may reassert its rights either by an impact from without, which interrupts the game, or by an offence against the rules, or else from within, by a collapse of the play spirit, a sobering, a disenchantment.[38]

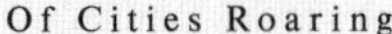

The *Stimmung* of play is thus constantly threatened. But one may, while being faithful to the original formulation, rephrase this statement, by turning it around: the function of play is precisely to keep its community attuned, to keep its *Stimmung*, as if in 'intoxication' [*roes*] [or, in German, *Rausch*].[39] It is a thesis that is not unlike the one Plato advanced in his *Politeia*, according to which the ideal rigorous distribution of bodies and roles had the sole aim of creating harmony. But where the Greek philosopher aimed at formulating the principles for the ideal constitution of the city, the Dutch historian moves away from the principles of play towards a critical diagnosis of his own time. A time that extends back 'far into the nineteenth century', that is, we may add, a time in which the modern *metropoles* began to emerge.

7

Huizinga's negative estimation of processes that we normally group under the name of 'modernization' becomes especially clear towards the end of the book, when its mood has changed. Moving away from the Ancients, Huizinga must concede that in modernity play increasingly disappears. At first, he writes, it seems as if something has 'compensated' for the disappearance of forms of play in social life. Huizinga is hinting at the increased importance of sports in modern society. Throughout the nineteenth century, sports have become a matter of increased systematization and discipline, Huizinga writes, and have thereby lost the connection that play maintains with the archaic cult. 'She is', we read, 'more of an autonomous expression of agonal instincts than a fruitful aspect of sense of community [*gemeenschapszin*].'[40] Sports games, whether the Olympics or the national leagues at American universities, no longer possess the capacity to create culture. He then extends the signalling of the decline of play in matters of sports to all spheres of modern life. From the hazard game and the play of cards to contemporary politics, they are all diagnosed as becoming more systematized and hence lacking a play element.

> In the politics of our time, which must always be ready and always be prepared to start a war, it is difficult to recognize a touch of a play-attitude [*spelhouding*]. Everything that attached play to celebration and cult has disappeared with our present war. With this estrangement [*vervreemding*] from play, play has also lost its place as an element of culture.[41]

Whereas Plato excluded play from politics, here politics is excluded from play. And what, then, became of the polis, i.e. the city?

8

Now, the city is not mentioned in this major work of cultural critique, but the time of modern urbanization is without a doubt characterized as a time in which play disappears. Indeed, in Huizinga's diagnosis the modern world is a disenchanted world. That is to say, we moderns have, through the passage from a closed world to the infinite universe, lost the ability to sense our place within the cosmos. As Huizinga writes at the beginning of the book: 'The very existence of play continually confirms the supra-logical character of our situation in the cosmos.'[42] But with the decline of the play element of culture this connection with the cosmos also seems to have gone irretrievably lost. Huizinga's treatise is marked by an explicit longing for a past in which the world was still in tune. But the modern world is one that could best described as a 'demusicalized world' as Leo Spitzer, who once planned to write a *Stimmungsgeschichte* of the concept of *Stimmung*, calls it.[43] In Huizinga's history of modernity the rhythm and roar of machines is taking over every sphere of everyday life. In such a world, a world full of noises, the music of a community attuned to its own rhythm and harmony has become impossible. Despite modern man's 'aesthetic sensibility',[44] there is no 'cosmic insight' any longer. It is something that many a modern author has observed. Baudelaire, for instance, wrote in his *Le peintre de la vie moderne*, about trivialities and noises that prevented the moderns from a return to that old harmonious world. And occasionally, one finds a more favourable mentioning of 'noises' in the letters of Gustave Flaubert. In a way, noise became the characteristic of modern city life. As Huizinga himself writes in a book that is of crucial importance for his critique of modernization: 'The roaring world is stupefying and shrivelling us [*De dreunende wereld verdooft en verdort ons*].'[45]

9

The book from which this line stems is Huizinga's second book on the United States of his days. He first started to write on America during his work on *Waning of the Middle Ages*. But the work on his *magnum opus* was soon paused when it became clear that the US were going to play an important role in the Great War. Huizinga decided to give a lecture course on the United States today.

The notes for this course were quickly developed into his first book on America: *Mensch en Menigte in Amerika*. Already in this book he deals with the 'mechanization of communal life'. But the inspiration for the book came from a tremendous amount of recent writings on America, not from personal experiences overseas. It would take him eight years before he finally had the chance to visit the country on which he had written his first book of cultural critique.

In 1926, he went on a two-month trip around the US. It was the first time that he really experienced modern urbanization. The modern city is otherwise virtually absent from Huizinga's writings, but there is one exception: his writings on America, and his diary in particular, offer us some of his most poignant observations of modern-day city life. His journey through the United States brought him from New York City to Princeton, Washington, Baltimore, Chapel Hill, Chicago, Madison, San Francisco, Stanford, and Kansas City. Throughout the 61 pages of his diary, Huizinga moves from a strong aversion to the process of modernization to an outspoken admiration and finally back to a somewhat milder criticism.

There is, however, one constant factor: his dislike of the modern American cities. In New York he finds 'cultural excrescence, superfluous and harmful weeds, everything is covered with bad culture, friction and a waste of time'. The innumerable shops leave him with only one impression: '*waste, waste*. All those shoes that will never be worn, all the wilted flowers, all the word that will never be read, the lights burning for nothing, the power that is wasted.'[46] And take his impressions of the city's traffic, phrased in terms of one of the Old World's most famous poets: 'Seen from above, the swarming busses and cars look like a somewhat mild Inferno. But in its direct surrounding one sees a furious Inferno! Not to speak of the ugliness and wretchedness.'[47] Judging the images of NYC found in old drawings, Huizinga jotted down: 'From old drawings of New York – 1791, 1830 – one could tell that the city, back then already, was certainly not beautiful or harmonious: tight, messy, neglected, without shape; in 1797 just a few stepped gables.'[48] Particularly striking in this comment is the use of 'back then already', which may also be read as a commentary on the cities of the present: 'it still is ugly and still lacks harmony'. After his visit to Johns Hopkins in Baltimore he noted: 'Those American cities are offensively ugly.'[49] Other negative examples include Chicago ('one should not see this as a city, but as something that has the potential of becoming a city' – 'a despicable city and a disgrace for humanity') and Detroit, in which Huizinga found the clearest example of the 'modern tragedy': 'so much material, so much ingenuity, so much labour for such a poor result as, for instance, an American newspaper'.[50] And Kansas city – 'again a big city' offers 'no improvement'. The only exception to this inventory of negative city impressions is Washington, the city designed by a Frenchman! It is not surprising, then, that Pierre Charles L'Enfant's city reminds Huizinga of the Old World, 'a touch of Paris and Vienna'.

10

However tempting it may be, one should not read Huizinga's negative impressions of life in the American cities as an example of the typical anti-American mood that was prevalent among European intellectuals of the interbellum era.[51] Huizinga's writings on America are marked by a curious ambiguity, or, as Thomas Macho puts it, dialectics. Always careful in weighing his argument, Huizinga often considers both the negative and positive aspects of his judgements. Huizinga, Macho writes, is always also critical of his own criticism.[52] Yet, this seems less the case with his personal impressions of the modern city. The Dutch historian – who saw himself as an ethnographer on this trip[53] – consistently judges the modern cities in terms of aesthetics: ugliness and lack of harmony are what prevail. In that sense Huizinga's criticism is not altogether different from that of modernity's greatest poet: Charles Baudelaire. In his *Le Peintre de la vie moderne* one finds descriptions of modern city life in terms of *tumulte* and *cacaphonie*. Like the Dutch historian, the poet claims that the modern world – a noisy, tumultuous world – makes us blasé. In the modern city our senses grow weary. The modern city, we learn from him, offers its citizens a world that can no longer be conceived in terms of harmony. But where the French poet is famous for his writings on urban modernity, the Dutch historian is seldom read for his thoughts on the modern metropolis. One has to search quite a bit to find a theory of the modern city, but the fact that there is only a few instances in which hints of such a theory can be found should not deceive us.

Upon his return, Huizinga used his diary to write a new book on America: *America. Levend en Denkend.* In those 'loose remarks' traces of his city observations can be found. His observations on

New York have resulted in a reflection on waste. The modern city becomes the place where all developments grouped under the header of 'the mechanization of culture' come together:

> The big city is no longer a dwelling place, but an instrument [*werktuig*], an instrument of traffic, transport and communication. It has become completely dynamic. It doesn't serve in the first place as a special place for dwelling, but as a place instead for moving through, both bodily and mentally,. Its actual organism comprises the means of transportation, the elevators, the telephone, the radio, the presses and calculating machines. The houses only form its skeleton.[54]

Huizinga could not be clearer. The modern city is literally a depersonalized city. Human beings come and go there, they pass through, but they no longer seem to dwell in what once was a 'special place'. To put the matter somewhat bolder: the city has given home to a new organism, namely that of technological means. That is to say, human beings are excluded from the city. And with them being gone, play has gone, too.

11

And thus Plato's dream of a city without play has finally been realized, but in a way that the Greek philosopher could hardly have imagined. 'Technological progression', Huizinga writes, 'pushes the economic process to run its course of concentration and total levelling of everything in an ever faster pace.'[55] Or, as Baudelaire once wrote: 'la marée montante de la démocratie, qui envahit tout et qui nivelle tout'.[56] The city no longer mirrors the organization of the cosmos. Instead, it has become a noisy – in the terms of Huizinga: *dreunende* – world, in which machines seem to have become its sole inhabitants. Anaesthetized (*verdoofd*), literarily as well as figuratively, modern man has grown blasé.

Huizinga was certainly not the only cultural historian who has signalled the loss of harmony and the disappearance of 'cosmic insight'. When Huizinga wrote that despite his 'aesthetic sensibility' modern man had lost this insight, readers of no one less than Walter Benjamin could have recognized this observation. At the end of his *Einbahnstraße*, the German critic describes the difference between the ancients and the moderns. The way the ancients related to the cosmos, he claims, was through *Rausch*; a communal rapture, so to speak. And this is where modern man errs: he 'regards this experience as unimportant and avoidable'.[57] Modern developments in warfare or astronomy make him think he is able to control nature, where in fact he is not. On his way 'to the planetarium', modern man discovers he is oblivious of his situation in the cosmos. But where for Huizinga this loss of this 'cosmic insight' coincided with the disappearance of harmony and, more importantly, with the decline of play in Western societies, for Benjamin it was a reason to formulate new bodily and mental requirements that modern man needed to guard himself against the process of modernization.

12

For Huizinga it was impossible to conceive of modernity as a ludic modernity. But Benjamin clearly objected to this possible impossibility of a ludic modernity. Instead of further lamenting the loss of harmony, Benjamin went looking for the ideal attitude to cope with the process of modernization. This attitude he found exactly there where Huizinga thought it to be gone. It is precisely, as we will see in a moment, in play that modern man is able to endure the continuous bombardment of the senses. Benjamin came to this diametrical opposite estimation of play through a different genealogy. Part of this genealogy has been thoroughly investigated by Heinz Brüggemann. Through a close reading of several chapters from *Berliner Kindheit*, such as the one on shadow play and one on word play, Brüggemann reveals by what books Benjamin must have been inspired in conceiving his ideas on play. Many thoughts on the education and play of children seem to have been influenced by Jean Paul's *Levana, oder Erziehungslehre*.[58] Among the other works that have inspired Benjamin are Tom Seidmann-Freud's *Spielfibel* books, of which Benjamin wrote several reviews. Also, and perhaps of even greater influence, was the work by Karl Groos, *Die Spiele der Menschen* (1899), which presents a physiological and psychological classification of human play. This classification itself is based on a theory of 'impulses', as the English translator rendered the German *Trieb*.[59] Groos distinguished between 'first order impulses' and 'second order impulses'. With the first he meant those impulses with which the individual tries to gain control over his own 'psychophysical organism;' impulses that control its 'sensory and motor apparatus'. Those of the second order are impulses with which he regulates his relationships with other living beings. One could think here of a '*Kampftrieb*', a '*Nachahmungstrieb*', or a '*sexuellen Trieb*'. Of the two, the first order impulses attract Benjamin's attention in particular. The exercise of those first order impulses, which Groos also called 'playful experimentation'/'*spielendes Experimenteren*'.[60] The way a child discovers its sense of touch, of sight or taste, for example, is by testing and a repeating of this testing. But also the way an old man rediscovers his sense of touch by holding a walking cane may be taken as an example of playful experimentation. Now, Benjamin takes up on this 'experimentation',[61] but gives it a decisive twist.

Benjamin started to work on his theory of play in the second half of the 1920s, most notably in his reviews of children's books and his writings on proletarian theatre. He built his thoughts on anthropological and pedagogical literature from the nineteenth century and pursued that line further into the twentieth century. Not without, however, giving a twist to that line. He took up Groos' theory of the *Spieltrieb* and confronted it with Freud's analysis of the death drive in *Jenseits des Lustprinzips*. Before we get to Freud, however, we must pause to reflect on the line that connects the Austrian neurologist with Groos.

In his review of Karl Gröber's *Kinderspielzeug aus alter Zeit*, Benjamin claimed that the theory of play as proposed by Groos must be supplemented with the '*Gestaltlehre der Spielgesten*' of which Willy Haas wrote in *Die Literarische Welt* from May 18, 1928. Based on the same premise as Groos' work – namely that children repeat the gestures of the animal world – Haas found three basic *Grund-Gesten* or forms of play: (1) cat and mouse, (2) a mother animal protecting her child (e.g., goalkeeper or tennis player), and (3) a battle between two animals for gain or over a love.[62] Haas found those forms also in the *Kriminaldrama* and *Kriminalbuch* of his day. In fact, criminal fiction does nothing but repeating those *Grund-Gesten*. And here, we touch upon the fundamental law of play – 'dem großen Gesetz' that presides over all rules and rhythms of the world of play[63] – which is: the law of repetition (*Wiederholung*). Children like to repeat their games endlessly, Haas claimed and he explained this drive for repetition by referring to Freud's *Jenseits des Lustprinzips*. This compulsion to repeat is, as Freud argued, a means for the child to mitigate the sensuous impressions in order to master his or her situation. The great example here is, of course, the *Fort-Da* game in which the throwing away and retrieving of a wooden reel helps the child to triumph over his mother going away without protesting.

In 1928, still writing about the world of children, Benjamin gratefully borrowed Haas' suggestion and wrote that 'every profound experience [*tiefste Erfahrung*] longs to be insatiable, longs for return and repetition until the end of time, and for the reinstatement of an original condition from which it sprang'.[64] Repetition is the key to prevent oneself from becoming numb (*Abstumpfung*) and to relive one's triumphs. Not pretending or 'acting as if', but 'Immer-wieder-tun' is the true aim of play: i.e. 'the transformation of a shattering experience [*Erfahrung*] into habit'. While this was all phrased in the context of the play of children, Benjamin already also understood the potentiality of this theory for his investigations of Western modernity. He wrote that 'play is the mother of every habit', thereby clearly hinting at an understanding of play as the basis for all social intercourse (as one finds in Huizinga). And in his 'Notizen zu einer Theorie des Spiels' one finds the unfinished plan for a 'Psychologische und ontologische Betrachtung des Spiels'.[65]

13

Yet, in 1928 the time was not right for him to transpose his theory of play from the child's world to that ontological level. One had to wait some ten years for a new elaboration of his theory of play. This theory, then, was presented within the framework of that great project that Benjamin was working on throughout the 1930s: his *Baudelaire-Buch*. In his discussion of Baudelaire's poetry in his 'Über einige Motive bei Baudelaire' Benjamin returned to Freud. *Jenseits des Lustprinzips* becomes the keytext for Benjamin's ideas on *Chock-Abwehr*. Freud had argued that consciousness has an important part to play in the protection against (external) stimuli. Benjamin translated this external threat in terms of '*shock*'. To survive in the modern metropolis, Benjamin claimed, one must learn how to deal with the continuous bombardment of the senses. With an overload of audible and visual stimuli, one must train one's defensive mechanism that protects against the shocks, which otherwise would deform consciousness. In his writings on children, Benjamin argued that play would be the best way to prepare oneself against a traumatic experience. It is a similar idea, but phrased in different terms that reappears in 'Einige Motive'. And indeed the figure of the player appears in this essay on Baudelaire too:

'Das Bild des Spielers wurde bei Baudelaire das eigentliche moderne Komplement zum archaischen Bild des Fechters',[66] we read. The player appears as the 'heroic figure' in modernity.

English translators consequently render the German *Spieler* as gambler, and indeed Benjamin had the player of a hazard game in mind. To be sure, gamblers are players. But they are certainly not the only ones who play and Benjamin was well aware of this when he conceived his ideas on *Spiel*. In Benjamin's work a whole typology of different play figures is to be found. An extensive reconstruction of all the instances in which Benjamin uses *Spiel* or related terms would show that children, prostitutes, cinematographers, or flâneurs need *Spielraum* too.[67] Miriam Hansen has shown how cinema offered a 'room for play' in which modern citizens were trained to cope with the experience of shock. For the other playful figures this still needs to be done. If cinema is one such place where *Spiel-Raum* is found, the arcades of the modern metropolis may be another. It is the place where one would have liked to see Benjamin and Huizinga going for a stroll. What might have happened, then, under the glass rooftops of the arcades, is left to our playful imagination. But of one thing we can be sure: Benjamin would have asked the Dutch historian to open his eyes and to look around him. What he would have seen there, in that enormous room for play, is not difficult to imagine: Harmony may be gone, he then concludes, but we are playing nevertheless.

Notes

1 On the curious history of this word derived from Latin see Benveniste. He argues that history has precisely reversed the Latin model, in which the city is not the entity that defines the citizen but precisely the other way around. In fact, this reversal leads straight back to the Greek model in which the city is postulated as something that comes before the citizen. Please see: Benveniste, 'Deux modèles linguistiques de la cité.'

2 And similarly, André Jolles argued that the art history of Ancient Greece is a history of the city: 'Der Mittelpunkt, um den sich alles dreht, ist die *Architektur*, und die Architektur ist die *Stadt*. Um die griechische Kunst zu verstehen, muß man eine griechische Stadt beschreiben können, die Kunstgeschichte is die Geschichte der Städte.' Jolles, *Ausgelöste Klänge*, p. 11.

3 Benjamin Kline Hunnicut has rightfully observed that 'many of Plato's dialogues such as the Phaedrus, Symposium, Republic, Parmenides, and Laws begin or take place outside the city walls: beside streams, in the fields, in temples around Athens, or on streets and country roads.' Hunnicut, 'Leasure and play in Plato's teaching and philosophy of learning', p. 216.

4 Statkiewicz, *Rhapsody of Philosophy*, p. 41.

5 Rancière, *The Philosopher and His Poor*, p. 4.

6 Plato, *The Republic*, II 370c.

7 Ibid., II 374c–d.

8 Rancière, *The Philosopher and His Poor*, p. 13

9 Rancière, *The Emancipated Spectator*, p. 5. For a modern example of such a 'choreographic community' please see: De Vugt, 'Dandyism as Monumental-Political Ethos'.

10 Rancière, *Disagreement*, p. 71.

11 E.g. *Politeia*, 396e, 425a, 547a; *The Laws*, 636e–674c, 643b–c; *The Statesman*, 268d–e; *Timaeus* 59d; *Phaedrus*, 265c, 276–278.

12 Voegelin, 'Homo Ludens', p. 180.

13 Plato, *The Republic*, 425a

14 Huizinga, *Homo Ludens*, p. 191.

15 Voegelin, 'Homo Ludens', p. 181; Cf. Plato, *The Laws*, 653e.

16 Morris, 'No Learning by Coercion', p. 110.

17 Cf. Statkiewicz, *Rhapsody of Philosophy*, p. 48.

18 Huizinga, *Homo Ludens*, p. 160.

19 Voegelin, 'Homo Ludens', p. 184.

20 Koyré, *From the Closed World*, p. 2.

21 Cf. Remi Brague, *The Wisdom of the World*, p. 32.

22 Voegelin, 'Homo Ludens', p. 184.

23 Ibid.

24 Huizinga, *Homo Ludens*, pp. 3–4. Translation slightly modified. It should be noted that the English edition, based on the German translation, originally reads: 'The very existence of play continually confirms the supra-logical nature of the human situation.' For reasons that remain unclear to us it leaves out precisely that what makes Huizinga's meditation on play so interesting: its emphasis on the relationship between play and the cosmic order.

25 I borrow the term 'Untranslatable' from Emily Apter. Please see her: *Against World Literature*, pp. xvii-xx. Apter, in turn, took her inspiration from the French edition of *Dictionary of Untranslatables*. Please see the introduction by Barbara Cassin.

26 Cf. Gumbrecht, *Atmosphere, Mood, Stimmung*, pp. 4–5.

27 Fritz Saxl, Letter of January 20, 1936 to Johan Huizinga. In: Warburg Institute London.

28 Calvino, *Letters: 1941–1985*, p. 22.

29 Huizinga, *Kultur- und Zeitkritische Schriften*, p. 15–17.

30 Huizinga, *In the Shadow of Tomorrow*, p. 17.

31 Huizinga, *In de Schaduwen van Morgen*, p. 316.

32 Huizinga, *Homo Ludens*, pp. 7 and 10.

33 Ibid., p. 10.

34 Ibid., p. 9. *Italics mine.*

35 Ibid., p. 10. On the relationship between music and order, please see: Attali, *Noise*, p. 62.

36 Ibid., p. 22.

37 *Translation mine.* The original English translation reads: 'The joy inextricably bound up with playing can turn not only into tension, but into elation. Frivolity and ecstasy are the twin poles between which play moves.' Ibid., p. 21. It, again, fails to render some of Huizinga's key concepts (e.g. *spelstemming*) visible.

38 Ibid., p. 21.

39 Ibid., p. 47.

40 *Translation mine.*

41 *Translation mine.*

42 *Translation mine.*

43 Spitzer, *Classical and Christian Ideas of World Harmony*, p. 138.

44 Huizinga, *Homo Ludens*, p. 26.

45 Huizinga, *Amerika. Levend en Denkend*, p. 165.

46 Huizinga, *Amerika Dagboek*, p. 32. This and all following translations from Huizinga's *Amerika Dagboek* are my own. The original reads: 'cultuurwoekering, overbodig en schadelijk groeisel, alles overdekt met wancultuur, wrijving en tijdverlies'; and: '*Waste, Waste.* Al de schoenen die nooit gedragen worden, al de bloemen die verwelken, al de woorden die nooit gelezen worden, het licht dat voor niets brandt, de kracht die verspild wordt.'

47 Ibid., p. 37. 'Van boven gezien lijkt het gekrioel der bussen en auto's een goedige Inferno-scene. Maar vlak eromheen zit een grimmige Inferno, hier aan de buitenkant! Om niet aan te denken van leelijkheid en ellendigheid.

48 Ibid., p. 39. 'Aan de oude prenten van New York: 1791, 1830, ziet men, dat het toen al niet mooi of harmonisch was: strak, rommelig, onverzorgd, zonder vorm, in 1797 nog een paar trapgeveltjes.'

49 Ibid., p. 45. 'Die Amerikaanse steden zijn beleedigend leelijk.'

50 Ibid., p.86. 'een abjecte stad en een schandvlek der menschheid'; and: 'zoveel materiaal, zoveel vernuft, zoveel arbeid voor zoo'n pover eindresultaat als een Amerikaanse krant.'

51 Cf. Krul, *Historicus tegen de tijd*, pp. 177–207.

52 Macho, 'Johan Huizinga in Amerika', pp. 352–53.

53 Huizinga, *Amerika Dagboek*, p. 103.

54 Ibid., p. 17. 'De groote stad is niet meer woonplaats maar werktuig, een werktuig van verkeer, transport en communicatie. Zij is geheel dynamisch geworden. Zij dient niet in de eerste plaats, om in een bijzondere ruimte te vertoeven, maar om zich, lichamelijk of geestelijk, binnen en buiten haar te verplaatsen. Haar eigenlijk organisme zijn de verkeersmiddelen, de elevator's, de telefoon, de radio-installaties, de drukpersen en de telmachines. De huizen vormen slechts het geraamte.'

55 Ibid., p. 15. 'De vooruitgang der techniek dwingt het economisch proces, zijn richting op concentratie en algemeene gelijkmaking in steeds sneller tempo te doorlopen.'

56 Baudelaire, *Le Peintre de la Vie Moderne, II*, p. 712: 'the rising tide of democracy that invades and equalizes everything'.

57 Benjamin, 'One-Way Street', p. 93.

58 Brüggemann's presents a thorough philological reconstruction of the books that Benjamin must have had in mind while writing down his childhood memories. It is a commendable attempt. However, for Brüggemann play in Benjamin's oeuvre is first and foremost child's play. And hence he leaves out all the other instances of *Spiel* that do not directly relate to the realm of the child. It is my conviction that, although certainly most pronounced in his writings on children, Benjamin's theory of play extended far beyond that realm. In fact, the play of children was only the starting point for a project that throughout the 1930s should have constructed a 'Psychologische und ontologische Betrachtung des Spiels', as we read in Benjamin's 'Notizen zu einer Theorie des Spiels' (p. 190).

59 Groos, *The Play of Man*, p. 4.

60 Groos, *Die Spiele der Menschen*, p. 7.

61 Cf. Bratu Hansen, *Cinema and Experience*, p. 191.

62 Haas, 'Sommerschlager, Volksmärchen', pp. 1–2.

63 Benjamin, 'Spielzeug und Spielen', p. 131.

64 Benjamin, *Selected Writings: Part I, 1927-1930*, p. 120.

65 Benjamin, 'Notizen zu einer Theorie des Spiels', p. 190.

66 Benjamin, 'Über einige Motive bei Baudelaire', §9, p. 634.

67 'With Baudelaire, the image of the player became the truly modern complement to the archaic image of the fencer'. See for example §7 of 'Über einige Motive' in which Benjamin writes: 'doch gab es auch noch den Flaneur, der Spielraum braucht.'

Bibliography

- Apter, Emily. *Against World Literature: On the Politics of Untranslatability*. London: Verso, 2013.
- Attali, Jacques. *Noise: The Political Economy of Music*. Minneapolis: University of Minnesota Press, 1985.
- Baudelaire, Charles. *Le peintre de la vie moderne: Oeuvres complètes, II*. Paris: Gallimard, 1976, pp. 683-724.
- Baudelaire, Charles. *The Painter of Modern Life and other Essays*, translated by Jonathan Mayne. London: Phaidon Press, 1995.
- Benjamin, Walter. *Gesammelte Schriften, 7 Bde.*, edited by Rolf Tiedemann and Hermann Schweppenhäuser. Frankfurt am Main: Suhrkamp, 1991.
- Benjamin, Walter. 'Über einige Motive bei Baudelaire.' In *Gesammelte Schriften*, Bd. 1, pp. 605-54. Frankfurt am Main: Suhrkamp, 1991.
- Benjamin, Walter. 'Spielzeug und Spielen.' In *Gesammelte Schriften*, Bd. 3, pp. 127-31. Frankfurt am Main: Suhrkamp, 1991.
- Benjamin, Walter. 'Notizen zu einer Theorie des Spiels.' In *Gesammelte Schriften*, Bd. 6, pp. 188-91. Frankfurt am Main: Suhrkamp, 1991.
- Benjamin, Walter. 'One-Way Street.' In *Selected Writings*, edited by Marcus Bullock, translated by Michael W. Jennings, pp. 444-88. Cambridge: Harvard University Press, 1996.
- Benjamin, Walter. *The Arcades Project*, edited by Rolf Tiedemann, translated by Howard Eiland and Kevin McLaughlin. Cambridge: Harvard University Press, 2002.
- Benjamin, Walter. *Selected Writings: Part I, 1927-1930*. Cambridge: Belknap 2005.
- Benjamin, Walter. *The Writer of Modern Life: Essays on Charles Baudelaire*, edited by Michael W. Jennings, translated by Howard Eiland, Edmund Jephcott, Rodney Livingston and Harry Zohn. Cambridge: Belknap Press, 2006.
- Benjamin, Walter. *Werke und Nachlaß: Kritische Gesamtausgabe, Bd. 8: Einbahnstraße*, edited by Detlev Schöttker and Steffen Haug. Berlin: Suhrkamp, 2009.
- Benjamin, Walter. *Werke und Nachlaß: Kritische Gesamtausgabe, Bd. 16: Das Kunstwerk im Zeitalter seiner technischen Reproduzierbarkeit*, edited by Burkhardt Lindner. Berlin: Suhrkamp, 2012.
- Benveniste, Émile. 'Deux modèles linguistiques de la cité.' In *Problèmes de linguistique générale 2*, pp. 272-80. Paris: Gallimard, 1974.
- Brague, Rémi. *The Wisdom of the World: The Human Experience of the Universe in Western Thought*. Chicago: The University of Chicago Press, 2003.
- Brüggemann, Heinz. *Walter Benjamin über Spiel, Farbe und Phantasie*. Würzburg: Königshausen & Neumann, 2007.
- Calvino, Italo. *Letters: 1941-1985*. Princeton: Princeton University Press, 2013.
- Cassin, Barbara. 'Introduction.' In *Dictionary of Untranslatables*. Princeton: Princeton University Press, 2014.
- Freud, Sigmund. *Beyond the Pleasure Principle*. New York: Boni and Liveright, 1924.
- Groos, Karl. *Die Spiele der Menschen*. Hildesheim: Georg Olms Verlag, 1973.
- Groos, Karl. *The Play of Man*, translated by Elizabeth L. Baldwin. New York: Appleton & Company, 1912.
- Gumbrecht, Hans Ulrich. *Atmosphere, Mood, Stimmung: On a Hidden Potential of Literature*. Stanford: Stanford University Press, 2012.
- Haas, Willy. 'Sommerschlager, Volksmärchen.' *Die Literarische Welt*, 18 May 1928.
- Hansen, Miriam Bratu. *Cinema and Experience: Siegfried Kracauer, Walter Benjamin, and Theodor W. Adorno*. Berkeley: University of California Press, 2012.
- Hanssen, Léon. *Huizinga en de troost van de geschiedenis: Verbeelding en rede*. Amsterdam: Balans, 1996.
- Huizinga, Johan. *Amerika, Levend en Denkend: Losse Opmerkingen*. Haarlem: H.D. Tjeenk Willink & Zoon, 1926.
- Huizinga, Johan. *In the Shadow of Tomorrow*. New York: W.W. Norton & Co., 1936.
- Huizinga, Johan. *Homo Ludens: Proeve eener bepaling van het spel-element der cultuur*. In *Verzamelde Werken V: Cultuurgeschiedenis III*, edited by L. Brummel et al., pp. 26-246. Haarlem: Tjeenk Willink & Zoon N.V., 1950.
- Huizinga, Johan. *Mensch en Menigte in Amerika: Vier Essays over Moderne Beschavingsgeschiedenis*. In *Verzamelde Werken V: Cultuurgeschiedenis III*, edited L. Brummel et al., pp. 249-417. Haarlem: Tjeenk Willink & Zoon N.V., 1950.

- Huizinga, Johan. *In de Schaduwen van Morgen*. In *Verzamelde Werken VII: Geschiedwetenschap, Hedendaagse Cultuur*, edited L. Brummel et al., pp. 313–476. Haarlem: Tjeenk Willink & Zoon N.V., 1950.
- Huizinga, Johan. *Verzamelde Werken*, edited L. Brummel et al., Haarlem: Tjeenk Willink & Zoon N.V., 1950.
- Huizinga, Johan. *Homo Ludens: A Study of the Play-Element in Culture*. Boston: Beacon Press, 1955.
- Huizinga, Johan. *Amerika Dagboek: 14 april–19 juni 1926*. Amsterdam: Contact, 1993.
- Huizinga, Johan. *Amerika.* Munich: Wilhelm Fink, 2011.
- Huizinga, Johan. *Kultur- und Zeitkritische Schriften*. Munich: Wilhelm Fink, 2013.
- Hunnicut, Benjamin Kline. 'Leasure and play in Plato's teaching and philosophy of learning.' *Leisure Studies: An Interdisciplinary Journal* 12 (1990) 2, pp. 211–27.
- Jolles, André. *Ausgelöste Klänge: Briefe aus dem Felde über antike Kunst*. Berlin: Weidmannsche Buchhandlung, 1916.
- Koyré, Alexandre. *From the Closed World to the Infinite Universe.* Baltimore, MD: Johns Hopkins University Press, 1968.
- Krul, W.E. *Historicus tegen de tijd: Opstellen over leven & werk van J. Huizinga*. Groningen: Historische Uitgeverij, 1990.
- Macho, Thomas. 'Johan Huizinga in Amerika.' In Johan Huizinga, *Amerika*, pp. 349–68. Munich: Wilhelm Fink, 2011.
- Morris, Stephen R. 'No Learning by Coercion: Paidia and Paideia in Platonic Philosophy.' In *Play from Birth to Twelve and Beyond: Contexts, Perspectives, and Meanings,* edited by Doris Fromberg and Doris Bergen. New York: Garland, 1998.
- Plato. *The Laws*, translated by R.G. Bury. Cambridge, MA: Harvard University Press, 1961.
- Plato. *The Republic,* translated by Paul Shorey. Cambridge, MA: Cambridge University Press, 2000.
- Rancière, Jacques. *Disagreement: Politics and Philosophy.* Minneapolis: University of Minnesota Press, 1999.
- Rancière, Jacques. *The Philosopher and His Poor.* Durham: Duke University Press, 2004.
- Rancière, Jacques. *The Emancipated Spectator.* London: Verso, 2009.
- Spitzer, Leo. *Classical and Christian Ideas of World Harmony: Prolegomena to an Interpretation of the Word 'Stimmung'.* Baltimore: Johns Hopkins Press, 1963.
- Statkiewicz, Max. *Rhapsody of Philosophy: Dialogues with Plato in Contemporary Thought.* University Park: Pennsylvania State University Press, 2009.
- Voegelin, Eric. 'Homo Ludens: Versuch einer Bestimmung des Spielelements der Kultur by Jan Huizinga.' *The Journal of Politics* 10 (1948) 1, pp. 179–87.
- Vugt, Geertjan de. 'Dandyism as Monumental-Political Ethos: Van Deyssel and the Walking Utopia.' *Dutch Crossing* 37 (2013) 1, pp. 57–78.

Commonplaces on the (Spatial) Commons

Lieven De Cauter

Approaching the Commons

The commons are under threat. Both Nature (the ecosystem we share) and Culture (language, expressions, cultural tradition, art, cultural heritage, and media we use and share without ownership, knowledge, free research) are under severe pressure. The impending appropriation by states and multinationals of the North Pole is symbolic of the vulnerability of the 'natural common', as Negri and Hardt call it in their Commonwealth.[1] The patenting of seeds by Monsanto and other multinationals is equally symbolic: it constitutes the appropriation and privatization of what was shared by farmers for 10,000 years. The battle over the privatization of knowledge (and research) in the knowledge economy is proof that the 'artificial common' (to stay with Negri and Hardt's terminology for the time being) is endangered as well.

As the commons are under threat, we become aware of the commons. But we have forgotten what it is. Or we know what it is (it is pretty common, we have things in common, et cetera), but it somehow remains alien, it is not an obvious category of our discourse. From newspapers to the history of philosophy and theory: discourse on the common is marginal. (Even if it has become a buzzword lately, in sociological and media terms this attention would still have to be considered as a marginal phenomenon – something for alternative people, ecologists and leftist thinkers such as Agamben, Žižek, Badiou, Rancière, Virno, Harvey and of course Negri and Hardt). The absence of the idea of the common, both our stuttering and our swooning when we use the word is therefore symptomatic. If we want to reactivate the common, we will have to start from its absence, its forsakenness, its oblivion, its abolition.

Particularly in relation to space, we are used to think in terms of public versus private: a space is either public or private. If we find a space that does not fit this dichotomy, we call it semi-public or semi-private. But the common is a third category. But what is this forgotten third category, which we are rediscovering after it had almost completely been forgotten? As we have forgotten the common, forgotten what it is, and in order to approach the commons in spatial terms, the 'spatial or territorial commons' it is maybe wise to start with some basics, some commonplaces – in search of the link between common and place. If we look for the most commonplace definition of the common it could sound like this: *The common is what is neither public (state owned) nor private.*

But what does the word common actually mean, where does it come from? According to the *Online Etymology Dictionary* the adjective 'common' was introduced in English around 1300, and means 'belonging to all, general'. Easy: common is another word for general. It is not particular. Belonging to all (in general) means also belonging to nobody (in particular). Interesting tautology and paradox at once... The word is derived form the Old French *comun* 'common, general, free, open, public' (that is dated around the ninth century, in modern French *commun*). It comes from Latin *communis* 'in common, public, shared by all or many; general, not specific; familiar, not pretentious'. But it comes originally from the Proto-Indo-European (PIE) word *ko-moin-i- 'held in common', compound adjective formed from *ko- 'together' + *moi-n-, suffixed form of root *mei- 'change, exchange', hence it means literally 'shared by all'.

'The second element of the compound also', still according to the *Online Etymology Dictionary*, 'is the source of Latin munia "duties, public duties, functions", those related to munia "office". Perhaps reinforced in Old French by the Germanic form of PIE *ko-moin-i- (cf. Old English *gemæne* "common, public, general, universal;" corresponding in English to *mean*, which came to French via Frankish.' And then, without further ado, the entry concludes: 'Used disparagingly of women and criminals since c. 1300....' The linguistic *Aha-Erlebnis* of this short entry is that common (in Latin languages and in English) and *gemein/gemeen/* mean (in Germanic languages) have the same root and are in fact a deformation of the same (hypothetical) 'urword' (*Komoini*) – so the French '*commune*' and the German *Gemeinde* (or Dutch *gemeente*) are not only equivalent (for village, or community) but in fact the same word, differently (de)formed. Besides, we discover here that the common is always also the mean, the general, not only what is shared by all, but also what is despised as low and vulgar. The combination with duty (*munia*) points to a political task: taking up tasks in and for the community, but it is too early to go into that.

The *noun* common(s) the dictionary dates as late fifteenth century, 'land held in common'. That is of course the quintessence of what we are looking for: the spatial commons. In Dutch the common in its stark meaning of 'land held in common' would be '*meent*', but apart from the London commons, a street name in Rotterdam, and apparently some places in and around Bruges, and some other patches here and there maybe, very little is left of it. The real proof that the common in spatial terms has been almost totally appropriated, privatized or nationalized. Beside this the dictionary signals: 'Commons "the third estate of the English people as represented in Parliament", is from late 14c. The Latin *communis* also served as a noun meaning 'common property, commonwealth'. That is the concept of commons now used by the defenders of the commons. This dictionary entry seems a good starting point for our commonplaces, which may prove to be paradoxical platitudes.

The Enclosure of the Commons

The first common place, the commonplaces of common places so to speak, would be that Nature is common. Indeed, Nature is common by essence. It is the ultimate commons. It is that what we share; not only share with all other humans, but with all living and inanimate creatures, organic or inorganic matter. The cosmos, literally meaning gem, ornament (hence cosmetics) has revealed itself, since space travel, as the blue planet. This once vast and overwhelming wholeness in which the human species one day appeared in prehistory is now a fragile and awfully limited ecosystem. It is precisely this human species that has become so predominant and so all-encompassing that it has given its name to a new geological era: the Anthropocene. It is in the Anthropocene that the common is at the same time precious in a new way and under stress, squandered and appropriated.

All this leads us to another platitude: the commons, in spatial or territorial terms, like the famous, paradigmatic London commons, are leftovers (of premodern law, like the Magna Carta and the charter of the forests, of nomadic cultures, of even the state of nature?). We can think of Rousseau's proto-anthropology of the 'good savage' (*le bon savage*): it is when somebody, in an audacious gesture to fence off a patch of land, said 'this is mine', and found people stupid enough to believe him, that private property and after that regulated society and inequality started. Indeed, only for what anthropology has called the 'nature peoples' and for nomads nature is truly common. For them it is common by nature, as it were. That is maybe the real reason behind animism: it expresses this deep awareness in the most perfect way possible. Both children and rational philosophers, even scientists can understand this (sometimes): the mystical 'given-ness' of it all.

Given by nobody to everybody. Given to nobody by this ultimate body, Mother Earth, the cosmos.

Deus sive natura, said Spinoza: God or nature, implying God is nature. Pantheism was a more modern way to state the unity of everything and the 'gift'. It is this 'given-ness', this gift that is taken away from us, or it is a respect or gratefulness that we have lost. In nomadic culture you *use* nature, but you don't *own* it. Life is a (sacred) give and take, a fragile process that requires restraint and respect, for land, trees, animals, and especially for the balance, the harmony of it all (which is more than a statistical equilibrium in an ecosystem). The shepherds are respectful of the land. The hunter is grateful and respectful to his prey. The common is primordial, archaic.

Agriculture needs land. Sedentary cultures cannot move their turf, or only to expand or colonize. With the disappearance of nomadic culture – let's not think of it as a natural process: think wars, colonization, genocide – the commons shrink, becoming more and more a leftover zone, often arid or at least non-arable land. From 1500 onwards, the commons in Europe become a reserve, like later the reserves for the nomadic Native Americans in the US and Canada. This idea of the common as 'protected' and imprisoned in reserves is something to stress. Of course the oceans are still common, like the air, but as we write, the North Pole is under threat of exploitation, as states and multinationals want to appropriate and exploit it. The retreat of the icecaps is leaving the North Pole naked and vulnerable to rape, so to speak.

The common is weak. Seeds have, apparently, no defence. Neither has water. Nor has air. Even language is not safe. Without property, it is not easy to defend a territory, a space, place, an entity, a species. Wild nature is everybody's, so corporations can 'enclose' it, appropriate it, as they do with 'wild seeds'. In a sense only a world body politic, a radically reformed and strengthened UN could outlaw the privatization of seeds, like only a world body, like the UN, could really defend the Amazon forest, the North Pole, the ecosystem.

That is maybe the great lesson of Peter Linebaugh's *The Magna Carta Manifesto*:[2] the Charter of the Forest is a legal protection of the commons. The commons are in a sense instituted by law: the right to take dry wood from the forest, to take fruits and let a pig graze, all these practices of subsistence were stipulated in the charter. *The Magna Carta* (and its second part: the said charter of the forest) is a contract made up after revolt between the sovereign and the people. The King promises the people fair trial by their peers, and in the second part: access to the commons of the forests, and if he does not stick to the contract, it is stipulated by himself that the people have the contractual right to revolt. Habeas corpus, legal access to the commons, the right to revolt, it is all there in Magna Carta, a legal document of the year 1215. Alas, it has been forgotten.

Modernity opens up with the enclosure of the commons. From the sixteenth century onwards the (spatial) commons (as 'land held in common') virtually disappear in Europe. The first wave of these enclosures have been documented by Thomas Morus in the first part of his book *Utopia*. Indeed, it has often been overlooked that the first part of *Utopia* is a tirade against the enclosure of the commons by the ruling classes and landed gentry. It forced large swats of the populace, the 'commoners', into poverty and vagabondage. The expulsion from their homes and the closing of commons was followed by a ruthless repression and criminalization of the homeless and the poor. *Utopia* was written against the enclosures, and this seemingly accidental link cannot be underestimated. It feels like a hint. But what does it mean? What does this omen want to tell us? A premonition of causality? Is *Utopia* the defence of the common? Yes. *Utopia* was a response to the shocking injustice Morus could see happening before his eyes. Is the common a utopia? Also affirmative. It is because he was looking for a counter-image, an alternative, that Morus was tempted to conceive an undiscovered Island that was an expanded community of mixed cloisters, with common meals, common dwelling, uniform clothes, strict day order, and no private property, since his narrator points to it as the source of all evil. The cloister, this most medieval of heterotopias, became the modern paradigm of utopia (one could say all utopias have this 'claustro-phobic' tendency, which explain their totalitarian tendency). All this could lead to a redefinition of utopia, also to redeem some of its claustrophobic, totalitarian tendencies: utopianism is a radical response to the enclosure of the commons.

The fact that the book was published at the very beginning of the sixteenth century (in 1516) is telling: both Braudel[3] and Wallerstein[4] put forward 1500 as the beginning of capitalism. The rise of capitalism has been marked in an almost allegorical, but also very real way by the enclosure of the commons. Marx has documented this process in the last monumental chapter of the first volume of *The Capital* on the 'Original Appropriation', besides the walling off of arable land for grazing for sheep – given the rise of the wool industry in Flanders – there was a massive destruction of houses and even towns. The people lost in one moment their dwelling and their means of subsistence (ground around the houses and the forests for wood, et cetera). This expropriation was followed by a severe criminalization of the poor that lasted for centuries, like the encroachment; and, driven to the cities, they supplied the new proletariat for the first factories and moreover they formed a new internal market (as they lost all means of subsistence). This is the mechanism behind the 'original appropriation'.

One can say that in the course of five centuries capitalism has erased the commons, both its reality and even the very idea of it. Particularly in spatial terms, we do not think anymore in terms of the commons. A massive appropriation of the commons has happened from two sides: the rise of capitalism has privatized the commons and the rise of the (modern) state has nationalized the commons: all not privately-owned land is almost by definition state-owned. Not only capitalism erased the commons, but communism too: everything was nationalized. Both capitalism and communism destroy or annihilate, abolish the category of the common: capitalism by privatization, communism by nationalization.

Both tend to destroy in their own (opposite) way the equilibrium of the three spheres: the public sphere (politics); the private sphere (economy), the cultural sphere (what we have called the heterotopian sphere).[5] In capitalism everything is swallowed up by economy: nature, culture, privacy, politics. All is subjected to a ruthless commodification and economization of everything, a true metastasis of economy. In communism (or state socialism, as Negri calls it) or totalitarianism, the same happens by a metastasis of politics. Nature is ruthlessly appropriated, the private sphere is abolished, economy is subjected to political plans and culture is 'purged'.

Today the commons have indeed become a utopia: not only an illusion, but also a *non place*. Think of the commons in London, touchingly absurd cut-outs, poetic nothingness, almost total absence: not even a park, just a green, for nobody, for everybody. For everybody and therefore for nobody. This could well be the best definition of the common: *the common is that what belongs to nobody and therefore to everybody, or, what belongs to everybody and therefore to nobody.* This simple paradox spells the fragility, the ungraspable, enigmatic character of the common well. The common is mysterious in a sense... (like language).

The common as Community: Communion and Communication

What can the cultural commons teach us for our investigation of the spatial commons? Can language help us? The most important lesson concerning the commons that we can learn from language is probably this: we use it but never own it, we can only temporarily appropriate the common: when I speak I use a language that is not mine, to say or write words that *become* mine. But even more than that: language is the symbolic order that we inhabit. It is in a sense the 'anthroposphere'.

How to find a spatial equivalent for language. Air? Maybe: air is spatial but not territorial. It is the only element we cannot appropriate, domesticate, privatize (or nationalize). Oh yes of course, we have tamed the skies. We have national airspaces, but not the air in it. Of course even that is not quite true since the Kyoto agreements: clean air is translated into juridical and economic quantities, so countries can compensate their pollution by sponsoring clean air elsewhere. But if we muse on: are air and language linked? A clear hint: *flatus voci:* the commons is an empty word, like the empty space it tries to name. Everything is common, nothing is common. *The common is almost nothing that could become everything.* That makes it so precious. Let us walk again across Clapham Common: it is an empty space in London, because it is for everybody, it is for nobody. Like language in a sense. *The common is sheer but also mere potentiality.* Here language is again a potent paradigm (as the work of Agamben has shown us).

What can the social common teach us, the communities that all of us are part of (from family over clan, to tribe, club, village, organization, neighbourhood unto the networks and e-communities)? In search of common ground, I asked, while we were reading *Commonwealth* (Negri and Hardt) with international students, that people explain us the word common in their respective languages. Some Chinese students provided a revelation: the ideogram for common looks like something of two separated hands eating from one bowl (共). This Universal symbol opened up a transcultural universality of communion, the sharing of food as the ultimate basic gesture of community and communication. It is this basic anthropological act of eating together, of sharing food, that is the core of all acts of communing and communion. It is the basis of hospitality, it is the basis of the feast and the festival. The Christian eucharisty is a ritualized version of it.

One could go as far as speaking about social animism in this respect. The hypothesis (of Durkheim[6]) that all religion is the forgotten self-adoration of the commons, of the community, is and remains extremely beautiful and inspiring, beyond the positivist leanings, not necessarily in opposition to them. The common is the body without the politic, it is the 'body natural' of the 'body politic', it is not mechanical, not an artificial body, a machine man (Hobbes' baroque metaphor). The community always underlies the institution (the Polis, the political, the public), there is always community before the polis, before the institution, and besides it, and also after it. It is the pre-political or 'zoöpolitical' social body: mother and child, family, kinship, the clan, the village, the circle of friends.

It is this community, this communalism of the commune, that has been haunting all thinkers looking for an alternative to capitalism. One of the latest attempts is Agamben's enchanting book on poverty (*De la très haute pauvreté*[7]), to show how in the medieval orders, notably in the Franciscan order, there was a radical attempt to think of *use* without and outside of property. The question remains if the cloister can once more become a paradigm: a heterotopia, or a heterotopian practice, can be inspiring but it can never become a blueprint for society at large.

Here it is useful to once more remind ourselves of the distinction between the three spheres: the political (public) sphere, the economical (private) sphere, and the cultural sphere (as the common). There are three forms of utopia: the metastasis of politics/public: the private and the common are swallowed up by the public/political sphere, the state. This is the totalitarian utopia. Then there is the capitalist utopia (neoliberalism is utopian, as clearly shown by Hans Achterhuis[8]): the public and common are swallowed up by the private, the economization of everything as the ultimate solution. And then there is the heterotopian utopia: a cultural institution becomes the paradigm and swallows up the public (political) and the private (economical). The best-known is the theocratic utopia and these days, it is rampant in all forms of religious fundamentalism, political Islam or Islamism being only its most visible form.

The big question that leads to a lot of confusion is this: is the common of the community a political form, or even shorter: is the *Polis* the common? Here we get in trouble before we even start speaking. The common is *not* the body politic. It is humans as communities, the community is the common, the common is community. It is this communication and this communion that makes up the social common. The *polis* is always the other of the communities. It is the political form of these spontaneous communities. The 'state' body politic is never spontaneous, it is instituted, it is a system (of sovereignty, of law and order, of separation of powers, monopoly of violence, et cetera). This is the big lacuna of the thinking of the common today: the absence of a political form, a 'state' or 'post-state' theory. But then as soon as the common finds a political institutional form, it could be regarded as a betrayal of the commons, like nationalization of the commons by the state. The political form of the commons, is its Achilles heel. But let us delay this big question for some other time and return to our search for the spatial commons...

Paradoxes of the Commons

In our time, we discovered, the spatial commons are inexistent. As said, it is difficult to point to a real 'common place', a 'common ground', since at least in the Western hemisphere land is either private or public, private property or state property. Besides the London commons, and then some patches here and there in and around Bruges, there would be only some common ground left, and no doubt elsewhere. But these are relics, hardly relevant spaces.

Maybe there are some spaces that almost look like a common or feel like a common. I think of Tempelhof in Berlin. Tempelhof, a former airport almost in the centre of the city (built under fascism and still very beautiful as architecture) that is now used as an open space for all sorts of informal activities, only looks and feels like a common. There are some allotment gardens, there is skating, picnicking, even carpentry and other informal practices, but in essence it is not a park. It feels like an empty, open, vacant space. The pressure group *100% Tempelhof* wants to keep it that way, but the City holds a different view. It wants to build over part of it, with luxury dwellings in skyscrapers and transform the open space into a park, which will have a huge gentrification effect on the entire neighbourhood. As it is state-owned it is a commons that people can now visit from 8 am to 10 pm. But, according to eyewitnesses, it is still very special: a huge open space of 4 km^2. Visiting Tempelhof you get the feeling of a beach: a sea of space; or of a desert: the vastness of a gigantic urban void.

The common of Tempelhof is most probably just a temporary mirage. And yet Tempelhof seems to be able to give an idea of the common as utopia. Realized utopia. Informal, for everybody but belonging to nobody. Heterotopia, not even, the real common, the almost nothing of the common, and therefore awesome like nothing, a feeling of everything, like at the seaside or in the desert. Something almost cosmic, a gigantic void, a crater, a vastness of possibility, simply free space. But state-owned. A tamed, and soon a theme parked common.

There was a question – when I discovered Tempelhof in a long brainstorm with two young artists doing a project on this space and its appropriation, transformation and gentrification – whether there could be political rallies at Tempelhof. My instinctive answer would be: 'No politics on Tempelhof'. Common space is not public space. It is not the space for public, political acts; it is the space for informality, not for informed, formal action. Only a manifestation to defend Tempelhof would be appropriate, at home so to say, in Tempelhof Common. The common is and should remain this almost nothing, like air, language. The use of the Franciscans, a minimalist approach, a temporary appropriation, not possession (see Agamben on this). In another discussion (after a walk with the activist architecture group Stalker) somebody proffered another beautiful platitude: the most important thing you can share is time. This is again this almost nothing. Like the common should be defended against the economization (boiling down to privatization), it should also be defended against politicization. You cannot and should not politicize (let alone get state control or any other political control) on language, culture, nature, air, et cetera.

Tempelhof contains a paradox: if you let it happen, it will become a park with high-rise along the side and it will lead to a gentrification of the entire neighbourhood. If you defend it (by mobilizing Berlin, like *100% Tempelhof* tries to do) it will mean a gentrification of the neighbourhood anyhow, because you will draw attention to something that should just be there. The commons is threatened as soon as you draw attention to it.

The Universal and the Particular Commons

We maybe should make a difference between the Common with a capital C and the common with lower-case c: the universal commons and the particular commons. The Common with capital C, the universal commons, is what really is owned by nobody (and therefore by everybody, like air or language: it can only be used, not appropriated), the common without capital, the particular commons, is a community, a community property, or collective property, one could call it the 'cooperative property', like in the idea of a cooperative corporation, a factory run by the labourers for instance or even a collective ownership of an industrial building divided into lofts that are collectively owned (although that is somehow less heroic, it is just a way to share the burdens). The squatter movement has always been an exercise in 'commoning'. It is appropriation by use, by living together in a vacant or abandoned building. The communal gardens and urban farming in (pop up) parks have become textbook cases lately of this particular commons (which of course have a link to the universal common of the ecosystem).

Not all commons are the same. Every feast is a practice of 'commoning', a celebration of the communion, the community as such, but it often is, when all is said and done, a private party (a family party, a party of friends). The festive communal meal in many French villages one day (weekend) in the year (with attractions and *bal populaire*) is, in a sense, a better instance of this common with lower-case c. The real Common with a capital C, the universal commons, is not 'celebratable', not something you can celebrate, not really. We can invent water day, air day, language day, open source day, et cetera, but it remains artificial. (Maybe religions have served this function. Religion is again an appropriation of the common – God owns it all). The Common is elusive and fragile, almost nothing. Even if it is almost everything.

You might think I am getting into some mystic trance here, repeating some mantra. No. Take the example of the city, the liveliness of the city, its very heart; who produces it? Common inhabitants, artists, bohemians, shopkeepers, cafés, the lot. Who captures it and capitalizes on it? The market, the real estate market, developers, and not to forget the tourist industry, only to destroy the original spirit (Greenwich Village, Soho, and soon even the Graanmarkt in Brussels, my local square, will be overtaken by tourism).

The commons can and will be appropriated time and again. But then David Harvey is right too (in his *Rebel Cities*[9]): the urban commons are created time and again. We collectively produce a nice neighbourhood, a nice ambience, which is then most of the times gentrified. This vicious circle of original accumulation, of appropriation, privatization, enclosure, if not theft of the commons should be broken. Even if all acts of enclosures of the commons are responded with new 'disclosures'.

Maybe in the digital age at least the artificial commons are ultimately beyond privatization: we can and will hack them and share them time and again... Wikipedia, the largest and most used encyclopaedia ever is for free, and is for all, it is made by anonymous commoners. It shows how monumental the digital commons and the open source movement can become. It gives a very good idea of how a universal commons (of knowledge and information) is made by particular acts of communing, of sharing (knowledge in this case).

Conclusions

The spatial common is difficult, temporary, more a moment than a space (a moment of space). More a use than a property. It has vanished, has been appropriated (read: has been mostly stolen) with the colonization of the territory by big agriculture, the state, multinationals, et cetera.

As we are all becoming nomads in some way or other: migrant, commuter, refugee, global student, business class, etc., but also digital nomads, internauts, cyber shepherds et cetera – the human herds a tweeting swarm – we may have to reconsider the commons. We should maximize the common: open source knowledge (Wikipedia!) will be crucial against the ongoing privatization of knowledge and research. Defending the cultural or artificial commons is equally important as defending nature or the natural commons against exploitation and appropriation. I gave the examples of the North Pole and the privatization of seeds.

To overcome or bypass the dualistic distinction between artificial and natural commons, we should make a distinction between the universal commons (air, water, seeds, in short 'nature', language, traditions, art, et cetera, in short 'culture') and the particular commons, the sharing as practice in a society or community or network. Practices of commoning are always particular, there is no such thing as a concrete world community (humanity remains always abstract). This distinction between the universal commons and the particular commons (a squad, a feast, an action, a place) is more important than the distinction between the natural commons and the artificial commons (of Negri and Hardt), for the privatized seeds for instance are both: nature and patented genes (hence technology). We should, in a sense, give up the idea of Nature, as Latour tells us in his 'politics of nature'. Is this new distinction helpful? Maybe it is. What is at stake in a certain sense in the twenty-first century, is to defend the universal commons (in particular the eco-system, the freedom of seeds, open source knowledge, et cetera) by the proliferation of particular practices of commoning. We have to take lessons from *The Magna Carta Manifesto* (and the Charter of the Forest): the protection of the commons should be enshrined in law.

The case of the privatization of seeds proves that the 'original appropriation' (the theft that starts the capitalist process) is not, unlike some phrases in Marx' chapter on it suggest, something of the beginning of capitalism but is *ongoing* (even land grabbing is ongoing, like in South America where huge soy fields of the agro industry, called 'green deserts', have taken the place of small farms). In *Rebel Cities*, David Harvey stresses that the process of commoning is as continuous as the process of enclosures. It is an important point. One can think of the open source movement or even the illegal downloading and uploading of about anything from music to films to entire books. But Harvey is thinking about the city, the urban commons. And it is indeed true that there is a certain metabolism: besides gentrification (as original appropriation of the atmosphere of a neighbourhood) there are a thousand practices of commoning, from a simple pick nick in the park to urban activism. Acts of 'commoning', of re-appropriation of the commons are needed. Use, not property, is what counts. Like the people spontaneously cleaned up and swept the ground after the revolution, on Tahrir Square: a public roundabout had become their shared space. Indeed, a paradigmatic act, real and symbolic at once. We re-appropriate the common every time we reclaim the streets, every time we turn a park into a community garden. The common is commonplace each and every time we make a space common, a common place. Like acts of commoning are the core of the creation of the spatial or urban commons, civic activism is the true core of democracy, is the re-appropriation of democracy (as the ideal of the rule of those who are not entitled to rule, eternally those who are not in power or in parties, as Rancière points out in his *The Hatred of Democracy*[10]).

All this has convinced me more than ever that one of the connotations of the common is indeed (as the etymology dictionary suggested) also *munia*, a duty to the community: the struggle for the commons will be one of the most important struggles of the twenty-first century. It already is.

Notes

1 Antonio Negri and Michael Hardt, *Commonwealth* (London and Cambridge, MA: Harvard University Press 2009).

2 Peter Linebaugh, *The Magna Carta Manifesto: Liberties and Commons for All* (Berkeley: University of California Press, 2009).

3 See Fernand Braudel's succinct, *La dynamique du capitalisme* (Paris: Flammarion, 1985). See also his magnum opus: *Civilisation matérielle, économie et capitalisme, XVe-XVIIIe siècle*, 3 Vols. (Paris: Arman Colin, 1979).

4 See Immanuel Wallerstein's succinct *Historical Capitalism* (London and New York: Verso, 1983), an accessible commentary on his magnum opus: *The Modern World System,* especially vol. 1: *Capitalist Agriculture and the Origins of the European World-Economy in the Sixteenth Century* (New York: Academic Press, 1974).

5 Lieven De Cauter and Michiel Dehaene, 'The Space of Play: Towards a General Theory of Heterotopia', in *Heterotopia and the City: Public Space in a Postcivil Society*, ed. Michiel Dehaene and Lieven De Cauter (London: Routledge, 2008), pp. 87-102.

6 Émile Durkheim, *Les formes élémentaires de la vie religieuse* (1912) (Paris: Presses universitaires de France, 1998).

7 Giorgio Agamben, *De la très haute pauvreté: Règles et forme-de-vie* (Paris: Bibliothèque Rivages, 2011).

8 Hans Achterhuis, *De utopie van de vrije markt* (Rotterdam: Lemniscaat 2010).

9 David Harvey, *Rebel Cities: From the Right to the City to the Urban Revolution* (New York and London: Verso 2012).

10 Jacques Rancière, *Hatred of Democracy* (London and New York: Verso, 2009).

Performing the Common City

On the Crossroads of Art, Politics and Public Life

Pascal Gielen

> *'...certain kinds of disorder need to be increased in city life, so that men can pass into a full adulthood...'*
> Richard Sennett, 1970, xxiii
>
> *'Per-for-mance means a person who per-for-ates himself and his surroundings (it is simultaneously an analysis, a destruction and an honouring)?'*
> Jan Fabre, New York, 1982

Two things block the road to adulthood: families and communities. That at least was Richard Sennett's conclusion when he analysed the problematics of urban life, in 1970. According to the sociologist, human behaviour mostly remains stuck in adolescence. Such pre-adults are afraid of the breathing space of possibilities created by the city air. Adolescents typically shut out chaos or disorder to safeguard their individuality. By maintaining pure beliefs and by strictly adhering to principles, the subject safeguards its pure identity. Adolescents live in permanent fear of the threats that may come from an outside world. Their desire not to project an ambiguous self-image drives them to a kind of hyper-puritan behaviour and a rhetoric in which the self must be continually affirmed.

> ...the degree, to which people feel urged to keep articulating who they are, what they want, and what they feel is almost an index of their fear about their inability to survive in social experiences with other men. (Sennett, 1970, pp. 9–10)

Therapeutic sessions with like-minded friends, family members or care professionals perpetuate this tendency of self-articulation into adulthood. This is why the subject remains stuck in permanent adolescence. Today as well, many people engage in serious and prolonged discussions about their own feelings, qualities, likes and dislikes, both with people they know and with people they hardly know, on the Internet or in other media. In short, even today our social environment encourages a continual self-articulation in which subjectivity is shaped by an affirmative expression of the ego. An introverted nuclear family life and relatively homogeneous communities also shield the adult individual from disruptive interruptions that may come from a problematic outside world. Thus the contemporary subject hangs onto an identity. Identity stems from the Latin *identitas*, which indeed means 'sameness'. Through their bonds, families and communities constantly confirm this sameness, in which the unique identity of 'us' can only be expressed by opposing the Other or otherness (this of course doesn't contradict the exception that certain families and communities may have a very destabilizing effect on one's identity). Within the family or community the 'I' cherishes its own self and its own being-right.

Sennett makes an important point by stating that ever since Georges-Eugène Haussmann, urban life has also been spatially arranged in the same manner. In Haussmann's view, large avenues drew strict boundaries between neighbourhoods of different social origins. This rational urban plan not only generated a functional and efficient urban space, but also resulted in segregating the urban multitude into socially relatively homogeneous neighbourhoods of conflict-free communities. Simply put, Haussmann and his many acolytes made sure that city-dwellers could retreat into a relative sameness, thereby excluding the daily confrontation with the all too radical Other as much as possible. The lack of real challenges, irritation, dissensus and conflict brought about by such a segregation also means that biologically adult city-dwellers can continue to wallow in their adolescence. In other words, they can settle down purely and consistently in their own halted identity because no one in their immediate surroundings deals them a proverbial (or real) blow anymore. The social order in which these adolescents have been socialized is after all established and firmly protected and screened off by urban strategies that allow the 'I' to remain in a safe comfort zone, together with its own kind.

Although over the past 150 years, architects, urbanists, social geographers and sociologists have frequently contested Haussmann's views, it is astonishing to see that most contemporary cities still follow the example of the Frenchman's rational plans in some way or other. Even more so: young, enthusiastic architects and urban planners still dare to present fashionably looking plans with a strictly delineated creative urban zone, shopping zone, commercial hub, university campus and administrative zone, and especially a number of spatially well-cordoned-off residential areas (be it for middle-class families, single yuppies or the elderly) in specific urban zones. Ambitious gentrification plans of the past few decades also demonstrate a strategy in which one homogeneous group – usually the lower social class – is carefully deported on behalf of another homogeneous group – especially the middle class or higher income groups. (Sassen, 1991; Hamnett, 1984; Smith, 2002)

And even when such master plans are hard to implement fully because of a historically embedded urban layout, we can still observe how cities are segregated 'organically', often along ethnic lines. Jewish neighbourhoods have historically entrenched themselves within the *Eruv* and in order to meet Chinese people or people with a Muslim background, one needs to visit completely different urban zones. The higher autochthonous middle class will have settled in a recently renovated green neighbourhood. If anything, this begs the question of whether urban planners have actually left Haussmann behind. In any case, we can see, with Sennett, that many cities even today still cultivate the adolescent within us by blocking any adult contact with the Other. The non-intentional, the contradictory and the unknown are still smoothed away as much as possible through urban segregation and functional differentiation. The lack of confrontation in the rational organization of urban life also means that city-dwellers only rarely need to defend their own existence or claim their own space, as this has already been taken care of on their behalf in a well-calculated plan, especially if these citizens belong to the middle class. As a result, city-dwellers hardly need a truly public space in which to account for, argument and time and again legitimate their own individuality. Or, put differently: the segregated city-dwellers hardly need to engage in everyday politics any more. They no longer need to fight for or account for how they shape their own lives and their environment. When one's identity is no longer questioned or challenged, politics become a strictly private affair, which, in a democracy, can be taken care of in the voting booth. In other words, in the functionally ordered city, politics are banished from the street. When the public space no longer provides a platform to confront the alien, the strange, people with different ideas or beliefs, it is automatically neutralized in a political sense. Or: when the public space allows us to not meet others, but to ignore them or pass them by (as, for instance, with a simple click in the virtual space of the Internet), it simply ceases to exist. Politics then withdraw from daily life and the public space becomes depoliticized.

But why should a peaceful, secluded and apolitical existence within one's own family or community be a tragic thing? At first sight, it would seem to offer only advantages. However, the paradoxical consequence of living in conflict-free or at least confrontation-free zones, according to Sennett, is that it encourages explosions of violence. Those who anxiously hide in their adolescent, pure identity will quickly become violent when they are eventually interrupted in their routines by someone else. Because these adolescents, thanks to their permanent stay in the segregated community, are no longer obliged to express themselves constantly in conflictual situations, they no longer know how to relate to others in an agonistic way. Because of the strong social homogenization of delineated urban areas, the public space loses its function of expressing differences. In this segregated city, these encounters with the Other are suppressed in any case, which means there are no verbal confrontations either. Whether these places to meet the Other did exist in the past or how they specifically looked, Sennett does not clarify, but it is the reason why in *The Uses of Disorder* (1970) he argues for more anarchy in the city. Communities and homogeneous neighbourhoods should be broken open, purely rational divisions be removed, especially to prevent random violent eruptions and solve them in an 'adult' manner.

> It is the mixing of diverse elements that provides the materials for the 'otherness' of visibly different life styles in a city; these materials of otherness are exactly what men need to learn about in order to become adults. Unfortunately, now these diverse city groups are each drawn into themselves, nursing their anger against the others without forums of expression. By bringing them together, we will increase the conflicts expressed and decrease the possibility of an eventual explosion of violence. (Sennett, 1970, p. 162)

This statement also makes clear the primordial role of the public space in the city or, in a wider sense, modern society. It provides the possibility to express diversity, thereby banishing blind or random violence. A lively public space that always allows for otherness thus has the important political function to convert antagonisms into agonisms. According to philosopher Chantal Mouffe, this is the basis of every democracy:

> To revitalize democracy in our post-political societies, what is urgently needed is to foster the multiplication of agonistic public spaces where everything that the dominant consensus tends to obscure and obliterate can be brought to light and challenged. (Mouffe, 2011, p. 20)

It now also becomes clear what role art and artists may have in this context. After all, artists are particularly good at 'expression', at shaping and articulating opinions, images, beliefs, ideas, et cetera. If they also succeed in projecting curious, unknown and unexpected images and performances into the urban space, they will constantly pull the adolescent city-dwellers out of their comfort zones. By making them see, smell, feel and hear that everything that is can also always be different, artists, in other words, can time and again *make* the public space anew. It is precisely in the interruption of the daily routine and of the regular social intercourse in the city that the public space originates and is charged politically.

Clearly, an artist's 'message' absolutely need not be political. Simply by the act of pushing the otherwise conceivable, by lending it a possible expression, the public and the political emerges. This otherwise conceivable can be formal, ethical, ecological or political in nature. The point is that the artist introduces something singular, with the result that everything regarded as 'normal' before suddenly no longer seems to be so evident. Or, as has been pointed out many times elsewhere: the artist introduces a 'dismeasure' into the measure that is regarded as 'normal' by an urban culture at a given moment in history. (Gielen, 2015a and b) Precisely in this unforeseen 'dismeasure' lies the political character and the force to generate the public space. At the same time, this means that not all art in the public space is truly public art, in the sense that it creates the space and therefore charges it politically. In short, there is absolutely no need for art to 'interrupt'. On the contrary, the majority of art in the public space is anything but disruptive and so also anything but political. The interruptive character of artistic interventions happens to depend strongly on the contexts in which they are performed. Pictures, sculptures and performances, and other art in public space may both confirm or even fixate the place or neighbourhood in which they are planted, and confront them, open them up. Michel de Certeau has provided some insight into this complex interplay of art, urban publicness and politics with the conceptual work he did in the 1980s. This theologian also paved the way for a more analytical look at Sennett's urban problematic outlined above.

Planning and Use of the City

In *The Practice of Everyday Life* (1980), De Certeau unfolds an idiosyncratic sociology of everyday human intercourse by means of two binary oppositions, which will be presented here in a somewhat simplified form in order to describe the relationship between city, politics and the public space.

Michel de Certeau defines *strategy* as an instrument of those in power. Simply put, policymakers and managers design strategies for controlling social phenomena or running their companies, respectively. Things are put on paper in black-and-white or, with regard to the city, are cast in urban development plans. Ideally, the urban fabric is studied beforehand and the results are documented in reports. These reports then set the agenda for policy meetings which again produce written reports that in turn have an influence on recommendations, (urban) regulation and possibly legislation, which is then, in more recent years, followed by processes of monitoring. Just like Haussmann's plans, a strategy's goal is to define social intercourse in the long-term for a geographically clearly delineated area. Following a rational logic, places are given a permanent function via a 'grid' that is superimposed from the top down upon the urban multitude. However, the users of the city develop their own *tactics* to deal with these ready-made plans. In doing so, they bend the predesigned strategy to their own will. As opposed to strategies, tactics are short-term reactions and actions that can pop up anywhere in urban life. For instance, a city tripper may deviate from the prescribed touristic tour to explore a run-down but intriguing dark alley. This adventurer's voyeuristic curiosity leads him to other places in the city, places that the city government, tour operators and city marketeers would perhaps prefer not to be revealed.

In addition to the opposition of *strategy* and *tactics*, De Certeau posits a distinction between *lieu* [place] and *espace* [space]. *Place* then represents individuality, stability. In particular material or physical elements such as a building, a road or a statue occupy a place and they can only be replaced with something else if the place is ceded or taken. To this French thinker, a place is therefore a well-defined and strictly delineated domain. Think, for example, of the boundaries of a nation-state, but also the walls around a city, or, again, the Eruv around a Jewish neighbourhood. *Space*, by contrast, represents movement, temporality and change. Literary scholar Koen Geldof (1996) calls space the result of many simultaneous, sometimes contradictory operations. Sociologist Rudi Laermans (1996) adds that space is being continuously created by utilizing place, by actively controlling it. Space includes a verb, a process of continuous 'spatialization'. In that process, place is made fluid, entering a state of permanent transmutation.

When we cross both oppositions, the result is an axial figure that enables us to map the relationship between art, politics and the city in a more analytical manner. It gives us a, albeit ideal-typical, typology of urban models in which art, politics and public space each display a specific topology. Related to the art that such urban orderings produce, these are called the monumental, the situational, the creative and the common city, respectively. And, although these urban ideal-types are presented here chronologically, obviously all types may occur simultaneously. For example, today there are no longer purely monumental cities, but there may be several districts within one city that are more like a monumental city, whereas other parts are more like the creative or the common city. In short, the city is always in motion and any typology trying to capture this is missing the complexity of real life, including the schematic structure below.

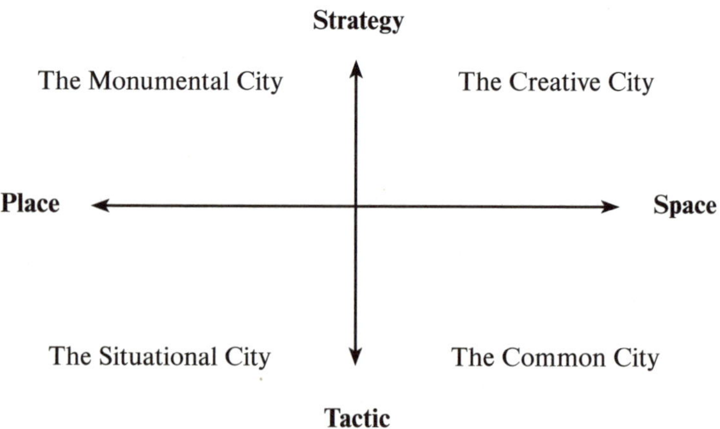

The Monumental City

The monumental city reflects Haussmann's ideal image: an urban organization based on the strategically developed rational plan in which every place is ascribed a well-delineated function. Such undertakings can be found in Paris and post-Victorian London of the late nineteenth and early twentieth century. Such urban arrangements actually do not in the first place represent themselves, but rather the nation-state. In a still young representative liberal democracy, this nation-state is governed by statesmen who make up an elite group of (former) aristocrats, rising bourgeois and liberals. Both literally and figuratively, these are Enlightened cities, in which rational bureaucracy has its Weberian heyday. The sociologist Luc Boltanski has described the political period during which this rational city was being prepared:

> The period in question was marked both by an increase in the state's ambition to control the populations residing on the territory where it exercised its power, that is, its power over what in the first half of the nineteenth century was beginning to be called society, as a grouping largely identified with the boundaries of the nation-state, and by the development of approaches to governance inspired to varying degrees of liberal tradition. These approaches found support – as Michel Foucault showed (2007) – in new administrative techniques for totalization through the use of statistics or accounting, and in techniques for identifying individuals – i.e., citizens – through the use of identity papers or through the use of physical indications (...). All these techniques were intended to address the problem of managing formally free individuals from a distance, either by making their aggregate behaviour globally calculable and predictable, or by making them individually controllable, that is by ensuring their traceability. (Boltanski, 2014, p. 65)

The city of the late nineteenth and first half of the twentieth century is the outcome of this tendency towards rational calculation on the level of the nation-state from the first half of the nineteenth century. This is why the public *sphere* there to a large extent coincides with what is called the public *space*, a strictly defined place that is 'made free' and organized by the state or city government.

The art found here is preferably a national monument, reminding the city of the grand momentum in which the nation and its people are rooted. This city is predictably interrupted by the art that resides in the semi-public spaces of equally monumental museums, theatres and opera houses. It is only strategically or calculatedly put on hold by regular parades, fun fairs or carnivals.

As Tessa Overbeek, in her interview with Jennifer Miller here, describes the ritual interruption by the annual arrival of the circus, likewise in the monumental city the artistic interruption is mainly of a ritual nature. This means that the artist may disrupt the everyday social order, but only to actually confirm it, as for instance in the symbolic inversion of carnivalesque artistic interventions (Bakhtin, 1981). Such inversions serve mainly as social vents (or sublimations) to prevent truly violent eruptions.

A symbolic inversion indeed remains only symbolic and also well-defined in time and space. Or, in De Certeau's words: the ritual interruption is assigned a permanent place in everyday urban life. The grandeur of the nation-state remains untouched by this kind of ritual art. Even more so: art primarily serves to socialize a population within the existing social order without questioning that order. Following De Certeau, artistic artefacts are assigned a permanent *place* in both the social hierarchy and in the urban zone where such art is allowed. The monumental city, in other words, is also the city of the class society in which monumental art defines the canon that must simulate a culture of national unity which glosses over persistent economic and social differences. Within such a context, art and education deliberately commit 'symbolic violence', in the words of Pierre Bourdieu (1979), as they must make the members of a lower social class believe that they too have one true culture, i.e. the national high culture that in fact legitimizes an equally high bourgeois lifestyle.

While art in the public space mainly confirms the social order during this period, the state controls the public space with the help of an army of sociologists and urbanists. It is against this rigidly strategically structured city of equally rusty functional places that the first seeds of protest begin to bud in the 1950s, seeds that will grow out to become mature counter movements in the decade to follow. And this brings us to another era with a different relationship between spatial planning and urban behaviour, and therefore to another city.

The Situational City

Among those starting to eat away at the rigid urban grid are the situationists, in the late 1950s. A strategically structured monumental city with fixed, assigned places slowly has to make way for other relations. The still permanent positions of hierarchical institutions, monuments and canon are confronted by a multitude of artists and young activists who reclaim the city through practical interventions and 'inappropriate' use of preordained urban zones and buildings. Revolution is frequently declared against both establishment and bureaucratic structures in volatile manifestos, pamphlets and posters.

Until late in the 1970s and even in the early 1980s, murals and primitive graffiti, together with squatters movements, continued the re-appropriation battle. The monumental city's authority is undermined by all kinds of movements that finally transform urbanity into a situational event. As De Certeau would say: place is directly confronted with tactics here. It may be someone walking down the street naked, or a crowd seriously reclaiming the street from King Car, only to disrupt it again with a playful happening. In other words, the situational city is the backdrop for unexpected events and encounters while that backdrop itself still remains rather firmly in place. The police sometimes act forcefully to maintain the existing order.

While the powers that be of both political and educational authorities cling to the traditional hierarchy, an orthodox art elite deploys reactionary strategies to safeguard its own position. The opposition between tactics and strategy, space and place, indeed appears to coincide for a while with the distinction between progressive and conservative, between heterodoxy and orthodoxy, or between left and right, at this juncture.

The institutional critique within the art world can also be understood within this chain of dichotomies. Often singular artists attempt to dislodge the museum and its historical canon with event-based and therefore tactical actions. At the same time, fellow artists break out of the institutional environment of white walls in order to create a new world in the streets and neighbourhoods. In the situational city, art often borders on politics in actions in which private and public spaces are made public at the same time. Or: time and again, these performances make existing places public by dropping unforeseen voices and unexpected images in them, sometimes by presenting and making concrete completely different forms of living together.

Social and artistic struggle, workers and students, proletariat and intellectuals, political and sexual revolution, creative and hallucinogenic transgressions or destructions find each other for a moment in a tactical undermining of authority and the state. However, as we know, the solidarity between the working class and the student movement, just like the lucid distinction between left and right, wouldn't last for more than two decades. The rebellious higher middle-class individuals who were still in school in the 1960s, would develop into a renewed specimen of the nineteenth-century progressive liberal over the next few decades. They did understand the message of the situationists, because they translated avant-garde art into design, politics into aesthetics, entrepreneurship into management, and ideology into lifestyle. In private-public collaborations they reached compromises with the state and municipal authorities to make the urban space truly fluid. Gentrification and real estate projects followed each other in rapid succession in a strategic change management that made the urban infrastructure increasingly flexible. Ever since the 1980s, the city has become increasingly fluid, exchanging place for space, and a planning approach made way for spatial or project-like approach of the city. In other words, we now find ourselves in a new urban era.

The Creative City

When, in the 1970s, money became no longer directly linked to gold, real and virtual economies became increasingly separated during the 1980s and 1990s. Money is becoming more and more liquid, while financial flows can hardly be stopped anymore at the borders of nation-states. Quite the contrary, governments are actively promoting the free transnational traffic of capital. But financial flows are quickly followed by streams of people – looking for fortune and happiness – and even by streams of companies, often in multinational conglomerates. Capital flow generates human flow, making the distinction between domestic and foreign policy more and more vague. Often, the nation-state can only watch all this traffic go by, seeing people come and go, companies settle and move, employment rise and vaporize.

Saskia Sassen (1991) is among those who say that the metropolis is becoming the epicentre of all this global traffic. The city now plays the leading role in political management while the nation becomes increasingly sandwiched between local government and transnational organisations, between small creative companies and giant multinationals. While migrants, illegal aliens and every now and then terrorists make the neatly delineated geopolitical place increasingly fluid from below, governments and capital join hands from the top in private-public collaborations that bring down the traditional spatial planning. In the 1990s, the city became a building site where real estate and project developers were sometimes given total freedom.

The so-called neoliberal city was born in the process that Gilles Deleuze and Félix Guattari (1972) would call 'de-territorialization'. Or, in their pathos: the war machines of migrants and illegals on the one hand and stateless multinationals on the other together 'squat' the geopolitical territory. Or, returning to De Certeau: the fixed *place* indeed makes way for an urban *space*. This urban space increasingly becomes a turntable for money and human trafficking, a transit zone for poor illegals and highly educated and hard-working but often poorly paid creatives. The so-called third gentrification wave provided a place for this last group.

By the end of the 1990s, after the relocation of social classes in previous waves, the creative class gets all the attention. The work of Richard Florida (2002) and others provide the necessary semi-scientific legitimization for these third-way politics. The creative city is born. While former socialists such as Tony Blair embrace entertainment and capital, civil servants and urban developers roll up their sleeves to design new creative zones. The industrial lumpenproletariat has to make way for a post-industrial creative precariat, the unionized labourer for the flexible freelancer, the artist for the cultural entrepreneur, the permanent job for the temporary contract, the welfare state for neoliberal power.

Here we immediately see the paradox of the creative city: while everything appears to become fluid, and mobility, flexibility, inventiveness and creativity are being encouraged by the government, that same – now urban – government tries to forge an alliance with the new capital. The artificial design of urban creative zones, fashion districts, flexible workplaces and lounge bars are all part of a truly political, urban strategy that desperately tries to tame the wild multitude of hip artists, hipsters and other creatives by offering them a fixed *place* within a well thought-out urban space.

From the Groninger Museum to the Guggenheim Bilbao, it is all part of a master plan to bring the city and its economy under control again. Once more, De Certeau: in the creative city, space confronts strategy. In this strategy, the public space – where ideally 'anything goes' – is carefully calculated. Although the square looks open, its use is organized by a tight time schedule. While the public space appears to be tolerant of some disorder, cameras meticulously register any possible real unrest.

Whereas mostly socialist, third-way politicians ruled the day with this new-fangled strategy until well in the 2000s, by the end of the first decade of the new century the torch is handed on to predominantly reactionary parties. In the process, the creative city becomes more and more a repressive city. Terrorist threats, in combination with the odd violent psychopathic case, help establish a new regime. Neoliberal and neo-nationalist forces join hands to build on the strategic methods of their political predecessors. This time not with hip rhetoric but with authoritarian vigour. More policing, and zero tolerance instead of turning a blind eye to soft drugs.

And if suddenly a too heavily armed individual appears in the urban commotion, there is always that last, desperate resort: the military. It is rather symbolic that it is precisely this exclusive representation of the nation-state that is called upon now. Driven by nostalgic desire for the monumental city, reactionary politics now re-establish the notion of the nation in attempt to control the uncontrollable multitude of city-dwellers and other hybrids. Indeed, the city has become an impure place within a purely nationalist rhetoric, a dirty stain on the nation-state, the Other within the own body.

And what can artists do in this creative but repressive city? As mentioned earlier, they had better become creative entrepreneurs, which also means not being recalcitrant or causing 'trouble', but rather help solve problems by thinking along constructively. The new artist is not a revolutionary as in the situational city, but a 'realist' and above all a pragmatist. Art in the public space then serves to mark the neighbourhood, too fixate it again with an identity. Or, again in the words of De Certeau: public art is deployed as part of a strategy to force space to become place again. And yes, in the creative-repressive city too, artists are welcome guests in problem neighbourhoods.

Community art is all the rage again. Both third-way politicians and conservatives are only too happy to enlist inexpensive artists to solve the problems caused by their own neoliberal policies. Community centres, small schools and medical facilities are dismantled under the guise of crisis and efficiency and artists may now try to repair the holes in the social fabric (see also De Bruyne and Gielen, 2011). While doing so, well-meaning artistic people often use methods that reinforce the internal feeling of oneness of Sennett's communities instead of promoting the open city which they themselves represent. In short, the only artists that are tolerated in the public space are those creatives that can cheer up a neighbourhood a little, both physically and mentally.

Or, this commissioned artist fits within a wider, indeed *strategic* marketing plan that distinguishes this city from the other one via a more or less phallocentric aesthetics. Grotesque museum architecture, megalomaniac light festivals and spectacular circus acts are supposed to replace the cathedral of yesteryear. The creative-repressive city is indeed first and foremost a touristic city and its public space a consumer-friendly shopping centre with tour operators disguised as artists, independent curators and art programmers. At the same time, this well-marketed and orchestrated creative image serves to gloss over and hide the urban confusion of growing social inequality and ethnic and religious conflicts, while an insidious, repressive – also sometimes biopolitical – approach tries to suppress violent eruptions. Together with multicultural local residents, the community artist is happily singing the hymn of social cohesion, thereby actually – as we know from Sennett – charging the violent eruption. Neither creative nor repressive urban policy can then stop the riots and unrest in the *banlieues* of Paris or the suburbs of London, emulated on a smaller scale in the Brussels municipality of Molenbeek or in and around the Schilderswijk in The Hague. Not a single artist – idealist or pragmatist – is capable of taming this 'common' multitude or predict when it will erupt.

One would need a crystal ball to know for how much longer the creative-repressive city can control the spatialized urban fabric with this strategic policy. Will it be able to permanently restrain the violent breed and will the creative entrepreneur be able to continue cheering up the public space in the long run? Or will the day come when the creative but rationally calculated and besieged city loses all control? In any case, this speculative thought opens up the theoretical possibility of a completely different city.

The Common City

Dystopia meets utopia when the urban swarming of global flows breaks up the strategic policy. When the cameras that are monitoring the public space in the creative city are smashed, two possibilities present themselves. Either the shards of the smashed camera testify to the criminal hordes, emerging gangs and other riffraff making urban intercourse unsafe, or they symbolize a desire for freedom, for a new social order that can deal with urban life without authoritarian, centralized control. The urban space, which is simultaneously made completely liquid by human flows from the bottom up and capital flows from the top down, opens up the field for a multitude of tactics. Just about anyone can try to appropriate space. When strategic control loses terrain, space and tactics are on equal footing. The city then belongs to everyone and everyone attempts to appropriate parts of it. Perhaps this is the utopia Richard Sennett dreamed of when he argued for more anarchy, in 1970. According to the American thinker, the dystopia of criminal and especially irrational violence will, on the contrary, not occur when the city rejects the strategically enforced order.

> ... the potential for 'irrational crime', for violence without object or provocation, is very great now. The reason it exists is that society has come to expect too much order, too much coherence in its communal life, thus bottling up the hostile aggressiveness men cannot help but feeling. These new anarchic cities promise to provide an outlet for what men now fear to show directly. In so doing, the structure of the city community will take on a kind of stability, a mode of ongoing expression, that will be sustaining to men because it offers them expressive outlets. Anarchy in cities, pushing men to say what they think about each other in order to forge some mutual patterns of compatibility, is thus not a compromise between order and violence;

> it is a wholly different way of living, meaning that people will no longer be caught between these two polarities. (Sennett, 1970, p. 181)

The new urban communities that Sennett advocates are special in the sense that they no longer need a 'we-feeling' towards the Other in order to emerge and survive. The constituting foundation for such communities therefore lies outside an identitary reflex. Not sameness, not coherence or consensus, but otherness, internal contradictions and dissensus form the ingredients of a new constituting force. Not 'being' but a continuous 'becoming' is the hallmark of the new social fabric.

As early as the 1970s, Sennett thus all but introduced the notion that is nowadays becoming all the rage again: the 'common', a concept that seems much more suitable than his notion of anarchy, by the way. Not the community but the common modulates the new urban fabric. Or, rather, it is the community of which this utopia dreams. The notion of the common has been expanded upon sufficiently elsewhere (see, for example, Gielen and Lijster, 2015). In short, the common is a space or area that can be both physical and symbolic, both material and mental and may serve as a resource for all.

Philosophers such as Antonio Negri and Michael Hardt (2009) or Hans Achterhuis (2010) define this space historically as a place or source of raw material that is free for anyone to use but to which everyone also makes contributions – both private and public players. According to Negri and Hardt, this common is required, not only to keep a culture and community simply alive but to keep it dynamic in the long run as well. This common, however, is not an anarchy in Sennett's sense but still a space that is regulated in order to safeguard its free use. In other words, the common cannot exist without strict rules that protect this space from being occupied by either the state or the market.

However, these philosophers do not specify how this common is to be enforced, which is why their plans have often been dismissed as utopian. This does not preclude convincing reports about the domain outside the state and the market, where the constitution of the common lies. Even more so, historical evidence demonstrates that this space has always only emerged from the interaction *among* people, i.e. in the social sphere. This may seem rather obvious, if it weren't for the fact that this sphere is regarded here as a fully autonomous domain that regulates its own laws and social intercourse regardless of politics and economy. The common therefore originates in an autonomous social space that doesn't submit itself to the laws of either government or capital. Somewhat predictably, the empirical examples of such social constitutions are mostly tactical in nature. This means, along the lines of De Certeau's thinking, that they are mostly of a temporary nature and attempt to appropriate or control the strategically primed space in their own special manner. Or, to formulate it in a way that befits this publication's title: the common is time and again newly constituted in the interruption.

In terms of the city, the plans of the Dutch artist-situationist Constant Nieuwenhuys come closest to such acommon city. We may in any case assume that with his New Babylon project he also envisaged some sort of common, as the major part of the urban fabric in it was designated for 'collective use' without any formal function. Besides, this Dutch visionary opposed Haussmann by presenting a disorienting urban space with a constantly transmuting, labyrinthine structure in which residents lead a nomadic existence and – while creating and roaming – constantly visit new parts of the city to stay there for shorter or longer periods of time. In other words, residents can always make tactical space, thus giving permanent shape to the urban fabric. Whereas Nieuwenhuys, paradoxically, still generated a somewhat Haussmannian global urban plan, today collectives such as Recetas Urbanas in Sevilla completely annihilate this illusion with their so-called 'temporary architecture'.

Fifty years after Nieuwenhuys' wild schemes, we see a multitude of initiatives emerge to constitute such a common. Just like Creative Commons aims to strategically redistribute awarded copyrights and patents, Occupy and communal allotments temporarily re-appropriate the pre-programmed urban space. Some attempts are more sustainable and of a more structural nature than others, but the important thing is that this 'movement' has been gaining force for a while now. New initiatives pop up everywhere, anytime. From the occupation of the University building the Maagdenhuis in Amsterdam to Teatro Villa Occupato in Rome, from Tahir Square in Cairo to Yo Si, Sanidad Universal and Recetas Urbanas in Spain, each time the urban space is occupied tactically with more or less long-term effects. It is not the lifespan of any particular initiative that counts, but the continuous popping up of time and again new movements. The common city is indeed only constituted in the continuous confusion of tactical manoeuvres, in confrontations and dissensus.

Although the administrators of the creative-repressive city prefer to dismiss these occurrences as 'meaningless', 'unguided' or 'hardly viable' because they would be 'little realistic', a growing army of philosophers, sociologists, economists and other scholars regard them as the signs of new forms of administration, even of a new democracy. Political scientist Isabell Lorey (2015), for example, speaks of a 'presentist democracy' which, unlike the liberal representative democracy, takes place in the here and now. Whereas the latter form only promises a better or more democracy for the future, the former is realized in current and everyday action. More pragmatically inclined thinkers, such as the political scientist David Held (2006), also regard a future democracy as possible only when social, cultural, political and economic forces continuously balance each other. Businesses, civilians, cooperatives and governments organise themselves in what he calls a 'democratic autonomy'. Many forms of self-government align themselves in this and often also grate against each other. Although Held does not disavow the state, with his point of view he does come close to a political desire that the Italian Autonomia movement already promoted in the late 1970s:

> Political autonomy is the desire to allow differences to deepen at the base without trying to synthesize them from above, to stress similar attitudes without imposing a 'general line', to allow parts to co-exist side by side, in their singularity. (Lotringer and Marazzi, 2007, p. 8)

It is precisely the common city that forms the basis for such a democratic autonomy. Cities have always been a melting pot of religions, cultures, classes, political and social contradictions. Urban cultures take shape at the cross-section of trade capitalism, fine arts and careless cosmopolitans as well as exploitation, prostitution, forced migration and deportation. Tensions can be found everywhere in the city. In this urban setting, we can detect the foundations for a rather strange ordinary lived democracy. This democracy could be called 'strange', because it does not fit with the rational organized liberal representative democracy we are used to in Europe and the U.S.

The latter form of political organization is based on quantitative representation and votes. It's a political form constituted in a nation state that claims to have built on a relative homogeneous identity of its population, called 'the people'. Big cities often contradict this myth of 'the people', because of their daily reality of a 'many', a multitude of heterogeneous cultures.

Urban spaces with a high social density are at the same time the playground of a lot of minorities that are not politically represented at all. Such cities are in that sense the Other, the stranger or sometimes the black spot in the sameness of the nation state. It's probably one of the reasons why they say that 'New York is not the United States', 'Amsterdam is not the Netherlands', 'Berlin is not the same as Germany' or 'Brussels does not equal Belgium'. It's a statement that is often made to indicate that the people who live in those cities, their interactions or, in general, their culture, are not at all representative for the country in which those same cities are located.

It are those crowded spots in the world which deliver the daily empirical proof that very different people can live relative peaceful together without a homogeneous (national) identity. Of course there are sometimes clashes, and even very bloody conflicts, but in general urban populations practice every day in learning to live with, or next to each other without having to fight with each other, even when they never make one effort to understand each other. That is the reason why it is probably allowed to say that those crowded spaces are the laboratories of a common city with a kind of daily lived – not peaceful, but agonistic – democracy. Or, again with Lorey: 'a presentist democracy'.

But who are the artists in this common city? Although they may still resemble their predecessors of the situational city, their social context is quite different. Whereas the artists of the 1960s and 1970s were fighting tactically against the rigidity of hierarchic structures and a superimposed, planned experience of the city, by contrast the artists in the common city navigate an extremely fluid domain in which movement and change are the rules. An important difference with the situationists is perhaps that in a fully liquid situation one cannot only criticize, confront and shock but at the same time one must build alternative platforms to stand on. Therefore, artists must be also partly 'constructive'. They must constitute new real worlds, real social, political and economic plateaus in the city from where that same urban fabric can be constantly irritated.

Today, artists only interrupt the city by slowing down its flows and freezing them completely every once in a while. Artists do not perform in the public space, but have to continually claim their place and in doing so *make* space public time and again. In other words, there have to constantly place beacons to demarcate where an autonomous zone is claimed for a shorter or longer period of time, or rather, where places are made autonomous. Artists who can not (or no longer) live off subsidies or off the state but who neither wish to offer their art on the free market, are left to rely on a social network to realize their art. As stated earlier, the social is the basis of the common. This is why artists will have to use the urban social fabric, sometimes even abuse it, to continue to make autonomous work. On the other hand, they will also be able to deploy their work tactically and generate (temporary) autonomous social spaces themselves.

In other words, artists become the cofounders of both artistic and social constructs and in this they may be different from the majority of their predecessors. Ever since the nineteenth century, artists have been able to behave hyper-individualistically. In the monumental city, their individual existence was covered by a bourgeois morality. And although the artists in the situational city increasingly resisted bourgeois institutions, paradoxically these still provided them with the logistic and financial safeguards for this hyper-individualistic attitude. In the creative city, it is the free market that supports the individualistic model of the artist-freelancer, whether in combination with indirect stimuli by various governments or not. This implies that in all these 'cities' they can go on nestling themselves in adolescence: either the artists are embraced because of their pure, consistent ideas, as in the monumental city, or because of their independent entrepreneurship in the creative city, or they can give full rein to their adolescent stubbornness in the situational city.

The common city, however, calls for 'growing up'. Here artists must adopt an attitude in and towards a world that is in continuous transmutation; a world that also asks of them to continuously redefine their artistic position. They will have to invent other models in order to survive, artistically as well. And they will not only have to invent them, but also test them in the urban reality. Those who wish to make personal and original work outside of the state and market will be forced into a collective model in which artistic ideas are tested experimentally all the time. It is as if Constant Nieuwenhuys is generating real experimental space in the city in order to effectively develop his New Babylon or at least empirically experiment with it. This experiment then no longer takes place in a secluded lab or studio, but in everyday social life. Besides, apart from Nieuwenhuys, many other artists in the same city are ready to launch their own singular projects: simply a matter of preventing him from any totalitarian or Haussmannian plans. Such experiments 'in real life' are however always hybrid forms between artistic and social settings, with all the risks such undertakings may include. For example, artists may lose their purely artistic ideas in the social process, rendering their ideal plans opaque. This is a risk they will have to take if they wish to bring both their own artistic practices and the common city to life.

Within the new urban context artists can no longer hide in the well-protected theatres or museums of the monumental city, like their bourgeois predecessors, but neither can they build a solid identity anymore by storming these monuments, as in the situational city, nor can they safely retreat into the hip district of the creative city. Their performances will only have meaning when they perforate the city and allow the city to perforate them. This requires a sharp analysis by these artists of the urban social fabric, as well as the courage to destroy it if necessary, but also the generosity to recognize and honour the most diverse social relationships.

When everything is liquid, artists can only work by first laying new ground to stand on. They will have to constitute the foundation for this themselves, emphasizing the 'con' of commune or 'together'. In other words, they will have to generate new institutions that can guarantee some stability or relative security on a collective basis, so that their singular artistic work may flourish. These new institutions in the liquid urban space hardly show any resemblance anymore with the rigid and hierarchic institutions of yesteryear. The autonomous social spaces, independent of state and market, are best understood as circus big tops, erected only temporarily and then put up again somewhere else later. In other words, these institutions are mobile units that only sporadically set up a perimeter. The area within this perimeter is not of a purely physical nature. It is a social domain in which social interactions are also shaped in a different manner. This shaping is more than a deviation from Haussmann's segregated city. Because of the actions of artists, homogeneous communities and neighbourhoods are constantly challenged and stimulated by experimenting with other ways of living and by demonstrating their viability. These lifestyles, by which artists crank up the common city, will in any case be highly hybrid. Just as in circus life, they will integrate private life and work, family and professionals, friends and enemies, celebration and creative production, art and economy. This same 'circus model' will break up Sennett's traditional family life. Only when, unlike the traditional circus, this itinerant company breaks open its own community and reflectively shapes itself in dissensus – in short, when this neo-tribal crowd becomes political – will the common city become operational. Or when, like the already mentioned Recetas Urbanas – which perhaps not quite coincidentally was once constituted around a circus tent – it deliberately continuously balances on the tightrope between legality and illegality and therefore cannot operate purely artistically or architecturally but is always forced to also think and act politically. Only in such a hybrid, open autarky can artists develop sufficient sovereign power to create personal work and constitute new social figurations. In short, only when they manage to shape such constitutions – that are both artistic and social – will they feed urban life as grown-up artists in confrontation with other residents and passers-by. Within this fluid urban space, artists themselves are the performers *of* a common ground on which they can stand high and dry for a while, together with others. They not only, like Nieuwenhuys, invent New Babylon but also bring it effectively to life in a New Babylon, a common city that is constantly in the process of becoming.

Although there are concrete examples such as Recetas Urbanas, it is difficult to predict exactly what tactics the artists of the common city will deploy. Anyway, trying to determine them already now would undermine their tactical potential beforehand. This is why this common artist for now remains vague and abstract. However, one thing can be said about his quest with relative certainty: it had better be both artistic *and* ecological *and* economic *and* political *and* social. Artists who play all these fields simultaneously certainly have a better chance of bringing the common to life. And only if time and again other artists project deviating images, ideas, visions and sounds about and of the world into the urban space, will they be able to outline the architectural common city, together with others. The common city only exists by the grace of the unpredictable performances in which a dissonant space of a multitude of voices and counter-voices emerges. Artists build fora of expressions in which they themselves only advance one of those singular voices. Because the common city is only becoming common in ongoing, dissenting singular performances of the common.

Bibliography

- Achterhuis, Hans. 2010. *De utopie van de vrije markt.* Rotterdam: Lemniscaat.
- Bakhtin, Mikhail M. 1981, *The Dialogical Imagination: Four Essays.* Austin: University of Texas Press.
- Boltanski, Luc. 2014. *Mysteries and Conspiracies: Detective Stories, Spy Novels and the Making of Modern Societies.* Cambridge, MA: Polity Press.
- Bourdieu, Pierre. 1979. *La Distinction: Critique sociale du jugement.* Paris: Les Editions de Minuit.
- De Bruyne, Paul and Pascal Gielen. 2011. *Community Art: The Politics of Trespassing* (Antennae Series No. 5). Amsterdam: Valiz.
- De Certeau, Michel. 1980. *The Practice of Everyday Life.* Translated by Steven S. Rendall. Berkeley: University of California Press.
- Deleuze, Gilles and Félix Guattari. 1972. *L'anti-Oedipe: Capitalisme et schizophrénie.* Paris: Les Éditions de Minuit.
- Florida, Richard. 2002. *The Rise of the Creative Class: And How It's Transforming Work, Leisure, Community and Everyday Life.* New York: Basic Books.
- Gielen, Pascal. 2015. *The Murmuring of the Artistic Multitude: Global Art, Memory and Post-Fordisme* (Antennae Series No. 3). Amsterdam: Valiz, 2009, 3rd ed. 2015.
- Gielen, Pascal, ed. 2015. *No Culture, No Europe: On the Foundation of Politics* (Antennae Series No. 15). Amsterdam: Valiz.
- Gielen, Pascal and Thijs Lijster. 2015. 'Culture: the Substructure for a European Common'. In *No Culture, No Europe: On the Foundation of Politics,* (Antennae Series No. 15), ed. Pascal Gielen, pp. 19–64. Amsterdam: Valiz.
- Hamnett, Chris. 1984. 'Gentrification and Residential Location Theory: A Review and Assessment'. In *Geography and the Urban Environment. Progress in Research and Applications*, ed. David T. Herbert and R.J. Johnson. London: John Wiley.
- Hardt, Michael and Antonio Negri. 2009. *Commonwealth.* Cambridge, MA: Harvard University Press.
- Held, David. *Models of Democracy.* Stanford: Stanford University Press, 1996.
- Laermans, Rudi and Koen Geldof. 1996. *Sluipwegen van het denken: Over Michel de Certeau.* Nijmegen: SUN.
- Mouffe, Chantal. 2011. *On the Political: Thinking in Action.* London and New York: Routledge.
- Lorey, Isabell. 'An Untimely Present in Europe'. In *No Culture No Europe: On the Foundation of Politics* (Antennae Series No. 15), ed. Pascal Gielen, pp. 183–94. Amsterdam: Valiz.
- Lotringer, Sylvère and Christian Marazzi. 2007. *Autonomia: Post-Political Politics.* Los Angeles: Semiotext(e).
- Sassen, Saskia. 1991. *The Global City: New York, London, Tokyo.* Princeton, NJ: Princeton University Press.
- Sennett, Richard. 1970. *The Uses of Disorder: Personal Identity & City Life.* New York, NY: Knopf.
- Smith, A. 2002. *The World' New Culture Meccas: Newcastle Gateshead from Coal to Culture.* http://stacks.msnbc.com/news/798868asp?cpi-1.

Contributors

Sander Bax (1977) is assistant professor in Literary Studies, Cultural History and Didactics of Dutch Language and Literature at the Department of Culture Studies of Tilburg University. In 2013, he published 'The Nobel Prize and the European Dream: Harry Mulisch's European Authorship from a National and an International Perspective' in *Journal of Dutch Literature* and in 2015 he published a Dutch monograph on twentieth-century authorship in the context of media and politics, entitled *De Mulisch mythe* (Meulenhoff, 2015). Currently he is working on a monograph on literary authorship in contemporary media culture. sanderbax.blogspot.nl

Bojana Cvejić (1975) is a performance theorist and performance maker based in Brussels. She studied musicology and holds a PhD in philosophy. Her latest books are *Choreographing Problems: Expressive Concepts in Contemporary Dance and Performance* (Palgrave Macmillan, 2015) and *Public Sphere by Performance*, co-authored with A. Vujanović (B-Books, 2012). Cvejić teaches at various dance and performance schools and is a co-founding member of TkH editorial collective. www.bojanacvejic.info

Lieven De Cauter (1959) is a Belgian philosopher, art historian, writer and activist. He teaches Philosophy of Culture in the Department and Faculty of Architecture of KULeuven and RITS, school of arts. He published some dozen books: on contemporary art, experience and modernity, on Walter Benjamin and, more recently, on architecture, the city and politics. He has also published poems, philosophical columns, statements, pamphlets and opinion pieces in newspapers and online. His latest books in English: *The Capsular Civilization: On the City in the Age of Fear* (NAi Publishers, 2004); *Heterotopia and the City: Public Space in a Postcivil Society*, co-edited with Michiel Dehaene (Routledge, 2008); *Art and Activism in the Age of Globalization*, co-edited with Karel Vanhaesebrouck and Ruben De Roo (NAi Publishers, 2011); *Entropic Empire: On the City of Man in the Age of Disaster* (nai010 publishers, 2012). He lives and works in Brussels.

Pascal Gielen (1970) is director of the research centre Arts in Society at Groningen University where he is professor for Sociology of Art and Cultural Politics. Gielen is also editor-in-chief of the book series 'Arts in Society' and has written several books on contemporary art, cultural heritage and cultural politics. Recent books are: *Being an Artist in Post-Fordist Times* (NAi Publishers, 2009); *The Murmuring of the Artistic Multitude: Global Art, Politics and Post-Fordism* (Valiz, 2009, 2010 and 2015); *Community Art: The Politics of Trespassing* (Valiz, 2011); *Teaching Art in the Neoliberal Realm: Realism versus Cynicism* (Valiz, 2013); *Creativity and other Fundamentalisms* (Mondriaan Fund, 2013); *Institutional Attitudes: Instituting Art in a Flat World* (Valiz, 2013); *The Ethics of Art* (Valiz, 2014); *Aesthetic Justice* (Valiz, 2015); *No Culture, No Europe: On the Foundation of Politics* (Valiz, 2015). His books have been translated into English, Korean, Russian, Spanish and Turkish. His research focusses on cultural politics and the institutional contexts of the arts.

Odile Heynders (1961) is a professor of Comparative Literature in the Department of Culture Studies at Tilburg University and was a fellow at NIAS (Netherlands Institute for Advanced Study in the Humanities) in 1998/99, and 2004/05. She has published books (in Dutch) on modernist strategies of reading, European poetry, Dutch public intellectual Paul Rodenko, and the history of literature studies in the Netherlands. Her current research project is on writers as European public intellectuals and celebrities. She has a book contract at Palgrave Macmillan for *Literary Writers as Public Intellectuals*. Heynders is Head of the Research Programme Literature and Visual Art in the European Public Sphere, and supervisor of the junior research team (PhDs & Postdocs) *TRAPS*: Transformations of the Public Sphere. She was member of the Core Staff of the Liberal Arts Bachelor at Tilburg University (2004–2010) and is the coordinator of the Tilburg Honours Programme European Discourses. www.tilburguniversity.edu/webwijs/show/?uid=o.m.heynders

Bram Ieven (1979) is a philosopher and cultural theorist whose research centres on Dutch and European modernist art and politics, literature in times of globalization, and contemporary French philosophy. He teaches in the department of Dutch language and culture at Leiden University, the Netherlands.

Vanessa Joosen (1977) is a postdoctoral researcher of children's literature at Tilburg University and a professor of English Literature at Antwerp University. She co-edited the new history of Dutch children's literature, *Een land van waan en wijs* (Atlas Contact, 2015, together with Helma van Lierop and Rita Ghesquiere) and is the author of, among others, *Critical and Creative Perspectives on Fairy Tales* (Wayne State University Press, 2011). Her current research is funded by NWO and focusses on the construction of adulthood in children's literature.

Jennifer Miller (1961) is the founder and director of Circus Amok, New York's only free outdoor on ring no animal queerly situated circus spectacular. She dances with Cathy Weis and Jennifer Monson. She is the author of *Cracked Ice* and *The Golden Racket*. She is a member of the Ethyl Eichelberger cover band The Eichelburglers and Professor of Performance at Pratt Institute. www.circusamok.org

Tessa Overbeek (1982) studied Arts, Culture and Media (BA) and Literary and Cultural Studies (MA) at the University of Groningen, the Netherlands, where she also taught courses in the sociology of art and academic writing. She currently works as a freelance writer, editor and researcher and has published articles in various books and magazines, as well as online. tsoverbeek@gmail.com

Gerald Raunig (1963) is a philosopher who works at the Zürcher Hochschule der Künste and at the eipcp (European Institute for Progressive Cultural Policies); member of the editorial boards of the multilingual publishing platform *transversal texts* and the journal *Kamion*. His books have been translated into English, Serbian, Spanish, Slovenian, Russian, Italian, and Turkish. Recent books in English: *Art and Revolution: Transversal Activism in the Long Twentieth Century* (Semiotext(e)/MIT Press, 2007); *Art and Contemporary Critical Practice: Reinventing Institutional Critique*, co-edited with Gene Ray (mayflybooks, 2009); *A Thousand Machines* (Semiotext(e)/MIT Press, 2010); *Critique of Creativity*, co-edited with with Gene Ray and Ulf Wuggenig (mayflybooks, 2011); *Factories of Knowledge, Industries of Creativity* (Semiotext(e)/MIT Press, 2013). Forthcoming: *DIVIDUUM*.

Machinic Capitalism and Molecular Revolution, Vol. 1 (Semiotext(e)/ MIT Press, 2016).

Gregory Sholette (1956) is a New York-basedartist, writer and activist. His recent projects include *Our Barricades* at Station Independent Projects Gallery in NYC, *Imaginary Archive* at the Les' Kurbas Centre in Kyiv, Ukraine and at the Institute for Contemporary Art, University of Pennsylvania, Philadelphia, and the forthcoming street performance *Barricade Ballet*, being produced in collaboration with the Workers Art Coalition and Aaron Burr Society. He is active with Gulf Labor Coalition and was a co-founder of the collectives Political Art Documentation/Distribution (PAD/D: 1980–1988), and REPOhistory (1989–2000). A Mellon Fellow at the CUNY Center for the Humanities, he is on the editorial board of FIELD, a new online journal focussed on socially-engaged art criticism. His most recent publications include *It's The Political Economy, Stupid*, co-edited with Oliver Ressler, (Pluto Press, 2013) and *Dark Matter: Art and Politics in an Age of Enterprise Culture* (Pluto Press, 2011). A graduate of the Whitney Independent Studies Program, the University of California San Diego, and The Cooper Union he teaches studio art and administers the new Social Practice Queens MFA concentration at Queens College CUNY, is also associate faculty at Home Workspace, Beirut, as well as at the Art, Design and the Public Domain program of Harvard University's Graduate School of Design. www.gregorysholette.com

Erik Swyngedouw (1956) is a professor of Geography at Manchester University. His most recent publications include *The Post-Political and its Discontents*, co-edited with J. Wilson (Edinburgh University Press, 2014) and *Liquid Power: Contested Hydro-Modernities in Twentieth-Century Spain* (MIT Press, 2015).

Since 2010, **Rennie Tang** and **Sara Wookey** have been collaborating on performance- and site-based projects for educational, cultural and non-profit organizations in the USA (Los Angeles), Canada and Europe. These projects bring together their individual expertise in architecture, urban design, dance and choreography. They recently completed a

commissioned work for the Van Abbemuseum in Eindhoven, the Netherlands. Their mission is to create collaborative performance and media works that encourage an awareness of the body and its relationship to the built environment. The works they create engage a curious, playful, and critical exploration of urban spaces making a case for socially focused creative possibilities.
www.rennietang.com
www.sarawookey.com

Sarah Vanhee's (1980) artistic practice is linked to performance, visual art and literature. Her work unfolds in different formats and is often (re)-created in situ, much on the brink of (in) visibility. Recent works include *The C-Project, Turning Turning (a choreography of thoughts), Untitled, Lecture For Every One*, and *I screamed and I screamed and I screamed.* Her work has been presented widely internationally, in visual art and in performing art contexts. Vanhee is co-author of *Untranslatables* and author of *The Miraculous Life of Claire C* and *TT*.
www.sarahvanhee.com;
www.lectureforeveryone.be;
www.manyone.be

Geertjan de Vugt (1985) is a cultural historian and literary theorist. He obtained his PhD *cum laude* from Tilburg University with a dissertation on political dandyism: *The Polit-Dandy on the Emergence of a Political Paradigm*. He has published on Baudelaire, dandy insects, Walter Benjamin, and Lodewijk van Deyssel. He is also the Dutch translator of Daniel Heller-Roazen's *The Enemy of All: Piracy and the Law of Nations* (Zone Books/MIT Press, 2009). Currently, Geertjan is working on the genealogy of fingerprinting as *Kulturtechnik*.

Arts in Society Series

Interrupting the City: Artistic Constitutions of the Public Sphere is the 20th publication in a series of books that map the interaction between changes in society and cultural practices. Inspired by art and critical theory, the series Arts in Society studies the possibilities of a repositioning of the arts and culture in society. The series is open for publishing proposals in the form of essays, theoretical explanations, practice-oriented research in the arts, and research studies.

Editor-in-chief
Pascal Gielen
p.j.d.gielen@rug.nl

Index

C

D

M

N

O

P

R

W

Y

Z

Colophon

Colophon

Interrupting the City
Artistic Constitutions of the Public Sphere

Editors
Sander Bax
Pascal Gielen
Bram Ieven

Contributors
Sander Bax
Bojana Cvejić
Lieven De Cauter
Pascal Gielen
Odile Heynders
Bram Ieven
Vanessa Joosen
Jennifer Miller
Tessa Overbeek
Gerald Raunig
Gregory Sholette
Erik Swyngedouw
Rennie Tang
Sarah Vanhee
Geertjan de Vugt
Sara Wookey

Antennae Series N° 20
by Valiz, Amsterdam

Part of the Series
'Arts *in* Society"

Translation Dutch-English
Leo Reijnen

Translation German-English
Aileen Derieg
(text Gerald Raunig)

Copy editing
Leo Reijnen

Literature and Proof Check
Els Brinkman

Index
Elke Stevens

Design
Metahaven

Paper inside
Munken Print 100 gr 1.5,

Paper cover
Bioset 240 gr

Printing and binding
Ten Brink, Meppel

Publisher
Valiz, Amsterdam, 2015
www.valiz.nl

ISBN 978-94-92095-02-2

This publication was made possible through the generous support of

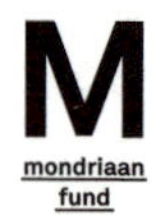

Mondriaan Fund
www.mondriaanfonds.nl

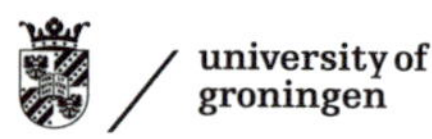

University of Groningen
www.rug.nl

Distribution:
USA /Canada/Latin America: D.A.P., www.artbook.com
GB/IE: Anagram Books, www.anagrambooks.com
NL/BE/LU: Coen Sligting, www.coensligtingbookimport.nl
Europe/Asia/Australia: Idea Books, www.ideabooks.nl

ISBN 978-94-92095-02-2
NUR 651

Printed and bound in the Netherlands

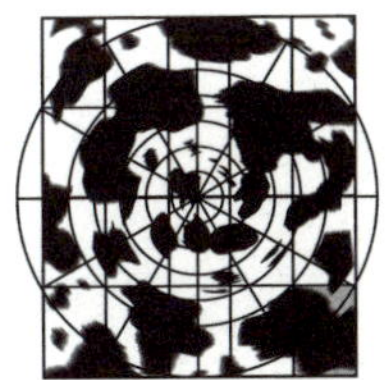

Antennae

Antennae Series

Antennae N° 1
The Fall of the Studio
Artists at Work
edited by Wouter Davidts & Kim Paice
Amsterdam: Valiz, 2009 (2nd ed.: 2010),
ISBN 978-90-78088-29-5

Antennae N° 2
Take Place
Photography and Place from Multiple Perspectives
edited by Helen Westgeest
Amsterdam: Valiz, 2009,
ISBN 978-90-78088-35-6

Antennae N° 3
The Murmuring of the Artistic Multitude
Global Art, Memory and Post-Fordism
Pascal Gielen (author)
Arts *in* Society
Amsterdam: Valiz, 2009 (2nd ed.: 2011),
ISBN 978-90-78088-34-9

Antennae N° 4
Locating the Producers
Durational Approaches to Public Art
edited by Paul O'Neill & Claire Doherty
Amsterdam: Valiz, 2011,
ISBN 978-90-78088-51-6

Antennae N° 5
Community Art
The Politics of Trespassing
edited by Paul De Bruyne & Pascal Gielen
Arts *in* Society
Amsterdam: Valiz, 2011 (2nd ed.: 2013),
ISBN 978-90-78088-50-9

Antennae N° 6
See it Again, Say it Again
The Artist as Researcher
edited by Janneke Wesseling
Amsterdam: Valiz, 2011,
ISBN 978-90-78088-53-0

Antennae N° 7
Teaching Art in the Neoliberal Realm
Realism versus Cynicism
edited by Pascal Gielen & Paul De Bruyne
Arts *in* Society
Amsterdam: Valiz, 2012 (2nd ed.: 2013),
ISBN 978-90-78088-57-8

Antennae N° 8
Institutional Attitudes
Instituting Art in a Flat World
edited by Pascal Gielen
Arts *in* Society
Amsterdam: Valiz, 2013,
ISBN 978-90-78088-68-4

Antennae N° 9
Dread
The Dizziness of Freedom
edited by Juha van 't Zelfde
Amsterdam: Valiz, 2013,
ISBN 978-90-78088-81-3

Antennae N° 10
Participation Is Risky
Approaches to Joint Creative Processes
edited by Liesbeth Huybrechts
Amsterdam: Valiz, 2014,
ISBN 978-90-78088-77-6

Antennae N° 11
The Ethics of Art
Ecological Turns in the Performing Arts
edited by Guy Cools & Pascal Gielen
Arts *in* Society
Amsterdam: Valiz, 2014,
ISBN 978-90-78088-87-5

Antennae N° 12
Alternative Mainstream
Making Choices in Pop Music
Gert Keunen (author)
Arts *in* Society
Amsterdam: Valiz, 2014,
ISBN 978-90-78088-95-0

Antennae N° 13
The Murmuring of the Artistic Multitude
Global Art, Politics and Post-Fordism
Pascal Gielen (author)
Completely revised and enlarged edition of Antennae N° 3
Arts *in* Society
Amsterdam: Valiz, 2015,
ISBN 978-94-92095-04-6

Antennae N° 14
Aesthetic Justice
Intersecting Artistic and Moral Perspectives
edited by Pascal Gielen & Niels Van Tomme
Arts *in* Society
Amsterdam: Valiz, 2015,
ISBN 978-90-78088-86-8

Antennae N° 15
No Culture, No Europe
On the Foundation of Politics
edited by Pascal Gielen
Arts *in* Society
Amsterdam: Valiz, 2015,
ISBN 978-94-92095-03-9

Antennae N° 16
Arts Education Beyond Art
Teaching Art in Times of Change
edited by Barend van Heusden &
Pascal Gielen
Arts *in* Society
Amsterdam: Valiz, 2015,
ISBN 978-90-78088-85-1

Antennae N° 17
Mobile Autonomy
Exercises in Artists' Self-Organization
edited by Nico Dockx &
Pascal Gielen
Arts *in* Society
Amsterdam: Valiz, 2015,
ISBN 978-94-92095-10-7

Antennae N° 18
Moving Together
Theorizing and Making
Contemporary Dance
Rudi Laermans (author)
Arts *in* Society
Amsterdam: Valiz, 2015.
ISBN 978-90-78088-52-3

Antennae N° 19
Spaces for Criticism
Shifts in Contemporary Art Discourses
Thijs Lijster, Suzana Milevska,
Pascal Gielen, Ruth Sonderegger
Arts *in* Society
Amsterdam: Valiz, 2015.
ISBN 978-90-78088-75-2